DIARY OF A YOUNG MISSIONARY

Diary of a Young Missionary

All This Freshness Fuming

by

Barry Martinson, S.J.

IGNATIUS PRESS SAN FRANCISCO

Cover art and design by Barry Martinson, S.J.

ISBN 978-1-62164-793-5 (PB)
ISBN 978-1-64229-357-9 (eBook)
Library of Congress Control Number 2025934382
Printed in the United States of America ♾

To My Fellow Missionaries

Morning Midday and Evening Sacrifice

This, all this beauty blooming,
This, all this freshness fuming,
Give God while worth consuming.

—Gerard Manley Hopkins, S.J.

CONTENTS

PROLOGUE

To say that Jerry influenced my desire to become a missionary in Taiwan would be an understatement. From the time my older Jesuit brother sailed from San Francisco to the Far East in 1967, his letters could hardly contain the joy and enthusiasm he had for his overseas assignment. These "epistles" were like the diary of a foreign missionary immersed in a new and challenging environment, fuming with the freshness of youth. Two years later, the Society of Jesus would appoint me to the same mission.

I had followed in Jerry's footsteps almost all my life—from becoming a Jesuit at eighteen to being assigned to the foreign missions six years later. But, although Jerry was my role model, I hadn't consciously decided to do whatever he did. We had both heard the "call", but we were two different people—two sides of the same coin, as some would say. The ways we chose to serve others were not always the same.

Jerry wanted to influence as many people as possible and accomplish great things for God. His ambition was to make a difference for good in the world. I had smaller ideals. Through the years, I had found that what made me happiest was to serve the poor—to share my life with them if I could. But even in this, it was Jerry who inspired me.

In a letter to his friends and family before departing for Asia, Jerry was clear and resolute on the reasons why he and his five companions were going to Taiwan as missionaries. He wrote:

> We believe that the principal way to world peace is through the *development* of nations. World peace, we think, is the highest of human goals. It is also Christ's special plan for the Church and the world.
>
> We believe that Christianity means *love*, and that love brings peace. We believe that nations must learn to understand and to trust other nations and that this can only come about through a plentitude of Christ-like interchange among these nations.
>
> We believe that as priests and *teachers*, we can contribute doubly to these conditions for world peace. Poverty, sickness, and national and personal avarice are the targets which Christianity aims to replace with prosperity, progress, and an entrenched concern for all other peoples as unique, personal, and irreplaceable creations of God.
>
> Obviously, six of us can't do too much. But still, we all feel something inside us that says "go" and something that tells us that our work as missionaries will have a place in God's plan of salvation.

I wish I had as much practical idealism as my brother. Of the three italicized words in his missive above, only *love* was a major factor in my desire to go to the foreign missions. I simply wanted to share my faith with others and serve the people in any way they needed me. I also hoped to make some friends along the way.

My desire to become a missionary sprang from meditating on the life of Christ during my first years in the Society of Jesus. Since then, this wish has grown stronger, and service in the foreign missions seemed to be the best way I could follow Jesus. Initially, I had wanted to go to Latin America, especially after a summer of laboring in the fields with

Mexican migrants. But it was Asia rather than Latin America that was asking for Jesuits from our province. And so, I was fortuitously sent from California to join my brother on the island of Taiwan.

Before arriving here, my imagination conjured up images of exciting adventures and challenging ministries. Hopefully, these will come in the future. But my first assignment is more mundane. I have to spend at least two years studying Mandarin, the official language of Taiwan.

I

CHINESE LANGUAGE SCHOOL

Noël Chabanel was a seventeenth-century Jesuit from France who was missioned to the Huron tribe in what is today called Quebec. Although Father Chabanel was unable to learn the native language and found everything about missionary life almost unbearable, he made a private vow to remain in the Indian missions no matter what the hardship. He died a martyr and was later canonized a saint.

Rather than naming the Chinese language school where I am now studying after a more successful figure, the Jesuits in Taiwan decided to call it Chabanel Language Institute precisely because of Noël Chabanel's stubborn perseverance in the face of apparent failure. From what I have heard about the difficulties in learning Mandarin, I can imagine Saint Chabanel would be a good example for me and the right person to pray to for assistance. This was made even more apparent to me when I first set foot in Chabanel Hall and learned that I was late for the beginning of the school year.

It was September 29, 1969, the day after I landed in Taiwan. After a leisurely three-week journey from the States, my brother Jerry had hurried me from Taipei to the Chinese language school in Hsinchu, only to be met at the door by Jean Chenut, the stern-faced director of studies, who scowled, "It's about time. Classes started two weeks ago!"

I reflected on the decision of Father Edward Murphy,

our mission director, to book me free passage on a merchant marine ship rather than pay for a plane ticket, which would have been much faster and allowed me to arrive in time for classes. The frugal mission director probably wasn't aware of when school would start. Anyway, it had been a pleasant sea voyage, and the short stopovers in Korea and Japan had made the trip more than worthwhile.

Standing in my room with Jerry in a new and strange environment, my thoughts went back six years to September of 1963, when my brother welcomed me to the Jesuit novitiate at Los Gatos, California. I was only eighteen then and just out of high school. Now I am twenty-four and on the cusp of my own missionary career. But it was always Jerry that I followed. And now he was here at the language school to show me the way. He taught me my first Chinese word, *gege*, which means "big brother", and told me to shout it out whenever I needed him.

After Jerry went back to his work at the social center in town, Father Bernard Chu, the young rector of Chabanel Hall, dropped into my room. Father Chu was originally from Peking and had only recently begun his new role as superior of the language school. He remarked that we were both in our "first year" at Chabanel.

When Father Chu spotted my guitar case, his eyes suddenly lit up.

"So, you play the guitar also!" he laughed. "I suppose you know how hard your brother fought to allow this so-called decadent 'Western' instrument to be played at Mass. Let me see it."

I pulled out the guitar and handed it to Father Chu, who sat down on the wicker chair in my room and began strumming a Chinese melody. He was quite good.

"Now you play something," he said, handing the guitar back to me.

I began singing a popular folk hymn called "We Are One in the Spirit" that I had sent to Jerry the previous year. The song is about how others will know we are Christians by our love. Father Chu soon joined in with a Chinese version.

"Your brother asked me to translate that hymn into Mandarin," Father Chu told me. "It has become popular at our Masses."

I could see right away that Father Chu would be a very friendly superior—and that singing and playing the guitar could be a valuable key for unlocking good relationships here in Taiwan.

~

The language school has over one hundred students from all over the world. For the first semester, we have been divided arbitrarily into classes of four or five. Later, we will be grouped according to our ability to learn Mandarin. My small class consists of two fast-learning Italians—Federico, a very talkative Salesian seminarian, and Roberta, a shy and scholarly laywoman—and two slow-learning, carefree Americans, Sister Patricia and me.

Our teachers gave us Chinese names. My surname is the same as my brother's—*Ding*. Since this character looks like a nail, it is associated with "workmanship". The other two characters of my name, *sung* and *ching,* come from the Chinese idiom "as evergreen as the pine tree". But many of our teachers just call me *Syau Ding* or "Little Ding" to distinguish me from Jerry, who is called *Da Ding* or "Big Ding".

My three classmates are about the same age, and most

of us, including our teacher, are prone to laughter. In fact, Ms. Luo, a heavy-set lady raised in Peking, spends half the class time giggling at our mistakes, her ample figure quivering with amusement. But she is also an excellent instructor, and we are slowly learning the language.

Slowly is the right word. There is no way to learn Chinese quickly. It has to be studied methodically. Since I was two weeks late in arriving, I missed the most basic step in learning a language: pronunciation. The first two weeks had been devoted exclusively to the intricacies of pronouncing Mandarin sounds, some of which sound unpronounceable.

Each Mandarin character must be spoken in one of four "tones". Mistaking the tone or word can change the meaning entirely. To emphasize this, Ms. Luo told us that one of her former students had regrettably exclaimed to the fat baby of a nursing mother, "Your horse must have good cow's milk!"

After our first prickly encounter, Jean Chenut, the polyglot Belgium scholastic who directs our studies, has generously tried to help me catch up with the other students. He told me one of the best ways to learn pronunciation is to visit a Taiwanese home, where I can hear spoken Mandarin.

So, one late afternoon, I climbed onto the tandem of Jean's black Honda and headed for my first dinner with a Chinese family. On the way, Jean sped from the entrance of the language school into a dark underpass while skillfully dodging the scores of food vendors who lined the passageway. I was soon hit by a blast of what smelled so much like rotten eggs that it almost knocked me off the Honda.

"What's that terrible odor?" I asked Jean, loosening my grip on the tandem to cover my nose.

"That's called *chou toufu*, or stinky bean curd," Jean yelled back at me, not missing a beat. "Do you want to stop and try some?"

"Uh, not now," I demurred. "It might spoil my appetite for dinner."

"Most foreigners can't stand stinky tofu, but the Taiwanese love it," Jean added. "*Chou toufu* is found in every night market in Taiwan, so you'll get used to the smell."

Emerging from the underpass, we encountered a busy intersection, and as we waited for the traffic light to change, row upon row of motorcycles lined up behind us, gunning their engines. When the light changed green—actually even before it changed—we were already far out into the narrow intersection with hundreds of motorbikes hot on our heels. It felt as if we were being pursued by a gang of hooligans. But it was also an exhilarating experience, and I was impressed by how well Jean weaved in and out of the traffic.

On the outskirts of Hsinchu was a barbed wire-enclosed enclave of small cement structures. Jean explained to me that these were settlements that soldiers had constructed soon after retreating to Taiwan from Mainland China in 1949. Before that, Taiwan's inhabitants had consisted mainly of Taiwanese and Hakka people spread out in the lowlands and aboriginal tribes in the higher mountains.

"When over a million Mainlanders suddenly relocated to Taiwan, compounds such as this one were quickly prepared for them," Jean explained. "Since the Jesuits and other missionary orders that were expelled from Communist China came to Taiwan about the same time as the Mainlanders, they built churches next to these communities. Mandarin was the common language, so they made many converts. You will soon meet one of the leading Catholic families in Hsinchu."

Before entering the little home, we removed our shoes at the doorstep and were greeted by a tiny, buoyant lady named Bernadette. Her husband, Francis, and two children, Johnny and Marianne, were equally short in stature but expansive in their warm welcome. There were two other Jesuits already reclining in the living room, Father David Reed, a friend of the family, and Father Albert Klaiser, the superior of the Jesuit community in Hsinchu.

When Bernadette introduced me to her son, Johnny, she remarked that he was the top student in his class. But she added that she always told her son that if he was ever tempted to be proud of how smart he was, he should remember how short he was. And if he ever felt bad about how short he was, he should remember how smart he was.

Bernadette sounded like a very wise woman. I learned that her main job was that of a catechist for Fathers Reed and Klaiser at their respective parishes. A catechist, Jean told me, was a kind of liaison between the priest and his parishioners, a necessary person to have when dealing with people of different languages and cultures.

That evening at dinner, I had my first taste of traditional Chinese culture by sampling a wide assortment of Bernadette's culinary specialties, artfully arranged on the circular table where we sat.

"Don't be polite!" Bernadette cried out, as she hurriedly brought in more stir-fried vegetables and braised meat hot off the wok. "I'm sorry there is so little to offer you. Eat more! Don't be polite." Jean translated these phrases for me, pointing out that they were called *kechi hua* or "polite expressions", which were always said to guests at a meal.

I hardly knew where to start. I noticed the other Fathers were first using chopsticks to pluck clumps of white rice from their bowls, so I did the same. Then I watched as Father

Reed deftly stretched out his chopsticks to grasp a slippery boiled dumpling from a plate on the middle of the table and delicately dip it into a small pan of soy sauce next to him before plopping the entire succulent morsel into his mouth. I attempted to do the same.

It seemed every eye at the table was upon me as I tried not once, not twice, but three times to enclose the reluctant dumpling within the forceps of my chopsticks. As I finally succeeded in catching my prey, there was an almost audible sigh of relief from the others at the table. Slowly, I drew the dumpling toward the little pan of soy sauce. But just as I was about to dip it in, the dumpling dropped into the soy sauce with a splash so virulent that both the table cloth (which fortunately was plastic) and the front of my new powder blue shirt (which unfortunately was cotton) were splattered with dark brown spots.

Hardly a moment passed before Bernadette was laughingly scrubbing my shirt front with a soapy towel and joking that she should have given me a bib for my first time eating Chinese food.

But an even more awkward situation occurred the morning after my visit with Bernadette's family, when Father Klaiser showed up at the language school demanding that I return his shoes. Vaguely, I remembered how Jean and I left Bernadette's home early, while the other two Fathers were still talking in the living room. At the doorstep, I slipped into what I thought were my shoes, which were black like the others. Although somewhat aware the shoes were rather loose, I had not realized I had taken the more sizeable Father Klaiser's footwear by mistake. He told me that when he left for his church, he could not get into my shoes and had to ride back on his motorcycle wearing only socks.

So, I have already learned a few important things about

Asian culture—for instance, not to wear a new shirt when eating dumplings with a pan of soy sauce nearby. And not to leave a family's home without checking to see if the shoes I put on are really my own. Obviously, I am on my way to becoming an "old China hand".

~

Although I have not seen much of Taiwan yet, I am gradually familiarizing myself with the fascinating area of Hsinchu, where I live. This has been facilitated by borrowing one of the many bicycles stored in the language school garage. Jerry helped me pick out my bike. I spotted a bright blue model, but my brother warned me it would be better to choose a more inconspicuous one. That way, I would not have to lock it, since no one would want to steal the bike anyway. So, I found a rusty old contraption that, despite its age and unappealing appearance, proved to be a trustworthy companion during my explorations of Hsinchu City.

The name Hsinchu means "New Bamboo". This is an apt name for the city since tall bamboos seem to sprout everywhere, even in crowded urban neighborhoods. Hsinchu is a very windy city, and when the long, hollow stems of the bamboos scrape against each other, they produce a crackling kind of music that is both haunting and delightful. It is common to see a farmer or two slowly hauling bamboos on water-buffalo carts along the narrow road in front of the language school, much to the consternation of motorcyclists trying to dodge the placid beasts.

Jerry accompanied me on his own bicycle as I made my first forays into the city. He brought me to the busy outdoor market area brimming with exotic fruits and vegetables, the sprawling temples where both Buddhist and Taoist monks welcome visitors and devotees, and the neighboring schools that disgorge their thousands of students in the late afternoon. The sights and smells are overwhelming. But even more awe-inspiring to me is Jerry's facility in communicating with the people he meets. His friendliness toward the Taiwanese and interest in their customs are probably the keys to his proficiency in Mandarin. I wonder if I will ever be as fluent in the language as he is.

In addition to the local barber, the bicycle repairman, the lady who sells fruit shakes, and the proprietor of a dumpling restaurant, Jerry has introduced me to some of the young workers who labor in small, congested factories and workshops scattered throughout the crowded city. In their free time, many of these workers participate in activities at the Catholic social service center where Jerry works.

The social service center was the brainchild of Father Louis Dowd, a zealous veteran missionary, who built the center to serve the most neglected segment of Taiwanese society. Indeed, there appears to be a wide gap between the more affluent, college-educated population and those who cannot pass the college entrance tests and end up laboring in factories or construction, often at a very early age. A group of leaders from these young workers make the social center their second home and conduct enrichment programs for the local working youth.

On Saturday nights, there are folk dances at the social center. I have ridden my bike there several times to watch and take part in them. Jerry told me that modern social dancing between young people of the opposite sex is forbidden by law (as is long hair and other suspicious "hippie-like" behavior). But traditional folk dances, not only of Taiwan but also from other countries, are encouraged. Still, the young workers appear reluctant even to hold the hand of anyone of the opposite sex. This leads to the disconcerting sight of boys dancing with boys and girls with girls. Even more unsettling is when one of the boys asks *me* to dance. I don't know whether to "lead" or to "be led".

Today, there was a "Day of Christian Community" held at the social center, with Jerry as the chief organizer. He invited priests, Sisters, and seminarians (including me) from all parts of Taiwan to join in the celebration. During the morning, we sat in groups on the auditorium floor, making posters and collages about challenging theological questions Jerry had thought up. In the afternoon, Jerry and I played the guitar together for hours in a rousing sing-a-long. Then we marched around the neighborhood in a colorful procession, displaying the posters and banners we had created. All this singing and good cheer as a profession of our faith had an added bonus for me, and probably for the other newly arrived missionaries as well—we got to know each other much better. And who knows what will become of that?

~

Since I have only recently entered into this completely foreign environment, making friends with the locals is a strong priority for me, yet very difficult to do. There is a natural tendency to spend most of my time in the familiar company of other foreign students with whom I study or older missionaries from Europe or America. So far, there has been little chance to find Taiwanese friends my age. This is probably because of the language barrier. I do not know enough Chinese yet to communicate with them.

And yet, I want so much to make friends among the people of Taiwan. I watch how easily Jerry interacts with the young workers, some of whom have become his good friends. But none of them speaks English, and, so far, my Chinese is limited to a few phrases accompanied by a lot of hand motions.

We do have classes in Chinese conversation. But these classes are not very practical. The first sentence we learned was *Matour dzai nar?*—"Where is the harbor?" When I tried that sentence out on a passerby, it was totally unintelligible. Gradually, I learned my teachers are all from Peking and add an "r" to many words. For instance, the Peking dialect pronounces "where" as *nar*, whereas the Taiwanese say *nali*.

This led Sister Patricia and me to devise a wicked riddle: "What sound does a Peking duck make?" The answer is "*quark, quark, quark.*" Unfortunately, when we told this joke to one of our teachers from Peking, he had no idea what we were talking about. So goes our communication skill.

The language students gather for lunch at the large refectory in the building where I live. The tables are circular and can seat ten persons each. With one hundred students speaking in a multitude of native languages, our refectory sounds like the Tower of Babel. Most students sit with compatriots who speak the same language. Thus, we have the Spanish table, the French, the Italian, the German, etc. There are also tables where the Americans and those from other countries sit, especially those who want to practice their English. But there is no Chinese table. And there are no local students or priests, except for our superior, Father Chu, who is also fluent in both English and French.

So how can I practice my Chinese outside of class? I want to love the island of Taiwan, but in order to do that, I need to know and love the people of Taiwan—and talk with them.

Father Chu suggested that I should be patient and wait a little longer. He said it is better to learn the fundamentals of the language correctly in class before attempting to converse too much outside of class. That way, I will not form bad habits of speaking. He also mentioned that teaching a few evening classes in English to young students each week might help me to make some local friends. I would not need to speak Chinese for that.

Our Jesuit community at the language school numbers about a dozen. Most are older than I, and all are from various countries in Europe. Only one of them, who is French, is a first-year Mandarin student my age. He is studious and quiet, as are the others in our community—quite a difference from the raucous, fun-loving Jesuits I was with during my years of seminary studies in the States. Sometimes, I look back on those friends and feel a twinge of homesickness. I wonder if I will ever see them again.

~

During our midterm break, I took a slow train to Taichung, only a few hours south of Hsinchu, to attend a workshop for foreign missionaries entitled "Indigenization: The Church as Living Community". About 170 priests, nuns, and seminarians discussed the hopes, problems, achievements, and failures of the Church in Taiwan. I was so inspired by the people I met. They were alive and forward-thinking—truly a "living community". By no means did they all think the same, but they were identical in their goodwill and dedication. They were an impressive group of both young and old—from newly arrived seminarians like me, who were struggling with the language, to veteran nuns and priests in their eighties, who were still attempting new approaches in evangelization.

We convened at a large high school, where the men slept in dorms and the nuns in nearby convents. The atmosphere of the workshop was something like a boy-scout camp, and the meticulous preparation similar to a presidential convention. Jerry was in charge of planning a "social night" for the last evening of the gathering. He printed songbooks especially for the occasion and enlisted three guitarists (including ourselves), a jovial banjo player, a Maryknoll priest with a trumpet, and an elderly Japanese nun who was a concert pianist. We were all looking forward to this opportunity to sing together. All, that is, except one—who unfortunately happened to be the bishop of Taichung.

During the afternoon of the last session of the workshop, when the bishop arrived to give his closing remarks, he said he was displeased to learn there would be a social night. The bishop, who was American, told us that in Taiwan priests and nuns do not socialize together, and even though we were all foreigners, we should abide by the same custom. Therefore, he told us to cancel the social night in the school auditorium we were planning for that evening. On hearing the bishop's unanticipated pronouncement, the crowd of religious in attendance uttered a collective groan.

After the bishop left, everyone crowded around Jerry and asked what they should do now. Jerry calmly replied that we could still have our planned social night—but not in the auditorium since the bishop had ruled that out. Instead, we would convene in the adjoining kitchen!

I do not think I will ever forget that evening. From beginning to end, our social night was an exhilarating, rollicking success. We sang and clapped and danced. Those who did not have musical instruments used pots and pans from the kitchen to accompany the songs. At the climax of our festivities, we formed a conga line behind the Maryknoll priest playing the trumpet and wove all through the nooks and crannies of the voluminous kitchen. But when all was said and done, the thing that made that evening the most fun was that we had found an alternate, though still daring, way to have our "outlawed" social night. And that helped us to get to know each other much better than by simply sitting in a stuffy auditorium listening to lectures.

When I was returning to the train station for the ride back to Hsinchu, a somewhat humbling incident occurred to remind me of my still fragile grasp of the Chinese language. Feeling a sudden rumbling in my bowels, I urgently asked a station attendant, *Tzeswo dzai nali*?—"Where is the toilet?"

The attendant stared at me, nonplussed.

Assuming I had mispronounced the word for toilet (*tzeswo*), I tried changing its tone from high to low to falling to level tones—all to no avail. Finally, with a desperate motion, I jumped up and down, grasping my backside.

"Oh, you mean *WC*," the attendant said.

~

I enjoy teaching English a few evenings each week. Since my students are smart and like to talk, I am learning quite a bit about Taiwanese customs from them while correcting their English. After class, we sometimes sing songs. On one warm Saturday, we went for an outing at nearby Green Grass Lake. The boys rode bikes, and the girls took motorcycles. At the lake we sang, played games, and did folk dances. We also rowed on the lake in small canoes. Next to the lake was a tall and ornate cream-colored pagoda and a temple cared for by elderly Buddhist nuns. If I understood my students correctly, it seemed this particular temple was venerated because it contained pearl-like crystals miraculously found in the remains of holy monks or nuns after they had been cremated.

Later, some of my English students brought me to Taipei for a visit. Although Taiwan's capital city is not too far away, I had only been there a few times. The students spent the afternoon taking me around to see the sights. Since I had not arranged for a place to spend the night, one of my students insisted I stay in a hotel room that his uncle (a fire chief) could rent for free. It was in a high-class hotel, and I felt like a foreign dignitary staying there. During my entire visit, the students would not let me pay for anything, not even a Coke. Paying the bill evidently gave them "face"—a highly regarded Chinese concept—or else they were simply very generous. More likely, it was related to the Confucian tradition of showing respect to their teacher and being a good host.

~

Although Mandarin is probably not harder to study than any other language, it does take more time to learn. The last few weeks of classes before Christmas break seemed particularly demanding since we were all getting tired. The big thrill for me was finally to begin learning how to write Chinese characters. Before, I was only able to scribble my name in Chinese. Now, I can write forty-five characters from memory. They are not easy to remember, but since writing them is a kind of art, I do not mind the practice. However, I have to be careful. One evening, I practiced writing so much that I continued during my sleep. All night long I dreamed I was writing characters. When I awoke, sadly there was nothing to show for my efforts, and I was exhausted.

As soon as classes ended and Christmas vacation began, I

rode across town on the back of Jean Chenut's motorcycle to accompany Father Klaiser and Bernadette as they visited all the Catholics in their parish. Some 3,500 members of the Taiwan Air Force and their families live in the large walled-in compound near the church. Their grey-cement block homes are positioned very close to each other and surrounded by barbed wire. The red gate in front of each home has shards of glass protruding from the top—not a very welcoming sight, but possibly necessary for security purposes. Anyway, once we entered their gates, each family was as hospitable as could be. During two days of home visiting, I picked up quite a bit of conversational Chinese, mostly just by listening.

One evening, we stayed so late talking and singing at one of the homes we were visiting that we didn't get back to the language school until the wee hours of the morning. As we rode back by motorcycle, Jean pointed out that the villagers were already bringing in vegetables—pulled by water buffalo—to be sold at the soon-to-open morning market. Some older men balanced bamboo poles on their shoulders, from which were suspended two wooden buckets.

"They are carrying 'night soil' from their toilets to fertilize the vegetable gardens," Jean remarked, as I became aware of the stench from the nearby fields.

The weather is getting much colder now, and the bracing Hsinchu wind makes it feel almost freezing. Father Chu gave me a bulky, red quilted Chinese jacket that wards off the cold air, and Bernadette found me some long underwear at the market that keeps me pretty well-insulated. Old Brother Mendiburo, the language school "jack-of-all-trades", spread a heavy cotton quilt on my rattan bed to help me sleep through the cold nights.

Buildings in Taiwan have no interior heating, and the terrazzo walls and floors of the language school soak up the freezing temperature, so we have to find novel ways to keep warm inside, too. Recently, I bought some boxes of little sugar cubes (normally used for coffee) that I pop into my mouth when I am studying on particularly cold days. They give me both warmth and energy.

For Midnight Mass the evening before Christmas, Jerry and I biked out to Father Klaiser's parish with our guitars and attended what Jerry described as "the first guitar Mass in a native parish church in the history of China." The congregation sang Christmas carols as we accompanied them on guitars. But the best part was when Jerry gave the sermon in Mandarin. I could understand most of what he was saying. Afterward, the parishioners clapped their hands to express their appreciation and encouragement to Jerry. I was sure they understood everything he said—and liked what they heard, too.

From Christmas till the new year, it was one big party. Every parish in Hsinchu City had a holiday get-together, and Jerry and I were asked to entertain at them all. At each party, we usually played our guitars and sang the same three songs, while the audience gathered in a circle around us, with the parish priest and his co-workers sitting up front. After one of the parties, Jerry told me that the old priest who was laughing and clapping the hardest after our rendition of "Love Potion Number 9" was none other than the bishop of Hsinchu. I guess that meant he approved of our entertainment.

On New Year's Day, beginning with a folk Mass at 7 A.M., we had five performances, including a rousing party for prisoners at the local youth prison, which is just a few blocks from the social service center. I've spent quite a bit of time at the center during the holidays, and this has enabled me to practice my Chinese with the young workers who congregate there. After three months of studies, I'm finally making a little headway in my communication skills.

Several of Jerry's Jesuit classmates also visited the social center, and I was able to have some nice talks with Paul, my former philosophy teacher, who had arrived together with Jerry on the boat to Taiwan. Some of the other classmates Jerry came over with have already left Taiwan because of various reasons. I think it saddened Jerry to have such close friends go back. In my case there won't be that problem since I had no classmates who came over with me on the boat. I was the only one.

During Christmas holidays, the Fathers at the Jesuit Church in Hsinchu, where most of the American Jesuits stay, invited me to a turkey dinner. Then they handed out presents, and I received a small transistor radio. It was not exactly a surprise because they had asked me beforehand what I wanted for Christmas. The radio is a practical gift since I can turn it on anytime and tune in to Chinese music. One station even plays Western songs, with news of the world in English. Otherwise, I do not get much news except what is printed in the skimpy China Post newspaper, which we all race for in the language school recreation room.

Being out of the country where I grew up gives me a better perspective on world affairs. I can view America from a distance now and see how it is only one of many countries, each important in its own way. I can also see how Taiwan has a significant role to play in the world today.

~

It is not easy getting back to the grind of classes once again after such a fun-filled Christmas break. But Chinese New Year will soon arrive and with it an even longer vacation. Taiwanese workers from the social center often visit me at the school, and this provides a welcome diversion from studies. A few of them might pop up unexpectedly in the evening and take me to town on the back of a motorcycle for a movie and street snacks afterward. I do not usually know what movie we are going to see. Most of them are historical dramas or Chinese kung-fu films, with people flying through the air on invisible wires.

One of Jerry's friends is named Hsiao. He is nineteen and getting ready to go into the Navy. In Taiwan, every male is required to spend at least two or three years in the armed forces. Hsiao is a wood carver who was trained at a workshop run by a Hungarian Jesuit Brother. One day, Hsiao brought me to his small home, crammed among others in a narrow alley, where he lived with his mother. Only a curtain served as the door. The rooms were full of partially carved statues of Chinese deities, Christian Madonnas and saints, and mythical beasts. Hsiao showed me a small and very delicate Chinese figurine he was working on that he planned to send to Jerry's and my mother. He is not only very talented in art, but he speaks Chinese slowly enough that I can understand some of what he says. Jerry is fortunate to have him as a friend.

Hsinchu City has a small American Club that was organized primarily for the U.S. military serving in Taiwan. However, others are welcome, too. Since it is not far from the language school, this club is a popular hangout for the language students and their friends, mostly because it is the only restaurant in Hsinchu where you can get a hamburger. Sometimes they also have ice cream, which is a better option than traveling all the way to town to get an ice cream cone at the only other place that offers one—the exotically named Venus Bakery. But the real attraction of the American Club is the chance to see a free Western movie. I don't go there often, because I try to integrate myself as much as possible into the local culture. But sometimes, on a Friday night, when I hear there will be a good movie, such as *Butch Cassidy and the Sundance Kid*, temptation prevails, and I relax there with my classmates from the language school.

Hans, one of my language school buddies from Switzerland, complains that whenever people in Taiwan see a foreigner, they always point and say *meigwo ren*, which means "American". Hans resents that since he is not an American. He told me about how he once passed a group of children playing marbles on a dirt patch, and when they saw him, they all cried out, "*meigwo ren*". Hans walked over to the children and bent down to draw a map of the world for them in the dirt.

"This is America," Hans said, pointing to one side of the map, "and this is Switzerland," he explained, pointing to the other side of the map. "I am from Switzerland, not from America. I am a *rueishr ren*—Swiss, not a *meigwo ren*—American. Do you understand?"

"We understand", the children replied.

"Good. Well then, goodbye", said Hans.

"Goodbye, *meigwo ren*", said the children.

~

Chinese New Year—the busiest, noisiest, and tastiest festival of the year—has already come and gone. A week before the holiday began, I rode my bicycle downtown to view the revelry, dodging children setting off firecracker rockets, stopping to watch dragon dances in front of temples, and mingling with the masses of New Year's shoppers that clogged the crowded streets.

It seemed all the people in the city were preparing to travel to their ancestral homes, wherever that may be. The Chang family, with whom Jerry lived last year, invited my brother and me to spend Chinese New Year with their relatives in central Taiwan. After taking a packed train to the city of Taichung, we first went to the home of the Changs' "Number Two Brother".

Number Two's real name was Abraham. He and his wife, Sarah, and their little son, Popeye (the only one with a non-biblical name), were devout Christians, members of the Holiness Church. Abraham told me the cornerstones of their faith were a personal relationship with Jesus and helping the needy. We sang hymns together in the early morning, including a Chinese version of "Amazing Grace".

From Abraham's home in the suburbs, we traveled to a chicken farm in the countryside, where Abraham's father was our host. We shared the New Year meal with their family, sitting at a round table with a steaming hot pot in the center, symbolizing family unity. In the evening, Jerry and I played guitars beside the emerald green rice fields under a bright orange sunset. I hope the chickens did not stop laying eggs when they heard us.

The next day, Abraham's whole extended family congregated for another feast at the home of the mother-in-law and her twelve children. I politely ate whatever dish was offered to me, even when I didn't know what it was. Maybe that was better since some of the dishes were a bit strange. Sea slugs, anyone? Then we crowded into the back of an old pick-up truck with youngsters from the family and chugged off to the brother-in-law's home, with the kids singing Taiwanese songs at the top of their lungs.

After traveling several miles from the city, we eventually reached a small valley that was encircled by hills and bordered by banana trees, tobacco plants, and the ever-present rice paddies. There, the matriarch of the family lived in a traditional farmhouse, along with three of her sons and their families.

When we arrived, the Chang brothers reverently introduced their grandmother to us. She was a small, thin Taiwanese woman with sharp, wizened features that commanded respect. She nodded politely and motioned for us to come into the farmhouse.

Feasting in the family compound was like being at a village bazaar. More relatives continued to arrive, children gleefully tossed firecrackers at each other, and turkeys gobbled around the tables, perhaps wondering if they would be next on the menu. Jerry and I were seated at the table of honor in front of the household altar, which contained the revered ancestor tablets. Outside, tables were set up for the other male guests.

The children had their meals in a separate area, while the women ate inside together after serving the others. By this time, most of us were too full to eat anything. But the men had foreseen this and brought plenty of rice wine, which livened up the group considerably.

Finally, it was time to go home. I felt ready to tackle the next round of language studies, refreshed by the humanism I had seen and the hospitality I had been shown. My only concern, I told Abraham as I was leaving, was that we had put our hosts to too much trouble. Abraham smiled, bouncing little Popeye on his knee, and replied, "Nothing can make Taiwanese happier than to have guests." Then he quoted the beginning of the Analects of Confucius: "Is it not delightful to have friends coming from afar?" And with that consoling thought, my memorable first Chinese New Year in Taiwan drew to a close.

~

For an extracurricular activity during this second semester, Father Chu suggested I take a course in Chinese watercolor painting instead of teaching English. Sister Monica Liu, a well-known artist of traditional "scroll" paintings, teaches classes in Chinese art at the nearby Teacher's College. On Friday afternoons, I have been biking over to the college to spend three hours practicing Chinese painting.

I was a bit nervous during the first session since I had never used a Chinese brush before and the class would be in Chinese with me as the only foreigner. But soon I felt right at home. Sister Liu placed the best student in the class next to me in case I needed assistance, and he helped me whenever I ran into difficulties.

There are thirty students in the class, evenly divided between girls and boys. They are all around twenty years old, but appear younger. When the bell rings at the start of class, they stand at attention and bow to the teacher. The students are very kind to me, with some of them explaining the various types of traditional Chinese painting. I am not having much trouble getting used to the Chinese brush. But what is most important is the "life energy" (or *chi*) that the brush strokes must transmit to the paper. This is more difficult to achieve and probably will take years to get right.

Sister Liu asked me to come a half hour before her class started, so I could watch her make a sample painting. Then, during class, I would spend two hours copying her painting, trying to remember how she did it. I liked to stand over her and watch as she painted. She was very fast but delicate. She did not speak much—her hands did all the talking.

In my spare time the past few weeks, I also completed an oil painting. It was of a young Taiwanese boy with his hands in his pockets, looking kind of lost. Perhaps it represented me during my first year in Taiwan. It is easier for me to express myself in oils than with Chinese watercolors. This is because the Chinese scroll paintings have to be copied exactly as they are. There is no room for innovation. That is part of the learning process.

Hsiao, with his hair completely shaved off, returned from the Navy for a week's vacation and he came to see me. He is almost like a younger brother because of his closeness to Jerry. Hsiao said he was pleased that Mother liked the statue he carved for her. In the Navy, he has no time to do wood-carving, so he misses it. He gave me some useful suggestions on how to improve my painting.

Recently, Jerry and I, Father Reed, and five Taiwanese parishioners from the Hsinchu Cathedral have been preparing a traditional Chinese folk song called "The Love Song of Kangding" for a TV talent show at the end of the month. Jerry and I are playing guitars while Father Reed accompanies us on the violin. A talented nun from the Philippines is directing the presentation. At first, we sounded so horrible that I was hoping something might go wrong so we would not have to go through with it. But now we are getting better. I am still uneasy, though, about being on live TV.

This show is quite popular on Sunday evenings, and it seems everyone in Taiwan tunes into it either during or after their dinner.

~

Before I came to Taiwan, I had heard that it is not easy to make good friends with the Chinese, but when it does happen that friendship goes very deep. I told myself then that I would give myself a year to see if I could make a good friend. During my first semester in Taiwan, I met many people and joined several activities, but was not able to find such a friend. Then recently, as my ability in conversation improved, I began chatting with the high school students that board in the student dorm adjacent to mine. They often play soccer with the seminarians and other language students who live there. In contrast, the Jesuit residence where I stay only has a small community of very quiet Jesuits, so it is easy to get isolated from other people.

Tai-hsin, one of the boarders in the student dorm, was recently baptized in our small school chapel. He is a few years younger than I, tall with hair as long as he could legally get away with and a lighthearted, mischievous sense of humor. Having finished high school, he is taking review classes to prepare for the college entrance exam, which he failed in his first attempt.

Tai-hsin invited me to the colorful opening ceremony of Taiwan's annual national athletic games that were held in Hsinchu's new outdoor stadium. We watched the towering figure of Olympic gold-medalist Chi Cheng hold the torch and lead the other runners around the track, her long legs catapulting across the field like an elegant gazelle.

After this outing with Tai-hsin, I went to visit his nearby

home, and he introduced me to his family. Soon, I was meeting his teenage friends, who taught me many slang terms the teachers would not dare let us use in class. Before I knew it, what had seemed almost unattainable was becoming a reality. I was making a friend.

Tai-hsin's parents migrated from Mainland China to Taiwan in 1949 during the great exodus of those fleeing communism, so they are called "Mainlanders". His father is a retired soldier from Hunan. The accents of his parents are very strong, so it is hard for me to understand what they are saying. Tai-hsin has told me all about his family history and showed me his photo album, which is something locals often do when I visit their homes. He spoke openly to me about his family problems and difficulties with studies, as well as the undercurrent of animosity that often exists between those of Mainland descent and native Taiwanese.

Perhaps it was our ease in using Mandarin to converse with each other about almost anything that drew us together. As I felt our friendship deepening, I also sensed a growing "belongingness" to everyone else in Taiwan—as if making one good friend proved I could make friends with others here as well. And that has meant everything to me.

~

I met a Christian lady from the States who has her own small church in Hsinchu. Stuart, an evangelical classmate at the language school, introduced me to her. I had become involved with prayer meetings before I came to Taiwan and have missed going to them for the past year. Stuart said that Helen Gilkerson, the Christian lady, had prayer meetings with university students in her home a couple of times a week. They invited me to join them.

Helen's "church" was simply a large *tatami* room in her Japanese-style home. Looking like a proud grandmother, with sparkling eyes and grey hair tied in a bun, Helen cooked a fried chicken dinner for us before the prayer meeting began. The prayer group consisted of only five students in addition to ourselves, but it was quite moving. Helen played the piano and led her congregation in old-time spirituals. It is hard to describe the atmosphere in her tiny home church, but I certainly felt the presence of the Holy Spirit. Helen said she had left California at an early age, just as I had, and had been ministering to university students for over twenty years. She also conducted English classes, so the prayer meeting was mostly in English.

Soon, Stuart and I began going to Helen's church every Sunday evening for a prayer meeting—and sometimes dinner beforehand, which was an added inducement. When I told our superior, Father Chu, about the prayer meetings, he suggested that I start one in our Jesuit community. After discussing the matter with the other Jesuits, they agreed that having a prayer meeting would be a good idea. So, we decided on the following Thursday.

I was excited about this and prepared some "prayer songs" to teach the others. I brought along my guitar and waited for them to arrive. And waited. But nobody came. I thought at least my superior might attend, but he had a pressing engagement.

After a while, Father Andrés Rabago came hurrying into the recreation room. He is a buoyant Spanish Jesuit, who recently joined our community after being exiled along with other foreigners from Timor in Indonesia, where he did medical as well as pastoral work.

"Am I too late for the prayer meeting?" Father Rabago anxiously asked me.

Dejected, I replied, "No. No one else has come. So, we can't have a meeting."

"Of course we can!" Father Rabago exclaimed, his passionate Basque face a mixture of joy and concern. "Did not Jesus say, 'If two or three are gathered together in my name, I am in their midst'? Well, you and I—that makes two! Let's begin."

I would not say that was the best prayer meeting I had ever attended, but it was certainly the smallest. I could tell Father Rabago was doing everything he could to make me feel the evening was worth it—and not to give up hope.

"Next week, there will be more of us!" Father Rabago assured me.

But, alas, there were not any more attendees the next week. Only Father Chu came for the prayer meeting since Father Rabago had to visit someone in the hospital that night. Father Chu delicately suggested then that we postpone prayer meetings for another time when the community was better prepared for them.

That was fine with me, as long as I could continue going over to Helen's church once a week. Eventually, I grew quite close to this self-effacing, single-minded missionary and introduced her to Jerry, who considered her a "walking Bible" because of her familiarity with the Scriptures. With hardly any funding, a simple home, an old piano, and some good food, she had led her little church for all these years—and only God knows the influence she has had on her students and what the future holds for them.

~

Our school has had several memorable outings. The first trip was to a well-known tourist area north of Taipei called

Yehliu, which has strange rock formations scattered along its coast. Years of waves lapping at the rocky shore have produced a series of eye-popping natural sculptures, each with its own name, like Lover's Peak or the Queen's Head.

Along with Sister Kathleen, one of the young secular-dressed Maryknoll nuns studying at the language school, we were viewing the Queen's Head, wondering how such a large "head" could rest on the slender slice of stone that served as the Queen's "neck". Unfortunately, our contemplation of this natural wonder was constantly interrupted by local women pestering us to buy postcards.

Trying to get away from the vendors, Sister Kathleen and I moved to the next rock formation, only to have the determined saleswomen trail us.

"This is really getting bothersome!" Sister Kathleen grumbled. "Let's walk over to Lover's Peak."

I followed along. But so did the postcard ladies. We tried to ignore them, but to no avail.

"I've got an idea," Sister Kathleen said. "Hold my hand."

"What?" I asked in surprise.

You'll see," Sister Kathleen continued. "Now put your arm around me like this . . ."

We only mimicked Lover's Peak Rock for a moment before glancing behind us to see the postcard brigade scampering away in embarrassment. Actions really do speak louder than words.

Our next excursion was to some Buddhist monasteries built on a high hill called "Lion's Head Mountain", several miles south of our school. Father Yves Raguin, a noted Buddhist scholar, who had done extensive research into Chinese religions, was our guide. I found this trip very interesting because we were learning about Buddhism by actually visiting temples and talking to the monks and nuns who lived there. For lunch, we were served a vegetarian meal. Father Raguin cautioned us to be sure to eat everything on our plates, so as not to offend our hosts or waste their food.

And finally, there was our trip to the talent show in Taipei. By the time we were set to perform "The Love Song of Kangding" on live TV, we had practiced it so much the music was coming out of our ears. But all the hard work paid off, and we tied for first place, with the prize money sufficient to cover the expenses of dinner at a restaurant. After reprising our performance on the dining hall stage at the request of a crowd of tipsy patrons, it will not be easy for me to forget that haunting ballad of moonlight and mountains in the Tibetan town of Kangding.

~

Father Franz Burkhardt, the superior of the Jesuits in southern Taiwan, invited me for a visit during spring vacation. As I rode a train to the countryside of Chiayi, where several Jesuit parishes are located, I watched the concrete homes and industrial factories of the north transform into the verdant rice fields and stately betel nut groves of the south. But the peace and quiet of this scenic ambiance did not last for long.

As soon as I got off the train at the small harbor town of Beigang and tried to find my way to the local church, I was swept up in a vast throng of devotees celebrating what I later discovered to be the annual homage to Matsu, a beloved ancient sea goddess especially revered by Taiwanese fishermen. Scores of red-robed men, some of them on stilts and sporting white-painted faces, ceremonially danced and artfully dodged a barrage of firecrackers tossed by enthusiastic onlookers. A trail of carved wooden deities on ornate thrones borne by burly youths bounced behind in a long, noisy procession. The ensuing smoke and blasts of fireworks were so intense I felt I was witnessing a battle rather than a religious ceremony.

Although viewing this spectacle of local folk religion was fascinating, it was also dangerous. Tightly packed within a dense crowd, there was no protection from the firecrackers that were bombarding me left and right. The other spectators had fortified themselves with motorcycle helmets. Eventually, spotting a cross in the distance, I squeezed into a narrow side alley and followed it until I reached the church.

For the next few days, I accompanied the Jesuits of rural Chiayi as they said Masses in nearby farming villages. I understood absolutely nothing because the dialect in southern Taiwan is Taiwanese, not the Mandarin that I am studying. What a contrast between those sparsely populated Masses, with only a couple of elderly Catholics in attendance, and the tumultuous ceremonies at the Matsu temple only a short, noisy distance away, celebrated by thousands.

"It is during these annual Matsu pilgrimages that I become aware of how few Catholics we have in our area," Father Ricardo Ferreira, a loquacious Argentinian Jesuit, told me. "There is a lot of missionary work to do here. If you want to come and help us in the future, you will be most welcome!"

Not quite ready to make that kind of commitment yet, I asked the Father, "How do you make converts?" It was probably a silly question because only God gives the grace and desire to become a Catholic. But I wanted to know how the missionaries here went about attracting others to the faith, and Father Ferreira had an insight into this.

"First, we make friends," he replied. "Since I like to talk, and God has given me a talent in languages, I speak to everyone I meet. Such unfortunate people—they are too polite to run away from me when I start talking! We become friends on an equal basis. Eventually, they share their problems with me. I share my faith with them. They see how my faith can help with their problems. Then they might want that faith for themselves. That is how converts are made."

It sounded so simple. But of course, it wasn't. Father Ferreira treated all he met as potential friends from the moment he met them. He did not just preach—he showed brotherly love. Although I could not understand what he said to others, I could readily comprehend his kindness toward them. That kind of love went far beyond language.

While taking the train farther south to the port city of Kaohsiung, I reflected on my past few days with the Jesuits in Chiayi. Despite a hard, unrewarding ministry with only a few parishioners, the Fathers there kept up their optimism. Every chance they got, they spent time with the people. But even without a language barrier, I felt those country folk, along with their complex folk religion, were probably not easy to understand. The most important characteristics of the Taiwanese people appeared to be housed deep within their souls rather than on the surface. It would take a long time and a lot of effort to get to know them.

I wish there was more of a chance for me to live with these people, so I could understand them better. At the language school, the students are all "foreigners" like me. True, I have a few friends like Tai-hsin, but I always return from being with them to an environment that is not Chinese.

I want to share more completely in the lives of the people—but I do not know how. This separation from others seems to be my main problem. Of course, such a distance is only natural in the beginning because of the language barrier, but it seems that it should gradually subside. Isn't it about time now?

Many of the churches here, even in the countryside, are often housed in compounds that look more like fortresses with high walls and forbidding gates. Sometimes I feel uneasy staying in them, especially when the simple homes and farms of the country folk are so open and inviting. I wonder if such a separation is really necessary.

~

Continuing my spring break, I went to see Hsiao at the naval yard located farther south in Kaohsiung City, where he was stationed. We walked around the seaport, which reminded me somewhat of San Diego, my hometown. Later, we visited a nearby night market and sampled Japanese *sashimi* and spiced plums from the vendors. Then Hsiao brought me to a worker's center run by the German Dominicans, where I spent the night.

Several Dominican priests lived at the center together with the young Taiwanese workers. During the evening, there was a camaraderie that I had seldom found in Taiwan. For once, there was no "separation". The priests and workers formed one community together. To me, this seemed like an ideal set-up, and I felt very comfortable sharing their lives even for a night.

But the next morning, I did not feel comfortable at all. A terrible pain gripped me in the bowels as I tossed feverishly back and forth on the bed. The young Dominican Father in charge of the center was alarmed and rushed me off to the clinic next door.

"You have a very bad case of food poisoning!" Sister Helga, a formidable, heavy-set German nun growled, without displaying even the slightest trace of sympathy. "What did you eat at the night market yesterday? Raw fish? Unpeeled fruit?"

"*Sashimi* . . . some plums . . . ," I mumbled.

"I thought so!" Sister Helga retorted, glaring at me. "You have to peel anything with a peel on it and cook everything that should be cooked. See that cot over there? You will lie on it for three days. I will prepare your IV."

What Sister Helga seemingly lacked in empathy, she made up for with efficiency. I was out of the clinic the next day—wiser now in the rules of hygiene, which Sister Helga had drummed into me over and over during the course of my short stay. Later, I heard that this highly regarded sister was the first to open a Catholic clinic in Kaohsiung. Lucky for me she was just next door when I needed her.

~

I am sitting on the little balcony of the Chang family's new home, gazing out at a green lotus pond with three lumbering water buffalo chewing on the grass beside it. Along the horizon, a flock of white egrets flies back and forth as if blown by the wind, expanding and contracting like a giant amoeba. The sky is a dark grey, promising rains, but the wind from the south is warm, giving assurance that spring is finally here.

Yes, after repeated invitations, I have finally moved in with the Changs, just as Jerry did two years ago. Although I was not too keen on moving out of the language school, where I have many friends, I will still go there for classes and lunch each day, so there will be some time to see the other students. The neighborhood I live in now is not far from the school. It is a fairly new housing development with about fifty homes. The Changs' house is made of unpainted concrete, attached to all the other identical houses on the same road. But at least there are green fields and a pond in the back—and more importantly, there is no separation from the life of ordinary people and my own.

Staying with a local family has certain psychological benefits since it makes me feel more a part of Taiwanese society than before. As a result, it is easier to identify with the people here. But there are not many advantages to learning the language. That is because the Changs speak the Taiwanese dialect at home among themselves rather than Mandarin. Moreover, Mr. Chang likes to use English to speak with me since he hopes my staying with his family will help him, as well as his three small children, learn English.

From the children, I can pick up some Chinese words and phrases, but not many. They are more intent on wanting me to play with them—and teasing me because of my faulty pronunciation—than helping me learn Mandarin.

Despite the benefits of living with a family, there are some disadvantages as well. For one, I seem to get lonelier here than at the language school. I miss the evenings spent talking with the high school students, who board at the nearby dorm, especially Tai-hsin.

In my heart, after a few weeks here, I am beginning to realize it was a mistake to move out of the language school. Father Chu had cautioned me beforehand that just because Jerry had lived with this family for a year did not mean it was the right one for me. Also, I somehow feel the Changs are disappointed that I do not spend more time speaking English with them. That is the opposite of what I am looking for. I want to practice my Chinese, not speak English. Anyway, there is less than a month before school ends for the year—so I should be able to last until then.

~

A few days ago, Sister Patricia, my usually cheerful classmate, had tears in her eyes during our morning class, and her Mandarin pronunciation was even worse than usual. Federico and Roberta, our other two classmates, who are far more gifted in the language than we, monopolized the class. During a break, I asked Sister Patricia what was bothering her.

"My little religious congregation has dissolved!" she wept. "I was the only one of our Sisters sent to Taiwan, and now the other Sisters in the States have all left the community. There is no one else but me. I will have to go back."

Soon afterward, I said goodbye to Sister Patricia. She had always been attired so properly in her nun's outfit of white and black. But now, as I saw her wearing an ill-fitting secular dress someone had given her, several sizes too big, and lugging her bulky suitcase to a waiting taxi, I too began to weep. I had not realized how attached I had become to this jolly, good-natured nun, who along with me had weathered such obstacles in trying to learn a language that we both struggled with. Yet we had had so much fun in class—and that was due to Sister Patricia. She was probably the reason I made it this far in my language classes.

Now what? I will be at the mercy of the two linguistic geniuses in my class, Federico and Roberta, until the end of the semester—lost without a partner to counter their skills in Mandarin. I am going to miss Sister Patricia. She had become my best friend.

~

School is out for the year—and not a moment too soon! Any longer and I would have had to be carried out of here on a stretcher. I breezed through my final exams by charming the teachers with clever jokes I had learned from Tai-hsin and the mischievous students in his dorm. My teachers laughed so hard that they did not seem to realize how poorly I answered their questions. When one of my private teachers saw how I was struggling with my written exam, she offered to help me write the characters. She said she was afraid she would "lose face" if I failed. Although I declined her proposal, how could I not be grateful for teachers like that?

The Jesuit scholastics at Fu Jen Theologate planned a vacation for us at Sun Moon Lake in central Taiwan, one of the nation's premier mountain resorts. Jerry, who is winding up his year at the social service center in Hsinchu, and his friend John Privett, a scholastic teaching at Fu Jen University, decided to travel to the lake by motorcycle. Jerry let me ride on the back of his beat-up Suzuki, while John fastened our backpacks onto the tandem of his classy Yamaha. The other scholastics in Hsinchu squeezed into the rear of the social service center's creaky old pick-up truck.

Sister Janet, the roughnecked Maryknoll nun who worked at the social center with my brother, drove the truck. As she backed the vehicle out of the center's parking lot onto the busy main road, she asked us to let her know when the coast was clear.

"There are still some motorcycles," I warned her, after a line of cars whizzed by.

"Motorcycles don't count," Sister Janet calmly replied, backing the truck into the street with such force that it sent a band of bewildered motorcyclists swerving for cover.

I remembered her words during our hundred-mile journey to Sun Moon Lake. Arriving in fairly good shape, I had nothing more than a sore bottom. But Jerry caught a bad case of conjunctivitis from the road dust. Fortunately, no trucks backed into us.

All twenty of the Jesuit scholastics and young priests, including theologians, regents, and language students like me, slept in one large room at a teacher's hostel next to the lake. After almost a year, this was the first time I had a chance to get acquainted with the group of Taiwanese scholastics who had been hidden away at the theologate while pursuing their final studies before ordination.

During the next few days, we bathed in the misty lake, hiked in grassy hills, and floated down pristine mountain streams. One day, some of us mustered courage to swim to distant Lalu Island, which rose like a tiny pearl at the dividing line between the "sun" and the "moon" sections of the lake. A worried scholastic paddled behind in case we did not make it.

Our week of vacation climaxed with a sailboat trip to a small Thao indigenous village on the other side of the lake, where we met the tribal chief and several local natives. This was my first time to visit with the original inhabitants of Taiwan, commonly called aborigines. The Thao tribe of Sun Moon Lake is the smallest of nine major indigenous tribes in Taiwan, which together comprise only a fraction (2.5 percent) of the total population.

The villagers I met were friendly and attractive, and I wished my visit with the aboriginal people could have lasted longer. But I will have another chance soon since I signed up for a month-long summer activity called the Mountain Service Program, which will serve a much larger aboriginal tribe called the Tayal. That will begin as soon as I get back from Sun Moon Lake.

Comprised of college students from various Taiwan universities, the Mountain Service Program was founded by a soft-spoken American Jesuit, Father George Donohoe, and organized by a dynamic French-Canadian scholastic, Michel

Marcil. The purpose of the program is to teach tribal children and assist villagers who live in the poorest and most remote areas of the Hsinchu mountains. Working with this group would be an opportunity not only to gain fluency in Mandarin but more importantly to serve the poor. That seems to be the mission to which I have been called.

~

I am here now in the village of Chingchuan, along with four college students from the Mountain Service Program. Getting to this faraway place was an adventure in itself. The only way to go up to the mountain village is by hitching a ride on the back of an empty, early-morning lumber truck heading to the hills to gather logs. Although travel time to Chingchuan from the nearest town should only be a few hours, it takes much longer because the bulky truck has to maneuver around sharp twists and turns on the mostly unpaved road. But I hardly noticed the time or distance. It was the breathtaking mountain scenery that captured all my attention during the journey.

As the truck rumbled deep into the hills, the forest of fir trees lining the road became more and more fantastic. Everything was fresh and green. The towering mountain peaks faded away into mist like real-life Chinese scroll paintings. I ducked my head as the truck swerved, dipped a bit, and then plunged into a narrow mountain tunnel.

After sloshing its way through the tunnel's mud and darkness for several minutes, the truck emerged from the passageway into a bright, sun-dappled rain forest. There, bathed in light and dotting the cliffs like bright flowers in the distance, were the brick and bamboo dwellings of the village called Chingchuan.

When the lumber truck finally pulled to a stop beside a narrow pathway leading down from the main road, the driver pointed to a picturesque church set precariously on a cliff overlooking the river valley below. The other four members of our mountain service team had already arrived at the church and were waiting for me. I pulled my bag and guitar off the truck and stood in the dust of the departing vehicle as it wound its way up to the higher hills.

Before I had a chance to find my way to the church, a bunch of children ran over to me, grabbed my hands, and led me to meet the other teachers with whom I would be working. Then I paid my respects to the parish priest of Chingchuan, who lived above the church where we were staying.

Father Aquilino Miguélez is a kind-hearted and energetic Spanish Jesuit in his early fifties, exuding hospitality. After giving me a tour of the attractive church grounds, he invited me upstairs for coffee. His little rectory only had the barest of essentials. It was plain to see that this priest was more focused on the well-being of others than his own comfort.

One of the first things Father Miguélez told me was how his former church had collapsed in a typhoon.

"Most of this village used to be located by the river. When Typhoon Gloria swept everything away, I was barely able to make it out of the church alive. Three men saved me with ropes, although many more claim now to have done so. We built this new church high on a rock, where it would be safe."

"What year did Typhoon Gloria strike the village?" I asked.

"1963. September 7th to be exact."

Nodding, I realized that was the very day I entered the

Society of Jesus as an eighteen-year-old. Was that a coincidence—or something more prophetic . . . ?

I asked Father Miguélez how he would translate Chingchuan, the name of the village, into English.

"It could be called 'Springs of Flowing Water'," he replied. "Another translation would be 'Fountain of Youth'."

It struck me that this priest appeared quite young for his age. Was this due to the purity of the air and water, the healing hot springs—the "fountain of youth" he had found here in the mountains?

Father Miguélez told me he was pleased that I had joined the Mountain Service Program for this month and assured me I was welcome to come back anytime. He certainly made me feel at home.

"*Mi casa es su casa*—my house is your house!" he said to me warmly in Spanish as I turned to go down the stairs and join the other teachers in our group.

The college students had already organized our classes for the children, so all I had to do was follow their instructions. Each morning, we walked across the swaying suspension bridge overhanging the river to the small wooden school on the opposite side of the village, where we instructed forty children in various subjects. I taught arts and crafts to primary school students and English to those in middle school.

I enjoyed art class and found the students to be very creative. Sometimes they could not follow my drawing example very well, so they used their own imagination. They are good kids—playful and laughing and singing, hardly ever crying or fighting. Maybe this comes from a lack of sophistication. Their lives are rather rough, and they do without a lot—so they probably find joy in little things.

Every afternoon, we went swimming with the children in the cool mountain stream. We fashioned a kind of swimming pool beside the flowing river by blocking part of it with stones. The way the children shouted and jumped off the tall rocks, you would think they would get hurt, but no one has been injured yet.

In the evenings, we visit families or have parties at the church and nearby villages. My happiest times up here are when I am with the youth. They have already taught me how to cook, how to sing their songs, and all about their lives in the village. Although many of them leave for the big cities, a good number still work in the mountains. Very few of the boys make it through middle school, and most of the girls are already engaged by the time they get out of primary school. If I have any charisma, it comes out when I am together with the young people. Whether it is hiking in the hills or swimming with the kids, I am doing things I have not done in years. It is like becoming a child again.

~

During the past few weeks, I have spent most of my free time with the Tayal villagers, exploring their land, learning about their culture, and trying to make friends. The college students, on the other hand, prefer to talk among themselves. Although they often criticize me for spending more time with the villagers than with them, I cannot help it. There is a mystical atmosphere in these hills that is unlike anything I have ever experienced before, and I want to immerse myself in it as much as possible.

Life is simple and natural here—poor, earthy, and real. There are certainly problems, notably poverty and sickness, but these seem to be balanced by the nourishing splendor of an unspoiled environment. The purity of mountains, trees, water, and air—and most of all, the people themselves—makes this an almost timeless place.

The mountains are a water and sunlight world for me. The river runs strong and clear. Children splash in the cool streams while their parents climb peaks to the forests above. Within a small cave, villagers bathe in a natural hot spring.

In the mornings, I watch the sky mingle with the mountain, as mist covers the lazy hills like white blankets over sleeping angels.

When evening comes, the hillside changes into a warm wine and firelight world. Families gather outside their homes to share stories and sing songs. There is always music—either Mandarin pop tunes or traditional aboriginal melodies. The Tayal are excellent singers, and this is most evident during the parties we have for them, which invariably turn into songfests, with the locals competing to see who can sing the best—and the loudest.

~

I met Yawee during my first week in the mountains while we were conducting a youth activity. He was standing outside the church window wearing a bright green shirt and holding a little brown monkey in his arms. He looked about twenty, with wisps of scraggly hair falling over his wide, almond-shaped eyes. I asked him if he wanted to come inside the church and join the other youth, but he replied that only good people went to church—and he was bad. But by the grin on his face, I knew he did not really believe that—and neither did I. So, I went outside the church, and we played with his monkey and talked for a while.

That evening there was a movie shown in the village.

Since television is unknown in these remote mountains, a movie is a momentous occasion, and the whole village was crammed along the main road to watch it. Too bad the film was so boring. Even the locals were snoozing. Soon, I noticed Yawee had come to sit next to me. He was holding out a small glass of rice wine and offered it to me. The wine was smooth but had a strong kick to it.

After a while, we went up to the church grounds and talked, and Yawee told me about his family and life in the mountains. His Mandarin was clear, and his stories were moving, and, like the wine, they had an intoxicating impact on me. I was making my first friend in the mountains.

The next day was a holiday so we had no classes. When Yawee came over to the church and asked if I would like to spend the day visiting the homes of his relatives in the higher mountains, I jumped at the chance. I had been curious about the more traditional life-style of villagers far up in the hills.

After packing a lunch, we climbed a steep path behind the church for several hours before reaching Yawee's ancestral homestead near the peak of a cliff called Bailan. Along the way, I could hear music each time we passed clusters of huts practically hidden away in the dense forest. The melodies wove in and out of the hills like tangled vines that swung from tree to tree. And from each home we passed, the people smiled at us and asked us to come in for a visit.

Yawee proudly showed me where he had planted mushrooms in stacks of old logs. Nearby, there were youngsters, hardly more than children, pulling cumbersome carts of freshly cut bamboo down dangerously narrow paths. We sat and chatted with a group of men working on a *makay*—a pulley machine that transports logs from one side of a mountain to the other.

One of Yawee's uncles welcomed us into his home, which was poor but clean, with a floor of packed dirt and walls made of smoke-blackened bamboo. Japanese *tatami* mats were spread neatly in the sleeping area and treated almost with reverence. Little dogs lay like rags before a small fire in the middle of the floor. Scrawny chickens pecked the earth around our feet. A new baby wrapped in old clothes fell asleep on her father's lap as we conversed in the gradually descending darkness of the evening.

I watched entranced as the firelight danced on the old, wrinkled, deep-souled faces of Yawee's grandfather and his great-uncles, etched with the knowledge of their land and the rhythm of its soil and the produce the earth brought forth. And I gazed in wonder at the gaunt, peaceful faces of the old women, tattooed with a black "V" from ears to chin, which must have been a traditional sign of beauty in the days of their youth.

There were the friendly faces of fathers and mothers, greeting us with a glass of hot water cupped in their calloused hands, offering a meal and a place to sleep after a long journey—and even toothpaste in the morning.

There, too, were the bright faces of youth, sparks of fire highlighting their freshness as they talked softly of their lives and loves and hopes—facing a world outside that would probably be much harsher than the mountains they had known. I thought of the courage they would need to confront such a world.

And their faces—the children's—were always there, always the first to be there, looking right into you and you into them and loving what you saw.

We were sitting in this way around the small fire on the earthen floor as the time passed (although there seemed to be no time) when somehow, from somewhere, a meal appeared. We moved to a round table overflowing with delicacies I had never tried before, such as flying squirrels, wild mushrooms, and rats (yes, rats!).

Yawee's uncle served us chicken boiled in rice wine, and soon once shy faces emerged from the dark corners of the room and joined us with songs and laughter.

I learned how to say my first phrase in the Tayal language: "When I am together with you, I am happy." But you do not need words to say that.

Yawee told me about his family. He said at one time his relatives had been fairly wealthy, but bad luck had caused his father to lose most of their land and money. They had become poor and now had to work hard hauling bamboo down from the hills in order to have enough money to live. After Yawee's father died, his mother remarried, and now most of the people in these hills were his relatives.

That night, I slept soundly on a *tatami* mat in one of the bamboo homes. Early the next morning, after a breakfast of leftovers from the night before, Yawee and I started hiking back down to the main village. We soon reached a spot where there was no trail—only a grassy slope in the midst of the fir trees.

"Let's go this way," Yawee said. "I want to show you something."

"What?"

"My father."

Yawee led me through some wet brush until we came to a clearing in the forest.

"There," he pointed. On the ground was a rectangular grave drawn with stones. A small wooden cross was at the head of the grave, and at the foot there was a beer bottle and a wine glass half-filled with rainwater.

Yawee stooped down to pull weeds from the soil around

the rocks. I helped him. After a while, he stood up, bowed his head, and prayed. Then he pulled out his cigarettes and lit one. We stood there for a few more minutes.

"My father . . . ," Yawee said softly as we turned to leave. Then he stopped, glancing at his cigarettes. Slowly, he went back to the foot of his father's grave and placed the pack of cigarettes next to the beer bottle and the wine glass. Then we walked down the hill together.

When we reached the church, the other teachers in our mountain service team were not happy about my trip. They said I had stayed too long.

"We only have a month here, and when it's over we won't return," one of the teachers said. "There is still so much work to do."

"Maybe I will come back here to live someday," I answered, almost under my breadth.

The teachers stared at me curiously and were silent. I wondered, too, at what I had just said. It was true; there was still so much to do, so much to learn. It could take a lifetime . . .

~

One day during our last week in the mountains, we were roused from a drowsy afternoon class by the sight of a familiar-looking creaky old truck barreling down the narrow dirt pathway that led to the church. It was the indomitable Sister Janet from Hsinchu's social service center, driving a truckload of young Taiwanese workers crammed in the back.

Alongside Sister Janet was a welcome figure I had not seen for some time—my brother Jerry!

When Jerry climbed down from the truck, we both laughed at each other's beards. Neither of us had ever grown a beard before—but now, unknowingly, we both had one at the same time. We thought this might help other people to tell us apart. Instead, we looked even more alike. Sister Janet said we resembled the Smith Brothers on cough drop boxes. Actually, my beard was fuller than Jerry's, but his had a red tint—so we did not look *exactly* the same.

Although Jerry only spent a day in the mountains, there was still time for us to sing for the children and go for a swim.

After bathing in the river, we sat on an overhanging boulder. Jerry asked me if the Mountain Service Program had gone well. I told him everything went fine, although my perspective was different from those of the college students. They were more focused on seeing concrete results than I was. For me, friendship with the people was the greatest priority rather than simply accomplishments.

Jerry reminded me that without being in a group, such as the Mountain Service Program, it would not have been possible to have such a successful summer school and do all that we did. The group helped us to achieve our purpose more than any individual effort could have done. As usual, my brother's words of wisdom gave me something to think about. But one thing was for sure, I would be coming back to these mountains—making more friends and trying to do something for the people as well—even if I came back by myself.

~

I am in the midst of my annual eight-day retreat at a church in Wufeng, not far from the village where I worked in the Mountain Service Program. It is the first time I have made a retreat on my own, and both my heart and soul are full of thoughts and inspirations. Today, on my twenty-fifth birthday, I want to gather some of these thoughts together.

It is impossible to express how much this summer with the mountain people has meant to me. I had the experience of falling in love, not with just one person or a few friends, but with a whole tribe. I learned much more from the people than I ever could have taught them. And I found the face of Jesus in them. Through their affection and goodness and simple way of life, these poor people radiate Christ, so gentle and humble and poor. In a special way, Christianity seems to be a religion for the lowly, the little ones who might feel their need for God more than those who are well off.

Now, from the bottom of my heart, I truly thank God for bringing me to Taiwan. He has given me—even for this short period of time in the mountains—something I had not counted on or expected to receive. I already knew I was attracted to the poor. But now, in drawing me so closely to such people, I see how God has truly called me to be poor like Jesus and his little ones, who are also poor.

The Mountain Service Program, besides being such a rich experience, also taught me my limitations. It was not easy working with the college students in my team or coherently expressing myself in Chinese. Now I feel the need not only to study more Chinese, but to deepen my prayer life so God can accomplish what He wants through me. It is not enough merely to draw people to myself. I can give very little. But Jesus, to the extent that He lives within me, can give so much more to others through me. I can only bring others to God if I am more aware of how He personally draws me to Himself.

Three Jesuits from Spain have been working in this mountain district for many years. Besides Father Miguélez in Chingchuan, there are also Father Gerardo Del Valle and

Brother Francisco Yerro here in the parish of Wufeng, where I am staying now. I am impressed by their total dedication to the people. From studying the local language to learning the Tayal way of life, these shepherds of the Faith have not only guided their flock but have become very much *like* them.

Maybe someday God will choose me to be a priest for the mountain people, although I could never fill these Jesuits' giant shoes.

~

Since my month with the Mountain Service Program, I have returned several times to Chingchuan, and each time has been a unique experience filled with unforgettable moments. It is such a joy to share the lives of such people.

A while back, after a big typhoon that washed out the winding mountain road leading up to Chingchuan, I wanted to bring some sacks of bread for the mountain people, but I dreaded the eight-hour trek. To my surprise, I met a group of some fifty villagers at the foot of the hill, returning with food from the city to take back home. Naturally, the people helped me carry up the sacks of bread. However, along the way, they helped themselves to the large Chinese buns inside the sacks. The sacks grew lighter as we grew nearer to the village, and by the time we reached Chingchuan, they were practically empty. But we had fun singing and laughing along the way, so it was worth it.

In early fall, I returned to the language school for my second year of Mandarin studies, boosted by a new motivation. The past summer had taught me how much more I need to learn. Class times are shorter this year, with more room for private study. Now, I only have three hours of private classes per day, but with six different teachers. Each has his or her own particular emphasis or accent. Most are quite sensitive and understanding. They have all invited me to their homes for dinner on various occasions.

Our Jesuit community this year includes Father Chu, the superior, a priest and two brothers from Spain, and one Italian priest. The five scholastics come from the Philippines, Spain, France, Mauritius, and the U.S. Compared with other students here, the Jesuits are probably the most studious. Except for me, they all excel in learning Chinese.

~

Last weekend, I visited both the Protestant and Catholic service centers for aborigines in Taipei. There are around three thousand young aborigines who come from poor and remote mountain areas to find work in Taipei. Often, they are exploited or cheated into doing the wrong kind of work. The centers help them get settled with a place to stay. I also took a short trip to an agricultural high school for aborigines located in the mountains of central Taiwan.

I wanted to take a look at these places so I could choose somewhere to work next year after finishing language school. It would probably be best to have a job that would help me to practice Chinese. I would like to serve the aborigines, but I am not sure where that should be yet. In the mountains, I could help the parish priest and also teach English in the junior high school for aborigines. In Taipei, I could work at one of the centers. In another mountain area, I could teach in an agricultural school. I still have time to look around. There are even poorer aboriginal areas I have not seen yet in the eastern part of Taiwan.

At the Protestant aboriginal center for students. I once

again met Kimbo, a young aborigine from the Puyuma tribe in southern Taitung. He was recovering from a motorcycle accident that had disrupted his studies. I had watched him perform a few weeks earlier at a folk concert in Taipei, so I was happy to see him again. Kimbo played his guitar and sang some aboriginal songs for me that almost left me speechless by the power of his deep and beautiful voice.

Jerry and I see each other every so often whenever I go to the Fu Jen theologate in Taipei, where he is now studying. He showed me a small book he wrote on group dynamics, which was translated into Chinese. His classmates are all friendly to me. My favorites are the five Taiwanese scholastics who are my age. I seem to fit in best with that group.

Recently, we finished two days of exams and are now enjoying a ten-day Christmas vacation. Everyone needs it. I want to use this time to write some stories and then go up to the mountains after Christmas.

We had a lively Christmas Mass at the language school, followed by an informal party and dinner. Father Chu said the Mass half in Chinese and half in English, while the students sang hymns in Chinese, French, Dutch, Spanish, Italian, and English. We had practiced a long time for the Mass, and it was very moving. For such a special occasion, I put on my father's old blue tie that I always wear whenever a tie is required, which has been about twice over here. At the Christmas party, I sang and debuted on an electric guitar.

~

I was in the mountains for four days during our Christmas break. When I crossed the suspension bridge leading to the primary school where I taught last summer, I was almost mobbed by most of the school's three hundred students. They came running over to me, shouting at the top of their lungs, "Good morning, Teacher Ding!" Later, I visited friends and families, which is always easy to do in the mountains because everyone welcomes me and nobody is in a hurry except for the parish priest, Father Miguélez, who was obviously overworked at Christmas.

I can get along with any priest if he loves God, loves his people, and at least *likes* me. Father Miguélez excels in all three of these qualities and has taught me a lot about "becoming a Father". In many ways, the priest is responsible for the happiness and well-being of his parishioners. For instance, on Christmas day, Father Miguélez juggled two weddings and two deaths, alternating between celebrating with the people and comforting them.

After returning to school, we had our final written exam for the semester. I wrote a five-hundred-character essay on the joys and sorrows of my Christmas experience in the mountains. Although the composition was neat and correct, I had to look in the dictionary to see how at least four hundred of the five hundred characters were written. That was frustrating. Too bad I do not have a photographic memory like Federico and Roberta.

~

An aboriginal boy I met from another mountain area other than the one I usually went to invited me to his village for Chinese New Year. He was the only aborigine from his district to get into college and was now in his last year of studies. I spent four days hiking with him and spending the night in different villages with poor families. At the end of the hike, I was getting tired and a little sick from all the food and rice wine. You have to be polite and eat what is offered since this is the one time of year that the mountain people not only have enough to eat but feast abundantly even if it takes the rest of the year to pay for it.

Later, I went up to Chingchuan, where I spent the remainder of the Chinese New Year's vacation, and that was more restful because I knew everyone and felt at home. All the teenagers returned for the New Year from their schools or jobs in the city, so the village was alive with merriment. I am getting closer now to these young people, and they are becoming like brothers and sisters to me.

The life of a country priest, or, in this case, a mountain priest—that direct pastoral work—is very appealing to me. Most seminarians or young priests over here do not seem very interested in such work, but I like it because it provides an opportunity to become closely involved in the lives of Taiwan's poorest people. The parish priest knows the names of all his parishioners, their relationships, their problems, where they are laboring and what kind of work they do. He is there when they are born, marry, get sick, or die. At various times, he can be a doctor, social worker, teacher, or counselor. I can hardly imagine a way of life as close to the hearts of the people as that of a parish priest, especially in such rugged hills as these.

When I go up the mountains, I usually hitch a ride on an empty lumber truck. On the way back down the hill, the truck is so full that I must straddle the logs piled on top. Rocking back and forth to the sway of the truck is like riding an elephant, I imagine, and sometimes as scary as being on a roller coaster, especially on the treacherous turns in the road.

In the city, I am more comfortable riding my trusty, rusty bicycle. It is slow, but it gets me to places in one piece. For longer distances I usually take the bus. Trains are often confusing, and I am afraid if I catch the wrong one, I will not be able to get off. But the trains here are very nice. They range from the cheap slow train (or the cattle car, as we affectionately call it) to the expensive fast train with wall-to-wall carpeting, soft music, and three choices of tea. (I have not taken the fast train yet, but that is what I have heard it is like.)

~

When Father Provincial Michael Chu came to the language school for a visit, I told him about my visits with the aborigines and how much I have treasured the moments shared with them in the mountains. He asked me what I would like to do when my language studies were finished, and I mentioned the possibility of teaching in a high school for aborigines. Since those schools were all government-run, not Catholic, I was afraid he might object. On the contrary, Father Chu thought it was a good idea and said if there was any way he could help me to secure a job, he would be happy to do so. (This provincial is so accommodating he makes the vow of obedience too easy!)

One of the reasons Father Provincial liked the idea of me teaching in a government-run school was because I would be able to influence the teachers and administrators, as well as the students, in their attitudes toward the Church. If this works out, I will be very happy. I have confidence the Holy Spirit will guide me to the proper place.

So far, this Spirit seems to be making it more clear what direction I should take. The life of a simple parish priest in the mountains is increasingly attractive for me, and my thoughts on this have been ratified by the positive response of my superior and the encouragement of friends. Some of the parishioners in Chingchuan said they hoped I would come back after my ordination and be their priest. If God helps me and I remain confident in Him, I hope to do that.

Jerry visited me for a few days, and we have had some long talks together. He told me how his deepening prayer life has led him to a closer relationship with others. We are both experiencing the depth of what friendship means—the love of God and people that merge mysteriously into one.

Someone said that the death of a Jesuit is never a sad affair. But for me and thousands of others, the death of Father George Donohoe was very sad indeed because he was so loved by the students he taught. Father Donohoe was the founder of the Mountain Service Program I had worked with last summer. He and around 120 students were taking a long hike over the mountains to the East Coast of Taiwan. On the fifth day of the hike, Father Donohoe was walking on the side of the road with two other students by his side when a logging truck came up the hill and either hit him with wood sticking out from the back or caused Father Donohoe, who was almost deaf, to back away and topple over the cliff to his death some seventy feet below.

The students gave the priest artificial respiration for four hours, but it was to no avail. At the funeral, there must have been over a thousand university students gathered at Taipei's biggest church. As the Mass finished, they broke into a song that was Father Donohoe's favorite. They had sung it on the hike, and now they sang it over and over and over again at the funeral. The song was called "Everybody Ought to Know Who Jesus Is". When I finally left the church, the students were still singing it.

There were also two other accidental deaths of priests. The Swiss pastor who had started the church on little Orchid Island died in a car crash on the east coast, and a young Spanish priest who had just been ordained was killed by a motorcyclist in Chutung. It is hard to understand why God would take these two priests—one so needed by his people and the other even before he could begin his priestly ministry. Hopefully, from these deaths there will arise new life.

~

There are only a few more months before I graduate from Chabanel Language Institute. I have added a short course in Japanese that will be useful for working with aborigines because the elders can still speak that language. In Mandarin, I am about at the level of a rather dumb seventh-grade Taiwanese student. We are studying the seventh-grade textbook now, which is very difficult. Many characters are only written but never used in speaking, particularly Confucius' writing. Even the characters are written differently from those used today.

My friend Yawee from Chingchuan just went into the Marines. Before he left, he invited me to a going-away party with his large extended family in the mountains. During the meal, all the older men gave speeches on the glory of serving the country. Yawee had to toast each guest with rice wine while being careful not to get too drunk in the process. At the end of the three-hour feast, everyone was tipsy, if not downright bombed. People sang all through the meal, which was served on *tatami* mats in every room of the sprawling family farmhouse.

Last week, Father General Arrupe came from Rome for his first visit to Taiwan. He talked to the younger scholastics, the parish priests, and those working in social action. Jerry and I had our pictures taken with him, one on each side. He turned to us and playfully exclaimed, "Oh, so you're those two brothers!" He said he wanted a copy of the photo.

Father Arrupe stressed the importance of our unity as Jesuits, our mutual acceptance of one another despite age, nationality, or ideas, and our personal prayer. I was most impressed when he told us, quoting Saint Ignatius, "We must do the best we can, and when all is done leave the rest to God." Then he added, "Now 'the rest' is everything!" He said he had total trust and confidence in God and in the Society's men. That made me feel very secure. Seeing how weak we are, and how much we must do, I think of Saint Paul when he said, "I am strongest when I am weakest."

For myself I would not want to do anything at all without first talking it over with Christ. I want to rely on God for everything, from the smallest thing to the biggest. To me, that seems to be what a life of obedience means—complete dependence on the action of the Holy Spirit. But although this is what I want to do, there are in fact so many times I am afraid I do not do it. Yet, without God in my life not one of my actions has any meaning at all.

Chinese studies seem to be getting harder as the time till graduation gets shorter, and the pressure is intensifying. Most of our classes are private now, so I spend more time alone in my room studying. Besides my transistor radio, there is little to distract me. The other priests and scholastics in the community seem satisfied studying alone and doing things by themselves and are not much company.

Several months ago, most of the Jesuits on my floor of the language school began moving out, one by one, to other churches or schools, leaving me alone in this wing of the building. And my room is at the very end of a long hallway. Believe me, the time of day I look forward to the most is when the maintenance man comes to sweep the hallway each morning. I rush out of my room to have a few words with him—the only human being around—before he goes on to the next hallway. It is a pretty lonely existence here.

Since my friend Tai-hsin failed his college entrance exam again, he had to go into the Army, and I do not have his companionship anymore. Although the high school students are only in the next building across the patio, I guess they are focused on their studies, too, since I rarely have a chance to be with them. Jerry is busy now studying theology in Taipei. My friends in the mountains are far away. And I am increasingly burdened with the seemingly impossible task of learning how to write and remember thousands of complicated Chinese characters, half of which are seldom even used today.

I am afraid I am losing touch with the present. My mind is increasingly crowded with memories of past experiences with the poor, or my future hopes of serving them. I am not sure I can make it through the next few months if all I do is study day and night by myself at the end of this abandoned hallway. There is something so powerful fuming inside of me, and sometimes I feel it is going to explode at any moment. I can hardly remember feeling such loneliness before.

~

Jerry and three other scholastics at Fu Jen Theologate formed a folk band with a Chinese name that means something like "Holy Wind". Last week, they invited me to go with them to Taipei and perform for an audience of orphans, disabled children, and elderly people. We wore fancy shirts and hippy beads. The stage was festooned with colored lights to give the show a more spectacular effect. Afterward, we sang again at a center for the blind. Then we went to a youth activity at the Jesuit-run Tien Student Center.

Tien Center's large, elegant auditorium was full of Taiwanese students dancing to folk music from different countries. Jerry walked over to some students and began talking with them, while I stood and watched quietly off to the side. I was tired from the band performances and worn out from Chinese studies. Moreover, I felt bored—as if the meaning of my life was slowly draining out of me. This now seems ironical, since we had been performing for the disabled, the orphaned, and the blind—people who were very much in need.

And then something disturbing happened to me.

The students began dancing a folk dance to the tune of *Cielito Lindo*, which had been a favorite of the Mexican migrant workers I had worked with during the summer I spent with them in Oregon—when? Only a few years ago, during a summer break from my philosophy studies. Sharing the lives of the migrant workers, picking crops with them in the fields, living the life of a poor migrant myself—that had been one of the happiest, freest periods in my life. And now? Where had it all gone? How had I gotten from there to here?

My heart became heavy with the desire to be back once again with those migrants. Why had I left them? Was it to be buried in endless Chinese language studies? To live alone in a half-abandoned language school like I had been doing for the past few months?

And now, as I watched the smartly dressed students dancing to a familiar Mexican melody, in my mind they morphed into poor, shoeless migrant children playing in the dirt of the campsite where I had once lived and worked. As the auditorium appeared to circle around and around in tune with the music, I felt dizzy and ready to collapse. Then, stumbling out of the auditorium to the chapel on the opposite side of the lobby, I fell to my knees and burst into tears.

Why am I here? I cried out to God. That was the question—the prayer—that consumed me. Why—when over half the world is poor—why can I not be with them? I felt shattered and lost. But most of all, I felt it had been a huge mistake for me to come to Taiwan. I should have gone to a poor country. Is that not what I wanted? Why did God bring me here? Why?

Sometime later, Jerry finally found me in the chapel, sobbing.

"Do you want to go with me back to the theologate?" he inquired quietly. He did not even ask what was wrong. It was as if he knew.

Two years of intense language studies can affect people in different ways. I had heard of one student who went mad in his second year of Chinese studies, only to be carried out in a straitjacket and driven to the airport, where he was put on a plane for home. At least that had not happened to me. And I would have been too stubborn to go back even if it had. But I felt like I must be having some kind of nervous breakdown. The loneliness and meaninglessness had been building up. Jerry saw it, too.

We took a bus to the theologate, and later that night I told Jerry how I felt. I just kept repeating that I must have made a mistake. I should have followed my heart's desire. I had wanted to be poor with the poor, but I was not able to do so. Jerry understood.

"There will come a time for that," my brother told me soothingly. "God will answer your prayer."

~

The first thing I did after getting back to the language school was to move out of it. I felt any community would be better than no community. So, I moved over to the student dorm next door. My only regret is that I did not do it six months earlier because it is so much better here. People are friendly and like to talk and be with each other. There are fifteen foreign students, mostly young priests or seminarians, and eighteen Taiwanese students in senior high school. It is like the difference between night and day. I am having fun here, and my spirits have improved. Even though there is more noise and many more distractions, I think I can get twice as much studying done as before.

The Taiwanese students are always in and out of our rooms talking, strumming the guitar, playing records, and asking us questions. I learn a lot from them, too, about what it means to be a youth in Taiwan. In fact, the idea of my moving to the dorm had come from the students themselves. They could not understand why I stayed over in the other building all by myself. Five of them had come over and helped me haul my belongings to the new building. Now it looks like my last few months of school here will be pleasant ones—and I will survive after all.

The second thing I did was to travel. To figure out the most suitable work for me to do during the coming year, I went all around Taiwan during Easter vacation, visiting with various priests working with aboriginal tribes. What impressed me the most was the beauty of the island, the incredible friendliness of the Taiwanese people, and the hard, challenging life of the priests and nuns as they work in often tough conditions, giving everything for the people and asking nothing for themselves.

First, I spent a few days in Pingtung, the most southern city in Taiwan. There was a hospital there for aborigines and also a national teacher's college, where a friend of mine from Chingchuan went to school. In his dorm, I sang and played the guitar and had a good time with aboriginal students I met from all across Taiwan. They said I was the first foreigner who had ever visited their school. That evening, my friend and his friends took me to a Chinese sword movie. Afterward, we ate fried snails and drank plum wine at a sidewalk café somewhere along the streets of the small town.

The next day I went to visit my friend Yawee, who was stationed at a Marine training camp in Pingtung. Some officers helped me locate him at the far end of the camp, where he was just finishing guard duty. As we were talking, Yawee asked if I would like a drink from his canteen. I took a small sip and quickly realized he had filled the canteen with rice wine instead of water. He told me that drinking wine made the long hours of guard duty go more quickly. Why do I feel Yawee might develop an alcohol problem later on—or maybe already has one?

In the afternoon, I took a winding, five-hour bus ride over the high mountains from Pingtung to the east coast of Taiwan. Upon arrival in the city of Taitung, I began looking for a church. Strange how I never search for hotels. There is always a place to stay in a church if you are a priest or seminarian. People welcome you as one of their own.

In each part of Taiwan that I have visited, priests of different nationalities usually live and work together. Their national characteristics and approaches are readily apparent to me. For instance, the Spanish like to be with other Spaniards and usually have their special "Spanish table" wherever they eat. Americans do not seem to be as cliquish as others and have much in common with Taiwanese. However, some of them tend to be insensitive and offensive to the local people. Germans appear authoritarian but are gifted in organizing big projects. Many of the French are passionate and philosophical. I find the Swiss to be the gentlest and kindest.

In Taitung, the main city on Taiwan's southeastern coast, the Swiss priests and brothers treated me wonderfully. They drove me around the town, proudly showing me their many ministries, such as parishes, tribal centers, and technical schools for aborigines. Taitung is one of the most beautiful and interesting regions of Taiwan, but few visit the area because of the difficulty in traveling on the mountainous roads and the time it takes to get there. It is sparsely developed, with hardly any factories and no television reception there yet. Six aboriginal tribes are spread across the various townships in Taitung, in addition to the much smaller ethnic Taiwanese population.

I spent a few days with Father Karl Stahli, a ruggedly handsome and charismatically cheerful Swiss priest, at his parish of Paiwan aborigines along the eastern shoreline. Father Karl cares for over a dozen villages scattered in the hills behind his main church, most of which can only be reached by walking. Only thirty-five years old, he is very close to his parishioners, often inviting them to his home for dinner so his church can have a family atmosphere. It would be hard to find a more challenging yet rewarding life than the one I witnessed in those inspiring days with Father Karl.

One evening during my visit, a parishioner asked Father Karl to drive him to Taitung City, which was over two hours away, to fill his propane gas tank. While they were gone, I played cards with the parishioners. For the first time, I learned about the southern aborigines' habit of chewing betel nuts, which not only turned their lips red but also stained the ground when they spit it out. Fortunately, during our card game, they spewed their scarlet sputum into plastic cups.

Soon, some men brought down a sick man from the higher mountains who needed to be taken to the hospital. When Father Karl returned from the city, tired and ready for bed, he saw the sick man. It was in the middle of the night, and probably the last thing he wanted to do was drive back to the place he had just come from. But Father Karl promptly took the man to the hospital, returning home at 3 A.M. He later told me it happened all the time. He said he sometimes selfishly thought of selling his car, but then the people in the higher villages would have no transportation when there were emergencies.

The next day, we had Mass in one of Father Karl's parishes, followed by a community lunch. After everyone had drunk a little rice wine, they began singing and dancing in a circle. Then a bunch of men rushed over to me, pushed me into an armchair, and tossed the armchair up into the air, cheering. Evidently that was their way of greeting a guest.

That evening, we went to another village of perhaps two hundred thatched houses covered with palm leaves. One family was raising silkworms, and I watched as they fed them. They placed mulberry leaves on top of the worms, and in a matter of minutes the silkworms had consumed them. You could even hear the insects chewing their leaves. I was told the worms eat for four days straight, then sleep for two.

Since this village recently got electricity, many homes have loudspeakers. Father Karl told me there is a black market for planting mushrooms in government trees, and sometimes the police come to check on this. When villagers spot the police approaching, they use loudspeakers to warn those who are planting mushrooms that the inspectors are coming. The warning is spoken in the Paiwan language, which the police cannot understand. As a precaution, the village nurse makes the announcement, so the police assume she is talking about health instructions—and the mushroom trade flourishes.

~

I think I have finally found a job for the coming year. If it all works out, I might be able to work on little Orchid Island, located some distance off the east coast of Taiwan and populated by several thousand aborigines, prisoners, and soldiers. It is said to be the poorest and most isolated region in Taiwan. Two years ago, a junior high school was begun on the island, and next year it will have 150 students. Perhaps I will be able to teach there.

At a church in Taitung, I met Father Hans Huser, who was assigned as parish priest of Orchid Island after the recent death of the former pastor. He was helping the principal find teachers for the island's new junior high school. When I told him I would like to teach there for a year, he told me that was the answer to his prayers. He wrote to the principal of the school, and I am now waiting for a reply.

What would make working on Orchid Island even more challenging is the fact that Father Huser would not usually be living on the island. He has other parishes in Taitung, where he spends most of his time. I would be there by myself. For some reason, this does not bother me. Maybe being alone would draw me closer to the people.

I am putting all this in the hands of God and my provincial because only they know the best place for me. But I am earnestly praying that God will choose me to be with these people and give me the wisdom and strength to serve them. If I should go, it would be like a dream come true. But I am fully aware of the hardship that is part of this mission. I do not fear the suffering because I know that God will be with me. My only fear is that I might not be able to give everything for Him. But I guess I don't really fear that either because I have placed my confidence in God.

After leaving Taitung, I continued by train up the east coast to Hualien and then to Taipei by bus, edging perilously along the narrow road above the ocean on the northern tip of Taiwan—a journey not recommended for the weak of heart.

This round-the-island trip gave me a chance to see some of the beauty of Taiwan and experience its different cultures. More importantly, I could witness firsthand the extraordinary work that so many priests and nuns were doing. The areas of Taiwan I visited during my trip were not those that most tourists see. I did not stop at any tourist sites or buy souvenirs. What I was looking for went deeper than that. I wanted to discover the heart of Taiwan. And wherever I went, Taiwan's people welcomed me—with their hearts.

Back at the language school, I am still enjoying the experience of living in a dorm with Taiwanese students. They are certainly a studious group, sometimes going to bed very late and then waking at 2 A.M. to prepare for their exams. Still, they know how to have fun and let off steam.

~

The semester is drawing to a close now, and most of us are getting tired of studying Mandarin, except Federico and Roberta, who are still as enthusiastic about the language as they were at the beginning. Unable to keep up with them, I left their class long ago. Although I am busy with studies during the day, after dinner my room has become a sort of social center for the Taiwanese students boarding here. I am beginning to notice an individuality in these students, who had before seemed so similar and drab in appearance, with identical short haircuts and military uniforms required by law. I am learning about their different personalities and feelings—and also their complaints.

The students have high expectations of priests, especially about how they should be kind to others, sensitive, and helpful. But they notice some priests who are just the opposite, acting so high and mighty that they scare the students. I realize these young Taiwanese do not expect a lot from the Church in terms of what can be done for them—but a smile or kind word from one of the Church's representatives might help. When people in Taiwan talk to me, most of them smile. Even if their pleasant countenance might not always be completely sincere, such an endearing custom shows respect for others. The locals can be critical of foreigners who display a bad temper or lack of courtesy.

A few days before school ended, I went to Taipei again to perform with Jerry and his band. We sang Peter, Paul, and Mary favorites along with our usual "love potion" song. The performance was a fundraiser for this summer's Mountain Service Program. Unlike before, I was in high spirits after the performance—because I was pretty sure of my future.

After returning from Taipei, I took my final exams and bid a fond farewell to my teachers. During the next few days, several teenagers I knew in the mountains came down to see me. Invariably, they would want me to take them to a movie since there are no theaters in the mountains. So, to celebrate my graduation from Chinese language school, I watched four kung-fu movies in a row, which wore me out even more than my final exams.

~

Father Provincial gave me the final okay to teach this coming year on Orchid Island. At first, he thought it would be better for me to work where there were other Jesuits, but after explaining how I desired to live with the poorest people in Taiwan, he agreed to let me go. In fact, he said he wished he could go with me! I know it would be easier for him if I remained in mainland Taiwan. That is why I could hardly believe it when he agreed to my request.

Although I am looking forward to this experience as something very challenging, right now I am still a little scared. I guess it is the fear of launching into the unknown. But if I let fear guide me, I will never do anything. I want to trust in God, who has guided me to this point. Once I get settled on the island and make some friends, I know I will be all right. The aborigines on Orchid Island are said to be even more friendly and welcoming than the other tribes in Taiwan.

The only other foreigners on Orchid Island are an elderly Protestant woman from Canada, who has lived there for a number of years, and a young Swiss volunteer named Elizabeth, who does medical work and teaches the islanders how to carve souvenir boats for tourists.

About two years ago, before I arrived in Taiwan, Jerry visited Orchid Island on a fishing boat, along with some priests, seminarians, sisters, and nurses. He mailed me photos he had taken of the people of Orchid Island, and I was struck then by their poverty and still primitive life-style. At that time, the government restricted most visitors, and the island has opened up to non-residents only during the past year. A typhoon had prevented Jerry's medical team from returning to Taiwan on schedule, so they ended up rationing food till the waves were smooth enough for a fishing boat to come and take them back. Later, a runway was constructed on the island, with a small plane flying there whenever weather permitted.

~

To my chagrin, after I had packed my belongings and traveled to the Bethlehem Mission Society's center in Taitung, Father Huser sadly informed me that the teaching job I had been looking forward to at the Orchid Island junior high school was no longer available because the principal did not want a foreigner teaching at their school. It seems he felt I might unduly influence the students to prefer my country and its way of life over their own.

I was unhappy to hear this decision and confused about what to do next. I prayed to God for guidance. Later, the Sisters at Saint Mary's Hospital, next to the Bethlehem Mission Society's center house, helped me realize that the most important "work" I could do on Orchid Island would be just to be with the people, understand what their needs are, and eventually serve them in some way.

So now, despite the obstacles, there is still a strong voice within me that says "Go!"

I wrote again to Father Provincial, to assure him that I would like to go to Orchid Island even without a teaching job. He replied that although I was not acting in the "classical" manner of most other Jesuits, he respected my desires and agreed with my hopes to live and work with the poor. But he wanted me to feel a part of the Society of Jesus even when I was alone on the island. He also said that he would like to visit me there during the coming year, if possible.

Father Provincial added that if at any time I felt my time on Orchid Island was over, or if things did not work out, I could assist at a Jesuit student center in Tainan City, which would welcome me with open arms. That gave me a feeling of security. Our provincial certainly is open and kind. It is hard to explain, but *I know* when someone trusts and believes in me, and this intuition makes me never want to do anything that would offend or lessen their trust.

I am now waiting for a boat or plane to Orchid Island. The Swiss priests and brothers have adopted me as one of their own and said they will take care of me when I return from the island for a break. Together with the Medical Missionary Sisters, I could not ask for a more caring community.

The Sisters have given me medicine and supplies that I will need for the islanders. They also paid me $30 for a set of paintings on hospital hygiene they had asked me to make. Other than that, I do not have much money—only enough for transportation to the island and some canned goods to take with me. Later, I will have to find some means of support.

At a church hostel nearby, there are around twenty Yami aborigines from Orchid Island, who are also waiting for a boat or plane to the island. Each time I visit them, they seem more like my new family. I am looking forward to sharing in their lives for the coming year.

2

SONG OF ORCHID ISLAND

Like a fading dream, my year on Orchid Island has long since come and gone. Now I am at Fu Jen University, winding up my first semester of theology, the last stage of formation before priestly ordination. The dry and intellectual atmosphere of the theologate in a colorless industrial suburb of Taipei could not be more different from the symphony of humanity and nature on achingly beautiful Orchid Island.

Shortly after arriving at Fu Jen, as a much-needed diversion from theology lectures in Chinese, I started writing a story about my year on Orchid Island. Of course, I could never express in words how intensely alive the earth, the sea, and the sky became for me during that time. Nor could I ever do justice to the kind and remarkable Yami people, who welcomed me on to their island. I could only hope that these reflections of mine might help me remember and someday share with others one of the best and most blessed years of my life.

My story of Orchid Island—a song, perhaps—begins in the magical summer of 1971 . . .

~

Toro, the Filipino pilot who flew planes from Taitung to Orchid Island, put the Cessna five-passenger into automatic, leaned back and gave me a Coke. Below us, the silky blue of the Pacific stretched forever, undisturbed by the changes and wars and discoveries of man. The ocean would flash and smile whenever the sun caught the tip of a wave—as if it knew that after the earth had given birth and grown and fought and died, its waters would yet remain, timeless and indifferent to it all.

In the distance, a lone velvety lotus leaf floated casually in the vast sea of blue. It was the island called Botel Tobago by the first explorers and later renamed Orchid Island, or Lanyu in Chinese. About forty-nine nautical miles from Taiwan, we arrived there in a little over half an hour. The plane flew low over the island now, and I could see the tall emerald mountains formed by volcanic eruptions in some distant past. The coast was rugged with gnarled rocks jutting up from the breakers. Toro pointed to one of the tiny villages—little brown houses clustered together as if seeking refuge from the elements—then miles of emptiness. We circled for a landing.

Only a few moments after settling on the short, bumpy runway, the pilot took off again and was gone. On a clear day, he might make two or three trips from mainland Taiwan. But when there was rough weather, often lasting for months, there were no flights at all. The other passengers, mostly elderly soldiers stationed on the island, stood in the shade of a betel nut tree and waited. I did the same. It was very hot and quiet, like a desert.

A three-wheeled motorcar broke the stillness. Its puttering sounded like a jackhammer. The driver was a tall, gaunt Taiwanese with a furrowed brow. He shouted orders to some boys on the three-wheeler to load the boxes delivered by the plane. Then a boy with long straight hair, bleached almost gold from the sun, smiled at me and said, "Let's go," and I climbed in with the others.

We bounced along on the back of the three-wheeler as it curved along the gravel road lining the coast. I could see the beach had no sand, only rocks and pebbles. On one side of the road, tangles of wild vegetation mingled with the sand. On the other side, taro fields stretched to the mountains, creeping up the slopes and fingering into the crevices. Along the road, women with baskets slung on their backs stared at us.

We approached an old village with stilt houses topped with thatched roofs, where children dangled their legs freely from wood-planked floors. Beside them were houses almost buried from view, with only their rooftops peeking shyly above the ground. Other dwellings of wood and rock were scattered along the hillside. The verdant green backdrop of mountains was highlighted by walls of white stones and armies of purple flowers marching up their sides.

A newer part of the village was composed of unpainted concrete duplexes arranged in rows, some with broken windows that had been boarded up. Through the open doorways I could see people sitting on the floor with their food spread out on leaves before them.

We were heading toward a military compound holding some five hundred prisoners from mainland Taiwan. Before reaching the prison, the three-wheeler made a sharp turn and stopped in front of a small store. The boy with the golden hair said, "The guest house is next to Old Ma's store." I told him I was looking for the church, and he pointed up a hill.

Some teenagers who were sitting around a grass-topped stilt house offered to help me bring my bags up the road to the church. Along the way, a handful of little children began to cluster around me, staring curiously. From the houses around the church a few of the men and women glanced at me while others reclined languidly on stilt houses and watched the ocean.

The church was built of grey concrete with wooden windows trimmed in red. There were no lights inside since the island still lacked electricity. On either side of the church was a room. I unlocked one door and found some *tatami* beds, benches, a table, and an oil stove. In the other room there was a small medical clinic. By that time each of the rooms was filled with people.

One of the teenagers who had brought up my bags sat down on a bench in the clinic and watched me silently as I unpacked my supplies. He had extraordinarily thick eyebrows that were pointed in a way that gave his entire face an angry, fearful expression. His bare feet were black from dirt, and his hair was long and stringy. He was shorter than the others but powerfully built. I felt he could not be as fierce as his outward appearance. In fact, he seemed more sad than angry.

"What is your name?" I asked.

"Molung," he replied. And then he asked me, "Did you know our priest?" I told him I had heard of Father Giger and his death in a tragic car accident a year before.

"He always helped us," Molung continued. "He would even scold the soldiers when their cows trampled on our sweet potatoes. He was afraid of nothing." The other boys sitting around Molung nodded as he spoke and stared listlessly at their sunbaked feet. "We miss him," they said.

I walked outside the church where I had a view of the entire village. The primary school stood near the road, and around it there were some old houses for the teachers. Farther on were the police station, post office, health department, and a few other concrete buildings. I counted forty Yami houses made from wood and rocks, though it was difficult to distinguish one house from an extension of another one.

As I was surveying the village, the little children were inspecting me. But when I spoke to them, they turned shyly away. So, I dug into my bag and brought out a sack of candy. Almost immediately the children gathered around and began asking questions.

"How far is it to your country?" one little girl asked. "Is it as far as from here to the harbor?"

"Even farther," I replied. "It is across the ocean. Try looking very hard, and you might see it."

"We don't see it," the children said, gazing at the sea.

"Then keep looking," I said. "That is how I found your island. When you search for something hard enough, you find it."

~

Elizabeth came to the church that afternoon. She was a tall and lithe Swiss lady in her mid-twenties with long, light brown hair, and she wore the same kind of red blouse as the Yami women. There were many questions I wanted to ask her, but we had little time to talk because the clinic was already filling up with patients. I watched Elizabeth as she tenderly patched up cuts and bruises. As she worked, she explained which medicines to use for what.

"If a boil hasn't opened yet, use the black goo," she told me. "But if it is already open, then use this yellow stuff. If that doesn't work after a few days, then try one of these red tubes. When people come with sore stomachs, first ask if they have had anything to eat recently. They might just be hungry. This is for diarrhea, and this is for constipation. Try not to mix them up. If you don't know what to give a person, just give him a vitamin. But don't give out aspirins to everyone who asks for them, because they taste like candy, and the kids will fool you into thinking they have a cold."

In the evening, we fixed dinner on the oil stove. Some little girls brought leaves that looked like spinach. They called the leaves "wild grass", and Elizabeth stir-fried them, adding peanut oil and soy sauce. We cooked rice and also warmed up a can of pork that I had brought. By the time we were ready to eat, it was already dark. I lit a candle. The glow filled the room and fell softly on the walls, which were lined with little children silently watching us.

"They look so hungry," I said to Elizabeth. "Should we give them some of our food?"

"You can if you like," she said smiling. "But you will have to give some to every child. And if you do, tomorrow there will be twice as many."

All the children had distended bellies, a sure sign of malnutrition and probably parasites. The little boys wore no clothes. The little girls had ragged dresses or simply a string tied around their waist with their swollen bellies overlapping the string. They kept staring at us, not saying a word.

"I think I'll give them the rest of this meat," I said. "I don't feel very hungry. I don't think I can eat with them just sitting there like that."

I got up and gave the plate of pork to one of the little boys and told him to pass it around. Immediately there was a panicky struggle as the children pushed and grabbed for their share. I turned uneasily to Elizabeth, who was still smiling. The candle flushed her face with light. She was strikingly beautiful and looked younger than she had that afternoon. It was clear she had a wisdom borne from experience.

"I knew the children would outsmart you," Elizabeth laughed. "You feel sorry for them and want to help, and

I'm sure you want to love them, too. But love means more than just giving things to people. Many people come here to 'help' these people. Develop them. But into what? Into a reflection of their own culture. Few people accept this little tribe the way they are. They 'help' without loving."

"But those little kids. Don't they need food?"

"Of course. And they have food. But yours is tastier. I've always eaten sweet potatoes and taro because that is what the people here eat. The more you can adapt to the Yami way of life, the more they will trust your efforts to help them. And you will know how to go about it. If you want to be with the Yami and share their lives, that in itself is a full-time job."

That was my last conversation with Elizabeth. She left the next day for Taiwan and soon after for her native home in Switzerland. But her wise words remained with me. Elizabeth had pointed out a way of serving others by sharing their lives. I was ready to begin that job.

~

Holding a tiny carved boat, a man about my age walked into the clinic. He wore a loincloth, and circles of ringworm disfigured his exposed buttocks. A scrawny little boy with sun-bleached blond hair followed him. He was a perfect miniature of his father. The man had sat with Elizabeth and me the night before as we talked and watched the moonlight playing on the ocean.

"This is for you," the man said, holding the boat out to me. It looked just like the bigger canoes the Yami used for fishing. The boat was painted white and carved meticulously with red and black designs.

I was grateful for the gift and wanted to give the man at least something in return. I reached in my pocket and drew out a pack of chewing gum.

"What is that?" he asked with a frown.

"Chewing gum."

"Is it like betel nut?" The man pulled an amorphous red wad of chewed leaves out of his mouth. "We call it '*man-mama*'. Do you want to try some?"

Before I could answer, the man unfastened a woven bag that hung from his loincloth. From the bag he drew out a cluster of yellow-green nuts and broke off one. Then he stuck a piece of vine between two halves of the nut and sprinkled white powder on it. Pressing the nut carefully together so the vine insert would not fall out, he handed it to me.

I took a deep breath, placed the nut between my teeth and began to crunch. My mouth quickly filled up with liquid.

"Do not swallow it," the man cautioned. "Spit out the liquid." I spewed out a long stream of red juice and chewed a few more times. Then I started sweating and feeling lightheaded. Finally, I spit out the whole wad.

"You are not used to it," the man said with a laugh.

After allowing me a few moments to recover, the man pointed to the blotches of ringworm on his buttocks and asked if I had any medicine. I used the brown stuff.

The man's name was Jayud. His son's name was also Jayud. The reason their names were the same was not because the boy had been named after his father, but because the father had been named after his son. Jayud explained that when a couple had their first child, the father changed his name to that given the child. He then replaced the prefix *Syi* before his name with *Syaman* to denote he was the father.

Jayud's son pulled at my leg and pointed to a cut on his

own tiny foot. After applying the red medicine, I glanced at the little boat his father had carved and recalled Elizabeth's words to me the night before. We had begun to share.

~

Molung handed me a large green leaf folded and tied with a straw reed. I opened the leaf and inside were three long, purple taro roots, still warm. Molung smiled, and for the first time I noticed that his teeth were black. He was chewing betel nuts and turned his head toward the door to spit out a long stream of the blood-red juice. I thanked him and sampled the taro. It was like a gooey potato.

"Taro tastes better with fish," Molung said. He hesitated and then asked, "Do you want to go fishing?"

A few moments later, we were walking to Molung's home, which was perched just above the rocky shore.

Molung lived with his family in a crumbling stone house built by the Japanese when they occupied the island. There were two rooms, one for cooking and one for eating and sleeping. A variety of fishing equipment—nets, poles, and oars—hung from the smoke-blackened walls. Molung took a spear gun from the wall and fingered its wire arrow.

"I made this myself," he said proudly, "but it is a little bent." Molung took a rock and began pounding the stiff wire until it was straight. A thick band of elastic joined the arrow to the wooden handle so that when triggered, the arrow would fly several feet before being halted by the band. When he had straightened the arrow, I followed Molung into an adjoining thatched hut with a doorway so tiny and a roof so low it was necessary to squeeze in on hands and knees. Molung removed a small net bag and a pair of water goggles from the wall. Tossing them to me, he said, "Let's go."

The underwater world was vast and beautiful. Molung swam ahead, moving through the crystal waters like a golden fish. We passed the children playing in the shallow foam, passed the men on the sharp rocks casting their nets, passed through the mountains of coral reefs and the silent blue valleys, and were soon a part of the deep and endless ocean.

Molung crouched behind a skeleton of pink polyps. On the other side, dancing in the shimmering lights and flowering corals, were the fish. Slim, fluorescent yellow fish darting here and there. Large grey ones lounging lazily with mouths agape. Splashes of orange and red fish scouting for food along the ocean floor. Molung's strong fingers fastened on a protruding rock, and he pulled himself deeper into their midst. Then ever so slightly, like a leaf falling from a tree, he separated himself from the rock and steadied himself into a sitting position. He pointed his spear gun before him and paused only a moment.

The fish must have sensed in that instant that he was there, for as the shadow of death fell upon them, orange and grey and red colors fled swiftly to safety. A lone yellow fish lay still, drifting slowly to the ceiling of the ocean, suspended on the tip of Molung's arrow. The silky blood from its torn side hovered like a crimson cloud over the emptiness below.

In a moment the rest of the fish returned. Orange and grey and red and yellow again peopled the blue waters. But their movements seemed quicker, more alert than before. The waters had brought new life, and the ocean went on and on and smiled at the life it had brought and laughed at the follies and boasts of men.

"Tie it around your waist," Molung shouted as he flung the fish and a thin cord over to me. And he dove again as

I fastened the fish onto the cord and watched from above. Molung's hair was tied around his forehead with a white striped towel to keep the hair out of his eyes. From his waist hung a net bag and a short knife—"for killing sharks". As he wandered through the mountains and valleys of the ocean—stopping, aiming, shooting—the cord around my waist grew heavier. Finally, his fierce eyebrows relaxed, and he turned to me and said, "Enough," and we swam back to shore.

We washed off the salt from our skin in a stream near the shore, and I followed Molung up to his house where we began to clean the fish. His thumb dug the fisheyes out of their sockets. He looked at me with a grin, then tossed the eyes into his mouth. "Umm," he said, "the best part." Most of the fish he cut in half, running a thin reed through their eye sockets and hanging them on a horizontal pole outside his house. Then he handed two fish to me and said, "Let's go to your house and cook these. They are 'men fish'."

"Men fish?" I asked. "How can you tell?"

"We just know. I don't mean that the fish are 'male'. We call them 'men fish' because only men can eat them. It is bad for a woman to eat a man fish. Besides, they have their own fish."

"What would happen if a woman ate a man fish?" I asked.

"The woman would get sick, maybe lose her baby, or even die. When we catch fish, we must be sure to catch some women fish, too."

"What about children and old people?"

"Children are the same. But old people can eat anything. There are some fish, though, that only old people can eat. Those fish are so tough no one else wants them anyway."

We began eating the fish. Molung had fried them in oil and ginger to a crisp golden brown. They were delicious.

And then Molung offered me another invitation.

"Tonight, we will go to the prison to practice our Yami dances. Why don't you come with us?"

~

The moon hovered lovingly over the ocean that night as if the two were friends. Molung and I walked down from the church to the road leading to the prison. As we went, other teenagers from the village joined us. No one spoke, and the stillness of the night was broken only by the beat of the breakers and the slap of our sandals against the pebbled earth. The group grew to about a dozen. Then Molung took a deep breath and began to sing. His music was like a call, a challenge tossed against the breakers and far out to the sea.

"*Ni syi yaden mo vavagut no ya . . .*" The others joined in and sang loudly from deep within their souls. Since their song seemed to hold everything they wanted to say, there was no need for words. The song passed along the village and the police station and the store. It went up a little hill, past the guesthouse and the post office and the health department. And everywhere it went it told the people all that it wanted to say.

But when it came to the prison, the song stopped.

The boys lingered around the prison store for a while. There were some Yami girls behind the counter, dressed prettily. When the boys tried to banter with them, the girls ignored them.

Soldiers and prisoners walked through the store and flirted with the girls, and the girls lowered their eyes demurely and smiled at them. After a while the boys left the store.

We walked into the compound toward the stage. No one bothered to check us as we entered. In front of the large outdoor stage was a sprawling courtyard with prisoners talking and walking about. On the stage a band uniformed in white accompanied a girl singing a popular Mandarin song.

"She is our best singer," Molung said, watching the girl.

"Are all of these men prisoners?" I asked, pointing to the scattered groups. "Doesn't anyone guard them?"

"They cannot get off the island. The soldiers are always watching them. In the daytime they work. This is their rest time. Those men in the band up there were all well-known gangsters who used to work in nightclubs in Taiwan. Do you want to meet them?"

"*Gokai*!" roared the bandleader, using a Yami greeting. "We have been waiting for you. Who is your friend?"

Molung introduced me to the members of the band. They brought out a chair for me. I sat on the side of the stage drinking green tea, watching the performance, and wondering what a strange prison this was.

While the singer was finishing up her number, a group of girls waited on one side of the stage, and a group of boys on the other. Then the girls began to dance. Their arms floated gracefully like the swelling of the waves, undulating and serene. When they completed their dance, the boys began theirs, and it was as if a tempest had broken the calm.

Beginning with their arms entwined in a snake line, voices soft and low, their steps soon became wilder and more intricate. Whipping across and around the stage, they were the waves thundering on the rocks; they were the arms and legs struggling with oars against a hostile sea; they were the iron spades churning the earth and subduing the elements. And they were like rhythm itself, alternating between crude bursts of frantic movement and a steady, restful beat.

As I watched the dance, I saw their lives unfold before me. Everything was reflected in the movements and the music flowing from their souls. Looking at Molung, his entwined arms pulling the others like a whipcord, his thick eyebrows with the look of the conqueror, I saw a clear message: at this moment, here in the prison, a group of Yami, who had been fought against and held back by the elements, on one hand, and the low opinion of men, on the other, were reigning supreme. In their dance they were absolutely invincible, the lords of the earth and the sea. Here in this prison, on a moon-filled summer night, they were the ones who were free.

~

The mountain in the back of the church had a path leading to the other side of the island. From the hillside, I had a panoramic view of my village of Imurud.

Below me were the dwellings, huddled together and separated only by a narrow road running through the center of the village. There was the stone house of Molung, watching over the vast sea like a dutiful sentinel. There were the underground houses and the stilt houses and the thatched workshops. And there were the pits for the black, long-nosed pigs. Some of the homes had roofs covered with black tar; others were topped with dry abaca grass. From the path above, the village formed a neat mosaic of black and brown houses scattered in a sea of green taro.

I was going to the village of Iranumiruk, famous for its peninsula of unusual rocks. It was Saturday. I planned to spend the night and attend the prayer service in that village the next morning.

The mountain was beautifully still. Clusters of purple morning glories, called *varinu* flowers, played among the stately betel trees on the soft and verdant hills. A group of cows sauntered along the path above and spilled over into the little valleys within the hills. On a distant peak was an old concrete dwelling. Coming closer, I could see it had once been burned; its blackened walls gave the look of dark, rich wood. A castle, I thought, but in fact it was a home for the cows.

From a point on the mountain where the road began its descent, I could see both sides of the island. Two oceans. The afternoon sun played hide-and-seek with the shadows on the mountain separating the waters. I walked farther down the road and came to a place where the wind blew furiously. Perhaps the contour of the mountains had funneled the various air currents into this one pocket. I felt that if I spread my arms I could surely fly. Out of the wind and into the stillness once more, the new ocean loomed in full view before me. Stretching out in a lengthy peninsula from a tiny inlet in the distance was a curious chain of dusky, jagged rocks.

A smiling young man carrying a stack of wood on his back shouted at me from a nearby hill. His hair had a reddish tint and stood straight up like a bush, and his skin was rusty with dark sunburned designs.

"What do you think of those rocks?" he asked me.

"They look as if they just burst from the sea," I replied.

"The Americans bombed them during the war," the boy told me. "Since they look so much like a ship, they thought the rocks were a Japanese submarine."

We had almost descended the mountain. The setting sun was bathing the rocky peninsula in a rich golden hue, and from level ground they looked higher, shielding the little harbor below. Breakers lapped lazily along the shore.

The young man's name was Katush. He said he had been to Taiwan three times and worked in various jobs. He liked Taiwan, "because you can earn money there."

"Do you need much money here on the island?" I asked.

"Not much. A few years ago, nobody had money. But now we must get jobs so we can improve our lives. When we have money, we can buy clothes and have nice things like they do in Taiwan."

We were approaching a village. The quiet inlet in front of the beach was dotted with brightly painted canoes. A few little children played in the water. Some men emerged dripping from the sea with their spear guns and nets filled with fish. Women were also coming back from the beach holding round, black buoys.

"The buoys are filled with sea water," Katush explained. "When we boil fish, we use half sea water and half fresh water. It makes good soup. The buoys come from the ocean. The ocean gives us many things. Once it gave us a TV set. But since we have no electricity in our village, we could not use it. We gave it to the police."

The sunlight was playing games now with the rocks. Soon, shadows painted the peninsula a dark silhouette, giving it a harsh, menacing appearance. It was already evening. Katush led me up a path to the village, where there was a small stone church. A herd of black, potbellied pigs scattered in all directions as we approached.

On the side of the church there was a little room with a *tatami* bed. Katush left and returned shortly, bringing a candle. He watched me unpack my bag.

"Is that a Bible?" he asked.

"Yes. Can you read it?"

"I can read the characters." Katush took the Bible and began reading a passage out loud. "But since I did not finish primary school, I do not know the meaning of what I read." Katush paused and asked me, "Are you a priest?"

"I'm studying to become one."

"How long does it take?"

I looked at Katush's simple face with the shock of hair on top sticking up like a bush. Should I tell him it takes over ten years to become a priest?

Suddenly in the narrow doorway, a shadowy figure appeared, ominously lit by candlelight. I jumped with fright, both from the form's abrupt entrance and by its ghostly appearance. An ancient woman with a long, massive face full of wrinkles stood there. Her mouth was drawn in a smile, and her shriveled eyes passed over me with curiosity. She wore nothing but an old rag tied around her waist, and her sagging breasts hung loosely behind a single strand of seashells fastened around her neck. Her gnarled hands held a large pot of steamed rice, and she handed the pot to me.

I accepted the gift with gratitude, and the woman left. Since I had had no dinner, I eagerly consumed the entire pot. Just as I finished, the old woman appeared again noiselessly at the door, frightening me once more, and she reached out for the empty pot. I thanked her again, trying to appear relaxed. It was a wonderful gift, especially since rice was a rare luxury on the island.

"Who was that old woman, and how did she know I was hungry?" I asked Katush the next morning.

"She is the shaman of our village. She talks with the spirits," Katush replied.

It was early Sunday morning then, and the village church leader came and greeted me.

"First, you eat these sweet potatoes," he told me, unfolding three warm yams wrapped in a leaf. "Then I will call the people for prayer." As I began eating, the church leader picked up a hunk of steel and went through the village beating the slab with a rock.

The ragged children were the first to arrive. When they

spotted me, they ran over and began pointing to their bruises and skin rashes. I opened my first aid kit and went to work. It was as if I were handing out candy—they fought to get painted with the "red medicine". Other villagers slowly trickled into the church. They squatted on low benches holding their babies and chatting with one another.

When the service began, the people stood and reverently sang the "Our Father" and "Hail Mary" in Chinese. Then the church leader began his sermon, and the people sat down and started chatting again. The leader's voice could hardly be heard above the din of the congregation. Adding to the general atmosphere of indifference, a dog wandered up to the altar, sniffing. When the church leader saw the dog, he gave it a powerful kick in the stomach, sending the canine howling in pain. Then he shouted and cursed at the dog. The congregation immediately fell silent, and the church leader finished his sermon with their close attention.

As I hiked back over the hill that afternoon, it seemed as though the sun was softly kissing the rocks once bombed by the warring planes.

~

Molung and his friends were sitting outside the church in Imurud, smoking and chewing betel nuts.

"We are going to the mountains to pick the dragon's eye," they said.

"What is the dragon's eye?" I asked.

"It is like the longan fruit in Taiwan but much bigger. Every summer we get them. The dragon's eye in Taiwan is sour. Here it is sweet. When we go to pick the dragon's eye, we do not need to eat lunch. The dragon's eye fills us up. Even if we eat hundreds, we never get sore stomachs."

I wanted to see this wonderful fruit. We set off around the coast of the island, past the prison and a garden lined with concrete, off to the barren beauty that twisted and struggled along the rocky shore. There were great bunches of green cacti that looked like pineapple plants, and between them and sometimes snaking along the silent path were purple *varinu* flowers. They seemed to lace the island like little orchids. Perhaps they were better than orchids. *Varinu* flowers were small and worthless, and no one ever bothered to pick them. But orchids would long ago have been taken and sold, and the island would have lost one of its colors.

"Will you teach me an American song?" Molung asked.

"I can teach you 'Oh, When the Saints Go Marching In'."

"Owella says go marshy no," Molung repeated. The other boys laughed, but Molung continued practicing until he sang it right.

We passed through three deep gullies at an area that was appropriately called "Three Gullies". Molung pointed to a high mountain peak in the distance and said, "That is where it all began."

"Where what began?"

"The first Yami man. That is where he landed."

"Where did he come from?"

"From the sky. Listen, I will tell you the story." We had just crossed the third gully. The mossy green peak watched calmly over the restless waters below it. Molung sat down, unfastened his net bag, and prepared a betel nut. The other boys did the same. When he had crunched the nut a few times, and the red juice was streaming from the corners of his mouth, Molung began his story.

"In the beginning, there was only the silent earth. Then, the *Taudoto*—the One Above—saw our island and knew that it was good. He sent a stone from the sky, and it landed on that mountain peak. The stone burst open, and a man crawled out. That was the first Yami man.

"The man started walking down from the mountain toward the sea. At the same time, a bamboo near the sea sprouted and gave birth to another man. This man started walking up toward the mountain. The two men met each other in a field of abaca grass and called themselves *tau*—Yami people. Then they separated. The bamboo man went over the mountain to the village of Ivarinu, and the stone man went along the coast to Iratai. There they raised their families." Molung spit out the dry nut, stood up, and said, "Let's go."

"There are the dragon's eyes!" The boys pointed to some tall, primeval trees. We had been walking through a deep ravine, and the sunlight danced on the yellow green leaves and made shadowy patterns on the boys' faces. Molung pulled up a stick of bamboo, squatted, and took out his knife. He split the end of the bamboo, then stuck in a small piece of wood to keep the halves separate. In only a few minutes he had constructed a device with which to pick the fruit. He tossed it to me, shinnied up a tree, and I threw the stick up to him.

Only a short distance away, Molung's mother and little brother were sitting on the ground, munching on dragon's eyes. I went over to join them. Molung's mother greeted me with a juice-filled grin and poured a bunch of the fruit into my hands. His little brother gave me a demonstration of the proper technique for eating the dragon's eye. First, the teeth bite down on the tough outer shell, cracking it open. This falls off, leaving the sparkling white fruit inside free to be sloshed about in the mouth, after which the large seed is spat out, gracefully. They were delicious.

"My grandfather planted these trees," Molung's little brother said proudly. He climbed up a tree to join the others, while his mother picked up the fruit he knocked down. I climbed up, too, and began picking and eating and swaying with the breeze. It was true. You could eat as much as you wanted and not get a sore stomach. And it was easier than cooking lunch. We must have eaten a hundred before we started home.

Before leaving, some of the boys went to the hills nearby and chopped firewood, which they piled neatly, bound, and slung on their backs. Molung filled his rattan basket with dragon's eyes. He placed a large leaf on his forehead, stringing it under the rope of the basket. This allowed his forehead to take the full weight instead of his shoulders. "It is more comfortable this way," he said. We sang "Oh, When the Saints Go Marching In" on the way home.

~

A short, plump, wrinkled lady rushed into the clinic dragging her whimpering daughter. She chattered excitedly and pointed to her little girl's leg, which had a small scratch on it. After I finished tending the wound, the mother rolled her eyes painfully, rubbing her little girl's stomach. I figured she meant her daughter was hungry, so I gave her some rice. Then her eyes fastened on a big jar on the table.

"Do you want some vitamins?" I asked.

The plump lady's face lit up. It was a full, jolly face, covered with tiny wrinkles so fine they could have been drawn with a pencil. She wore a red scarf around her tanned forehead, which gave her an uncanny resemblance to Aunt Jemima. I put a few pills in a small bottle and handed it to her. She frowned, unsatisfied, and pointed to the big jar of vitamins. "No," I said. "That is the whole supply!"

Aunt Jemima's eyes fluttered around the room like a butterfly and landed on my can of shaving cream. She examined the can curiously, squirting out a little of the cream onto her hands. She smelled it and looked delighted. She wanted the can. I explained it was used for shaving and she did not need to shave. Then her eyes brightened again as she spotted one of Father Hans' shirts hanging on a peg. I told her it was not mine, so I could not give it to her.

She saw my old tennis shoes and pointed sadly to her own shoeless feet. "No, they are the only ones I have," I said. Then she walked across the room and found a tube of hair oil, almost empty. She smiled with bewitching eyes as she held up the tube. In a younger woman, her look would have been flirtatious, but she must have been in her sixties. I gave her a little of the oil, and she rubbed it vigorously into her hair, then demanded the entire tube. When I refused, she walked out in a huff, clutching her rice and vitamins and pulling along her limping daughter. I said, "God bless", and she grunted.

~

Molung's family was preparing a special meal for his father, who was ill. According to Yami tradition, if a feast was held for someone who was sick, the One Above—the *Taudoto*—would be more likely to heal that person.

The feast was in Molung's workshop. I bent down on all fours in order to creep into the low dwelling. Inside, Molung's mother sat on one side of the floor with the women, her smooth face glowing like amber in the sunlight streaming through the tiny door. The women wore grey skirts and shawls made of woven ramie, and bells jingled from their ankles whenever they moved. Their long black hair was piled up high and tied with red ribbons. Long strands of polished agate beads hung from their necks down to their waists.

Molung's older brother sat on the opposite side of the floor with the men, clad in short woven vests that reached down just above their embroidered loincloths. Some of the men sported silver bracelets fastened tightly to their wrists, and one had a gold ring pierced into his earlobe.

The men watched as Molung's father divided chunks of cooked goat meat that had been piled on a round wooden plate. Several large "elephant ear" leaves were placed on the floor in front of each guest, and Molung's father put portions of the meat on each leaf. When he had finished, he brought out a plate of freshly boiled fish, which he also divided, placing the portions carefully on the green leaves. Finally, a plate of dried fish was brought out. "My favorite," Molung commented, and this too was divided.

Each of us now had a leaf "plate" filled with meat and fish on the floor in front of us. A metal container of yams and taro piled high and covered with leaves lay in the center of the floor. Molung removed the leaves like an artist unveiling a painting. Taking a sharp stick, he poked a large white tuber and handed it to me. "This is mountain taro," he said, "our best." Then his brother moved four earthen bowls next to the container. "Two are filled with fish soup and two with goat soup," he said. "Hurry and eat!"

It was like an eating contest. Molung stuffed the yams, taro, fish, and meat into his mouth with incredible speed. The white taro root tasted like a delicious baked potato. The yellow yam was tender and filling.

"Is that all you can eat?" Molung asked incredulously as he started on his seventh sweet potato. He grabbed a heavy soup bowl in both hands and slurped and then handed it to me. I took a gulp and puckered up because it tasted just like seawater. Molung saw my expression and laughed and said, "You have to get used to that one."

We finished eating surely in record time for the huge amount of food consumed. Molung covered the metal container with leaves and took it to a corner. As short as he was, he still had to bend over when he shuffled under the low roof. He put leaves over the remaining pieces of fish and meat and placed them on a high shelf next to the ceiling. "Wash your hands," Molung told me, and he reached out the doorway, tipped a black buoy with a hole in the top, and washed his hands. Then he held the buoy for me while I washed mine.

Molung's mother went to a shelf and pulled out a basket of betel nuts. In it were two fresh branches covered with green and yellow nuts. There was also the vine with which the nuts were mixed, plus the plastic container of powder—"made from sea shells which are crushed and burned," Molung explained.

"*Manmama*," Molung's brother announced as he selected a nut, sliced, and prepared it.

"*Manmama*," I repeated.

"That means 'betel nut'—Yami tobacco." He looked at me questioningly, then asked the by-now-familiar word, "Tobacco?" I pulled out a pack and passed out cigarettes to everyone.

"*Ayoi*! Thank you! God bless you," they said. Molung's mother stroked my arm as if I were her favorite dog. "*Ayoi*," she said and turned to the other women laughing hoarsely. Her black teeth were covered with dry betel nut. Then she spoke seriously to her son, and Molung translated for me.

"My mother says that whenever you have nothing to eat, come to our house, and we will feed you."

Some other boys crawled into Molung's workshop. We strummed the guitar for a while until the afternoon heat and the big meal began lulling everyone to sleep. Molung's mother pulled out two thin bamboo mats and unrolled them. She lay down, and her husband did likewise, and soon so did Molung.

Molung's grandmother, old and blind, was squatting just inside the doorway below the raised platform where we were sitting. She had been talking to Molung's parents, and after they fell asleep, she continued her conversation. Soon she must have realized the others were all asleep because she became silent as well. Then slowly she began sliding under the floor where we sat. There was only a sliver of an opening. I watched her with alarm as she slithered down into the darkness of the stones and dirt beneath the house.

"What is she doing?" I asked a boy who sat beside me softly singing with the guitar.

"She is going to sleep."

"Can't she sleep up here with the others?"

"It doesn't matter," the boy replied indifferently. "She is old and blind. She likes to sleep down there." He glanced at me for a moment and added, "Pitiful, isn't she?" Then he continued his song.

While the others sang or slept, I climbed up Molung's stilt house and watched the waves lap gently on the shore. There was so much about this strange and beautiful island that was still a mystery to me. So much I wanted to find out about the people, their environment—and myself.

Three weeks had passed since I first arrived on Orchid Island. I was learning about the livelihood of the Yami. I was making a few friends and handing out medicine. My heart was slowly sinking into the beauty of the island, and it wanted to go deeper and share all it could in the world about me. But sometimes my mind would say, "What about goals? What about serving these people? You have to plan. You have to help. You have to *do*." And then my heart would answer, "You have to *be*. Keep going deeper, and you will learn, and you will share, and you will love."

~

Molung sat with me one morning at breakfast drinking coffee and eating my instant oatmeal.

"When I build a new concrete house, you can come and stay there," he said.

"I like your house now," I replied. "It is made of wood and rocks and dried abaca. It looks beautiful."

"Our houses are no good. The tourists say they look funny. The soldiers laugh at them. I don't like to live like that. When I build a new concrete house, we can drink coffee there. And eat oatmeal."

Molung's friends came in and told us a typhoon was on the way. "Maybe even a tidal wave."

"There will not be any tidal waves," Molung stated confidently as he slowly finished his cup of coffee. "Why should there be? Over here no one does anything bad. There are no gangsters except those in the prison. We do not steal or shoot people. Well, we steal—but not so much. Not like bad people in other places."

"The radio says the typhoon will come this afternoon," one boy said.

"Ask the old people," Molung said. "They know." He

flicked his cigarette butt on the floor and put it out with the ball of his foot. "Let's go watch the waves."

I followed the boys down to Molung's stilt house and watched the swelling of the waves while Molung went to "ask the old people." The tall blue breakers came in at an angle from far out in the sea. The children ran down to the beach and jumped and shouted at the rising winds until their parents saw them and called for them to come home.

It was as if a huge dark hand passed over the waters and changed the color of the swells to a dark murky grey. I turned toward the hills and saw the masses of black clouds pouring from the mountaintops like smoke. The wind picked up suddenly, and mothers grabbed their children's hands and pulled them into the large winter houses set beneath the ground. The grey swells began to burst, and the frothy white spray danced wildly and fought against the winds.

We hurried back to the church, passing the teenagers with their ears pressed against transistor radios to learn where, when, how big . . . The men were on the rooftops hammering down the thatch with bamboo supporters and thick vines. The crackle of the radios and the hammering and the thunder of the waves and the crash of the winds blended into a new song, and within all this music was silence and waiting, and it was the silence of the coming typhoon.

In the afternoon, the typhoon arrived in all its fury. Soon, many of the thatched roofs had been blown away. From a window in the church, I watched as the men braved the wind to patch up each new onslaught to their homes. The waves battled against a tall rock in the distance. The white foam swept up the coral stone, then exploded like a spray of fireworks in slow motion. Inside the church, rain seeped through every crack, and the wind blew it all over the room.

Molung, Jayud, and his son stayed with me in the church that evening. Jayud passed the time by meticulously carving another little wooden canoe. They remained until daylight, because no one felt like fighting the wind on the way back to their own house.

Early the next morning, there was sunlight and calm again. The room in the church filled up with people. Some older men wove baskets out of split rattan. Jayud still concentrated on the details of his souvenir boat. Two teenage girls were playing the church harmonium. Molung carefully disassembled what was left of a pack of wet cigarettes, dried the tobacco over the oil stove, and wrapped it up for his father. I wondered why there were so many people sitting around—why no one was going to work.

"It is not over yet," Molung said. "When the south wind comes, then it will be over."

As if unsatisfied, the typhoon circled and returned for a further attack that afternoon. It lashed and howled and threatened, but it could not touch the people tucked away deep in their underground houses. Then at last, the south wind laughed and breathed on the people, and the typhoon went its way, and the island came to life once again.

~

Aunt Jemima trotted into the clinic, chattering away and scratching the collar of her ragged red sweater. She pointed to her bedraggled little daughter, so I gave her some skin cream. She made a sour face and coughed and sputtered, so I gave her some more vitamins. She scoured the room as if I were having a summer sale. Her eyes landed on my swimming trunks, and she looked over at me, but I shook my head. Then she saw an old dust rag and eyed me coquettishly. I told her it was just an old dust rag. She continued to plead until I told her she could take the rag. She squealed with pleasure, gave me an exuberant hug, and barreled out the door waving her skin cream, her vitamins, and her precious dust rag.

I sat in the clinic room for a while. That evening, an Army boat would be leaving for Taiwan, and I hoped to hitch a ride on it. There was a young man from another village who needed a heart operation. I had agreed to help him. I did not know when or even if I would come back.

It was hot, and the mosquitoes were out for blood. As I sat thinking and scratching, an old man poked his head through the clinic door and asked a familiar question: "Tobacco?" I pulled out a cigarette and mechanically gave it to him, and he bowed politely saying, "God bless" in flawless Mandarin.

Little Jayud wandered in the clinic and rummaged in the trash pan where I threw old bandages. He picked up a gooey piece of gauze, and I snatched it away from him and sent him outside. He hit his little brother who was standing by the door, and his brother sat in the dirt and bawled. I went out and gave him some candy so he would stop crying. He took the candy and threw it on the ground and kicked it with his feet. Then I walked over to Jayud's underground house and shouted down through the door that I would be leaving that night.

"Do you have any rice left?" Jayud's wife yelled up from inside the house, "Give it to us!" Then I heard Jayud's sharp voice reprimanding her. He came out, smiling apologetically and said he would help me carry my baggage.

"You will not come back?" Jayud asked slowly, fixing his wide-set eyes on mine. "Little Jayud will miss you. He is naughty and does not obey, but he likes you."

I looked down at Little Jayud. His face was black with dirt. He smiled, and his tiny teeth were rotten.

"He is a good boy," I said, and gave them the rest of my rice.

That evening Molung, Jayud, and some of the teenagers went with me to the prison, where they put me in a jeep with some soldiers, and we headed for the harbor. Our goodbyes were quick, and soon I was inside the Army boat, moving slowly through the dark waters toward Taiwan.

I thought of Aunt Jemima scouring my room for things I could give her, of all the people who asked for tobacco as if I were a cigarette machine, of my failure to find a job to support myself, of Jayud's wife greedily eyeing the remainder of my rice . . .

My mind, reeling with these thoughts, reprimanded me, "See, you did nothing for these people. You helped them neither spiritually nor materially. They took advantage of you. They are only interested in what they can get out of you. Why do you want to be with people like that? Why don't you do something useful?"

This time my heart said nothing at all.

Beside us, the silky black of the Pacific stretched forever, timeless, indifferent to the changes and wars and discoveries of man. Even now in the night, its silent waters would sparkle and flash and smile with confidence—as if the ocean knew better than all the rest.

There in the stillness I thought I saw a woman sitting on a stilt house combing her long black hair. Her head was tilted just a bit, and she sang a soft and lovely chant. And there was Molung as he talked in the candlelight, his face flooded with yellow and red colors . . . Jayud's eyes were wise and kind, and his son's hand felt so tiny when I held it in mine . . . I would go back.

~

My friend Lipasa was from the village of Ivarinu on the other side of the island where I stayed. He had two valves in his heart that were not functioning well. For a long time, he had hoped to have an operation. But since he had no money, it seemed impossible. Lipasa continued, however, to hope. He was twenty-five now and frequently sick. Unable to work or to fish, his future seemed bleak—unless he could get an operation.

The first time Lipasa asked me to help him, I shrugged it off. Heart operations cost thousands of dollars and the family of Lipasa had no money at all. But when I mentioned his problem to my brother Jerry and others in Taipei, I found there were those who wanted to help.

The National Taiwan University Hospital in Taipei offered to perform the operation for free if we would buy the artificial heart valves and supply the blood. Lipasa was very grateful. At last, there was hope. His parents would be overjoyed when he returned to his village, well and healthy.

The night before the operation, I sat with Lipasa and his little brother. A priest came to baptize him.

"I am afraid," Lipasa told me. "If the operation does not succeed, my parents will blame my little brother. His responsibility is too great."

"Don't worry," I said. "They should blame me because I am the one responsible for your operation."

When a carload of young students from Fu Jen University arrived to donate their blood, Lipasa's mood picked up. I nudged Lipasa and said to him, "See how much they care for you."

The next morning, the head nurse hugged Lipasa as the

orderlies put him on a stretcher. I noticed tears in the eyes of this warm Taiwanese woman when she turned quickly away. The other nurses on the hospital floor accompanied Lipasa on his way to the operating room.

"You look like a king," I told my friend.

"Now is not the time to joke!" he retorted. But then with a laugh he added, "The king of the sick, perhaps?"

I sat with Lipasa's younger brother outside the operating room and waited and prayed. I had never thought of the operation not succeeding. Busy with collecting money and blood donors, I had scarcely given a thought to the possibility the operation might fail.

But now as I prayed, I knew there was a chance Lipasa could die. And I would have had a part in his death.

As we sat and waited, more university students stopped by, wanting to do something—anything—for a poor boy they didn't even know.

Ten long hours passed. When the haggard doctor finally stepped out of the operating room, he told us simply and without emotion, "It is very bad. There is little hope."

A few moments later, the nurse brought us into the recovery room, where Lipasa's body was connected to a machine that had been keeping his heart beating for the past few hours.

"How long?" I asked the doctor.

"There is very little hope." The doctor's voice had sympathy, but his eyes showed nothing but fatigue.

I thanked the doctor with a few mumbled words and watched sadly as a nurse turned off the machine and covered my friend's body with an old white sheet.

Lipasa's little brother and I wheeled the body out of the recovery room. An orderly guided us to a sprawling building at the back of the hospital. It was dark inside, and there was the smell of incense. The orderly lifted up Lipasa's heavy body and placed it on a stone slab in a small, dimly lit alcove. There was a thudding sound when his body hit the cold concrete.

Lipasa's little brother—as if he were aware of the dead form for the first time—cried out in horror, "Big Brother!" and crumpled in my arms.

The operation had not succeeded. Consequently, I had a gnawing feeling of failure, of abandonment by God. It was almost like being double-crossed.

But then I thought of the compassionate students as they crowded into the hospital to give blood . . . the head nurse who turned away her head in tears . . . the doctor who tried so hard . . . the sad little brother who needed to be consoled with positive thoughts . . .

I knew Lipasa was with the One Above, the *Taudoto*, who cared for him in life as well as in death. And he was singing a song, not of abandonment, but of gratitude.

But, oh, how long it took before I was able once again to hear that song.

~

The crowded, puttering barge wallowed in the harbor like a water buffalo in a mud hole. Since the boat rarely made a trip to Orchid Island, every available space was crammed with boxes of supplies in addition to the animal, vegetable, and human life on board. I found a spot on the deck next to a pineapple plant and a cage full of nervous ducks.

There was laughter and excitement as we began the seven-hour journey. Young people were returning to the island after working in Taiwan, and their new clothes danced brightly in the wind. They held radios to their ears and sang the latest hit songs. Some of the older men fastened lines on the back of the barge, hoping to catch a few fish along the way.

I leaned back with my head on the pineapple plant and my feet propped up on the duck cage and soaked in the warmth and blueness of the sky. Only the ducks seemed at all uneasy over the coming voyage.

The lullaby-rocking of the boat had a narcotic effect on us, and in no time each passenger was curled up in his spot on the deck, dozing. The radios hummed, and the sea lapped playfully along the sides of the barge, and soon I, too, fell asleep.

About an hour out, the first spray of seawater splashed over the boat, disturbing our slumber and drenching our clothes. It was so sudden that we laughed as if someone had thrown a bucket of cold water in our faces. We settled down peacefully again into catnaps. But the sea must have been angered by our complacency, for she threw up a hard wall of water before us. The boat slammed into it with a force that sent us sliding into the boxes and the bags and one another. Everyone was now wide awake, groping along the watery deck for something steady to hold onto. The ducks at my feet were quacking loudly as if scolding us for not heeding their warning.

We were in the midst of the turbulent Bashi Channel, and the reluctant sea fought us and teased us every inch of the way, daring us to continue our voyage. Every few moments, she bucketed us afresh with her stinging salt water. We lay still in silent agony while the groggy boat struggled on toward the little island.

There was a large sheet of plastic under me that I had folded around my head for protection from the watery attacks. The boat rocked and swayed, and the sweat of weakness and nausea mingled with the seawater. People groaned and vomited and huddled for protection. Unsteady from exhaustion, I found it impossible to move. I held the plastic covering tighter—until the wind caught it and tore it from my hands. The plastic flapped in the wind, the remaining half of it still beneath me. I did not have the strength to reach up and pull it back down. Like the ducks at my feet, I shivered at each new onslaught of the merciless sea.

Through salt-soaked eyes, I saw the figure of Katush crawling painfully along the deck toward me. He crept inch by inch, waiting till after each slam of the waves and consequent tilt of the boat to make his moves. When he reached me, he threw himself at the plastic tarp, caught it in his sinewy arms and swung it over me, all in one motion. Then he collapsed on my chest and was so still I could feel his heavy breathing close to my heart.

The sea's anger left almost as suddenly as it had begun. The Yami on the boat began to sing. When the velvet hills of Orchid Island came into view, the voyagers' happiness at reaching home overpowered the emotions of the sea, and they laughed with joy. One man proudly displayed a fish he had caught on his dragline during the ordeal.

The families waiting at the harbor were decked out in their finest garments to meet the boat. The men wore embroidered loincloths, vests of coconut bark, and helmets of woven rattan, and held long pointed spears. The women were spangled in colored agate beads and conical hats made of banana leaves and bamboo. The arrival of the boat was a festive occasion.

Molung met me at the pier. His skin had reddened since I last saw him, and his hair was dark gold. He told me the news of the village—who had died and who had been born in my absence. When I reached the church, the children crowded around and talked excitedly. No one was bashful.

The summer heat had passed, and a pleasant breeze blew through the tall abaca grass and the purple *varinu* flowers scattered here and there.

Some little girls brought me taro and sweet potatoes. Jayud and his wife came over and gave me a bowl of clams. Molung's mother presented me with a cooked fish. I passed out pictures I had taken during the past summer, and the neighbors came hurrying over to see themselves in the photos. That night I slept soundly, and from my bed the next morning I heard Little Jayud and the children calling my name.

~

Little Jayud slipped in the door just as I opened it, and we had breakfast together. He was a clever five-year-old, whose baggy eyes could not conceal his interest in my food. Most likely he would have received more nourishment at his own home, but we enjoyed each other's company. After breakfast, Little Jayud swept the room. Then he grabbed the dishes before I had a chance to wash them and carried them outside to the waterspout. They were, of course, just as dirty as before washing, but I could not tell him that.

Little Jayud's grandmother was old and could not walk very well. Her main responsibility was to care for her son's children while he and his wife were out working. In the daytime, she sat in the shade of the church eaves and watched the little ones playing under the waterspout.

Jayud's family had moved into a new concrete house on the other side of the village. But the grandmother refused to leave their old underground house next to the church. This was because of the sacred wooden *tamok* column, which was not only the main support beam for the home but also its soul—and the repository of her ancestral memories. She told me that in the evenings she would lean back on the *tamok* board and remember her dead husband and sing the ancient songs. I even heard her speak to the *tamok*, which must have heard and understood because it was sacred.

Sometimes when I went out to the waterspout, I could see the old grandmother hobbling along and tapping the hard earth with her staff until she came to the edge of the cliff. She would gaze at the ocean for a long time before shuffling back to her house and the sacred *tamok* inside.

Little Jayud's grandmother came to the evening prayer service in the church. The church leader chanted the Rosary in hypnotic Chinese, and the children and a few old women sang along. Their voices harmonized naturally, a wellspring of richness from weary bodies. The music floated in and around the church and down to the village, then up into the hills and skyward to the heavens. The *Taudoto* must have heard the song and known it as His own as He smiled down upon the church and the children and the old women.

~

After the prayer service, I took Little Jayud and some other children to the prison compound to watch a rehearsal for the prisoners' next show. As we walked into the courtyard where the band was practicing, I heard a shout, and some prisoners came running over to me.

"Can you sing? Come and join us!"

They pushed me onto the stage, and there—with the band's guitars and drums in the background—I rendered my version of "Oh, When the Saints Go Marching In". Little Jayud sat patiently on the side of the stage while a growing crowd of prisoners clapped and sang along with me. Soon the prisoners were dancing. The band played louder, and the music grew livelier until one of the prisoners yelled in English, "Cool it!" And the grey clad figures vanished from the stage.

"Guards," a prisoner whispered as he rushed by me. "Time for the saints to go marching out!"

When we went backstage, the bandleader, who was also the prison cook, brought me a big bucket of noodles. I ate what I could, then motioned to Little Jayud, who literally buried his head in the pail, slurping up the noodles at breakneck speed while the cook stared at him in amazement. "He looks like he hasn't eaten in ages."

"Jayud has a bottomless stomach," I explained.

The Yami girls had finished their songs. Backstage, I listened as the prisoners flattered them and offered them food. Across the sea were places they could hardly imagine. There would be money and nice clothes, and they could travel as they wished. The girls looked away shyly and said nothing. But their eyes wandered beyond the bare-chested boys watching and wanting them as they came in sweating from their dance, past the taro fields where their mothers worked in rags, past the tiresome island and the changeless waters to the lights and music and comfort.

~

"All he talked about this morning was the big pail of noodles he ate at the prison," Little Jayud's mother told me the next morning. Little Jayud grinned broadly, displaying a full set of decayed teeth, and watched his mother sling her rattan basket over her shoulder and head for the distant taro fields.

Later, as the restless clouds were preparing for the sun's evening performance, Little Jayud's father invited me to his new house for dinner, setting the food outside on a stilt house. Jayud's youngest child was barely a year old and had huge black eyes. She seemed, in fact, all eyes, the rest of her body fading away into stringy arms and legs and a distended belly.

"Is she sick?" I asked Jayud's wife as she passed me a sweet potato.

"She has worms, a bad cold, and boils," the mother answered slowly. "So I guess you could say she is sick."

For a while, the little girl simply stared at me. Then she turned to her mother, grabbed a long breast, and placed the nipple in her mouth. With her eyes still fastened on me, she tossed her head back and stretched out her arm—such a little string—to me.

The rainbow colors of the spectacular sunset looked insignificant to me behind the little girl's saucer eyes and outstretched arm and her nursing mother gazing silently at the sea.

~

Every afternoon, two girls from the primary school came to the church to prepare a tasty meal of yams, wild vegetables, fish—and mud snails. I could eat everything except the mud snails that were gathered from wet-taro fields. The two girls would painstakingly break the tails off the little snails, boil them, and then fry them in peanut oil, adding soy sauce and hot peppers. They smelled delicious. Unfortunately, I could not acquire the knack of sucking the snails out of their shells. I wondered if something was wrong with my mouth.

The neighborhood children enjoyed the colorful picture books I had brought from Taiwan. When it came time to eat, they moved their books from the table to the benches along the wall. By now, they knew what I ate was not very different from their own food. This made things easier for all of us.

After dinner, the children continued reading stories by

candlelight. They had a custom of reading out loud. It did not seem to bother them if a dozen voices coming from a dozen different books filled the room at the same time.

In the mornings from six to seven, I was busy at the clinic applying the yellow medicine or the black goo and tending to a variety of ailments. I had two regular customers. The first was a gaunt old man with a cane who came every other day. He smiled broadly when he saw me, then cringed with arthritic pain. Reaching to hold onto my arm, he slowly eased himself onto a bench. Then he sighed and pointed to his legs. After rubbing them with Ben Gay, I treated a boil or two he was sure to have somewhere on his body. As an afterthought, the old man invariably pulled out a plastic bag from his loincloth and handed it to me. "*Mugis*?" he asked. Rice. I always gave him a few bowls.

My other regular customer was a sour-faced old woman who visited me on the days the old man did not come. People said she was a bit crazy. She was not as subtle as the old man and would simply hand me her plastic bag with a drawn, hungry face. I always gave her a few bowls, too. It was almost three months before I found out those two were married.

A boy named Gakrang came to the clinic one morning. Usually a happy-go-lucky fellow, that day he sat with his head drooping and looked very sad.

"This morning, blood flowed from my father's bowels," Gakrang said. "I took him to the health department, and they gave him some pills. But we are going to pound millet and boil it for him. This will please the *Taudoto*."

Gakrang and his brother brought sheaves of millet heads with their stalks still attached to the church area because the eaves of the roof protected them against possible rain that would spoil the millet. First, they threshed the millet heads in a shallow basket to separate the chaff from the grain. Then they brought out a wooden mortar in the shape of an hourglass and took turns beating the grain with a carved pestle. Their sweaty bodies were soon caked with the yellow dust of the millet as it blew in the wind. In the afternoon, they boiled the millet and gave it to their father to eat.

The *Taudoto* must have been pleased. The next day Gakrang's father was well again.

~

The Lee brothers were very different. Big Lee was a tall and quiet Taiwanese with an intellectual bent. He was not too keen about his job as third-grade teacher, a position he considered beneath his talents. Little Lee, on the other hand, was short and stocky, outgoing, and enjoyed teaching as well as playing with his fifth graders. I got to know the Lee brothers when they came from Taiwan to teach in the primary school. They lived with their uncle, the school principal, in a house near the church. We shared the same waterspout, as did half the village.

One day after taking a shower in the waterspout, Little Lee dropped in for a visit. Still dripping with water, he sat on the *tatami* mat for a while, thumbing through my old magazines. Some children were on the other side of the *tatami* looking at picture books.

Soon, Little Lee put the magazines down and said, "There are two hundred children in our school. But we have only three teachers. My uncle is in Taiwan now trying to recruit more, but no one wants to come here. We cannot manage all those children, so most of them just play in the classroom all day."

"If I could help . . ."

Little Lee jumped off the *tatami* and with a big smile put his hand on my shoulder and said, "I knew you would agree!"

"But . . ."

"Now, as far as teaching them, you can tell stories, draw pictures, sing, do anything you like. All the children can sing, but they can't read music. You can teach them the scales."

"But . . ."

"Don't worry; you'll do fine!" Little Lee went sprinting out the door, cheerfully tossing his wet towel in the air. "See you tomorrow!" he yelled from the distance.

I wanted to tell Little Lee that I did not know the music scales in Chinese. I spent the rest of the day trying to figure them out on the church's harmonium. The next morning, Little Lee introduced me to the students as a "foreign music expert". I pumped the organ as the class sang "do re mi".

Before long I discovered a method of teaching music that would save me from "losing face". Since each song had several Chinese characters I could not pronounce, I asked the children to read the words out loud first. As they read, I quickly scribbled in the pronunciation of the difficult characters. Then I sang with the children as if I had known the pronunciation all along. If I was not fast enough the first time, I would have the children read the song again.

My method worked well until we came across a character that not even the children knew how to pronounce. Then there would be dead silence. Humiliated, I had to go and ask for Little Lee's help.

The children loved art class. But when I complimented them on their pictures, they ignored my comments. Only after repeatedly telling the children their pictures were good did reactions come. First came smiles, then courteous denials in the Asian way. Soon, the children were dashing up to me to show their colorful drawings and unabashedly praising their own artworks.

Sometimes I wondered why Principal Chen had come to work on Orchid Island. He probably had the same question about me. I concluded the principal came here because he was a fighter. He had a passionate desire to improve and to build—and the island was waiting for him. He was a big, handsome Taiwanese with a square jaw and keen eyes. Nearing fifty, he still had boundless energy. Always busy about something, he would whitewash the peeling plaster in the classrooms, plant peanuts in the school garden, or organize the student body in constructing a new wall.

Principal Chen loved walls. His goal was to have the school completely encircled by walls, so that no unwanted goats, pigs, or naked pre-school children could wander in. He tried to get the parents of the students to help move rocks for the walls. But the more he exhorted the parents that it was their school, the more they felt it was his school, so none of the parents helped. Principal Chen then worked on the walls all the harder by himself, while the children, out of fear and not a little respect, moved the rocks.

The students were so excited about the school outing that they gathered in their classrooms a full two hours before it was time to go. Every semester the primary school held a field trip. For the smaller children in the village of Imurud, it would be a chance to visit the other side of Orchid Island. Although only an hour's walk over the mountain, most had never been there before.

As we began climbing up the mountain in back of the

church, we could see some of the old people on the road overlooking the village. At least two dozen of the mothers and fathers were going with us. The men wore rattan armor and carried spears to protect their children from evil spirits that could harm them.

"I wish they would stay home!" Big Lee shrugged as he hurriedly strode past the old people. We had been walking together, with Principal Chen slightly ahead of us.

"Why don't you want the old people to come with us?" I asked Big Lee.

"Because they always ruin everything with their old-fashioned customs and superstitions."

"I like their culture," I said, not consciously trying to start an argument.

"Culture?" Big Lee stared at me in amazement. "These people have no culture. Look at what they eat. Sweet potatoes and taro. They use their hands instead of chopsticks. No matter how much we tell them, they still refuse to change. Sometimes the children are so dirty and smelly I can hardly stand it. They never wash their hands before eating—only after. Do you call that 'culture'?"

"I was thinking more of their way of life. It's so simple and rich in traditions—especially when you compare it to ours. Why change all that?"

"So, you would like them to remain in their misery. Do you want to preserve this island as a reserve for anthropologists like the Japanese did—or as a zoo for tourists?"

Big Lee had caught me off guard. I recalled what Elizabeth had told me my first day on the island, "Most people who come here to help the Yami don't accept the way they are. They help without loving."

"Oh? And then there are those like you who come along

and say everything is perfect here. Orchid Island is a paradise, and the people are saints. They can do no wrong. They don't need anything."

Big Lee's retort stung, partly because it was so unexpected and partly because there was truth in what he said.

Was my attempt to love these people simply the idealistic quest of a wishful romanticist? I tried to respond to Big Lee but could not find the right words to express my feelings.

After an uncomfortable moment of silence, Principal Chen spoke for both of us in a positive way.

"Everyone has his own style. One likes to teach. Another likes to draw and sing. I like to build things. Each has his own way, and each way is the right way. If all of us tried to change the Yami, they would resent it. If all of us tried to accept them as they are, they would never improve. The right way is the way that is right for you."

When we reached the jagged peninsula near the village of Iranumiruk, Big Lee began to lead the children down to the shore to see a large donut-shaped rock formation. But the old people protested, waving their arms wildly. Big Lee grunted, "Superstitions! Taboos!" and told the children to follow him. As we made our way down to the rock, the elders crept sullenly behind.

"They say there are many spirits here," one little boy whispered to me.

The children climbed nimbly over the rocks and then gathered around their parents, who were squatting on the coral and pointing animatedly to a cave between the rocks and the water. They listened wide-eyed as the old people spoke.

"That is where those who once lived on a smaller island floated after a flood washed them away. Their bones still remain in the cave." The children looked at the donut-shaped rock with hushed awe.

"Always the superstitions!" Big Lee complained, shaking his head. "The old people should stay home." Then he climbed back up the road and turning with a grin called to me, "You better hurry—before the spirits get you!"

~

Principal Chen and the Lee Brothers had invited me to lunch at their home. They were intrigued by my inability to extract mud snails from their shells, which was so easy for the locals to do. The stubborn little mollusks would not come out no matter how hard I sucked. I was tempted to chew the snails, shells and all.

While we were still eating, Little Jayud rushed in the door and told me his baby sister had been caught by a spirit.

"Eat first," Big Lee said, shaking his head in frustration. "The spirits will wait for you. Always the superstitions!"

I ate as fast as I could without offending Principal Chen and the Lee brothers. Then I followed Little Jayud to his house. There were thin bamboo poles placed end to end from the road up to the village, and these poles led to the house of Jayud. I knew such poles were laid to keep away the spirits of the dead.

When I reached the house, I saw two elderly men, fully armored in wooden helmets and coconut vests, squatting in the doorway. They did not greet me as I approached. Little Jayud's frightened three-year-old brother sat between them, clutching a heavy dagger between his legs.

Inside, Little Jayud's mother, also brandishing a long knife, sang disconsolately, while the grandmother beside her beat a tin tub. Jayud squatted sadly in a corner, clad only in his loincloth.

Little Jayud's baby sister had already died. I was shocked by her death, but even more surprised to learn she had already been buried. According to their custom, the Yami bury their dead immediately after death. But I could not imagine that happening. Not to the little girl with the saucer eyes. I thought of how she had reached out to me with her tiny hand while she nursed at her mother's breast . . .

The armed men outside the door stood up and began shouting fiercely. Jayud rose quickly, put on his coconut bark vest and rattan helmet, and slung a sheathed dagger over his shoulder. Grabbing a long spear, he rushed out of the house and down the hill with the two other men.

I watched them march to an open field near the side of the village. Before them lay a fresh pile of green leaves and dried abaca. That was the grave of the little girl. The men approached cautiously at first, then rushed toward the grave, jabbing the fresh grass with their spears. They retreated as if chased by an enemy, then repeated their attack, screaming in high voices. After three such attacks, they marched single file back to the house.

Jayud's wife quickly gathered her children about her skirt and huddled in a corner, her knife stretched out for protection. The three men scrambled in and out of the house, screaming and stabbing the air viciously with their spears. I sat near the door, sad and helpless, with no idea what to do.

After a few minutes, the men removed their armor, sat down on the floor, and quietly chewed betel nuts. Little Jayud stood next to his younger brother, who still held fast to the dagger. None of them raised their eyes or even noticed me.

I walked down from the house along the path lined with bamboo poles. Molung called to me from his workshop. I went over to see him, and he asked me what I was doing.

"Just walking," I said.

"Do you have any skin medicine?"

"In my bag." I reached to open my medicine kit. But Molung's hand stopped me.

He stared suspiciously at me and asked, almost in a whisper, "Where did you go just now?"

"To the home of Jayud. His little daughter died."

Molung's mood changed abruptly.

"I will come for the medicine later," he said. "It is getting late. You better go home." He mumbled goodbye and pushed me gently in the direction of the church. Any other time he would have invited me into his house to eat sweet potatoes.

~

It was sundown. I sat down on the rocky shore, munching disconsolately on one of Old Ma's stale biscuits, and gazed for a long time at the still and silent sea.

"Where are you, Lord?" I prayed. "Where are you in all of this?"

Soon the wind blew softly. Waves hit the distant rocks and broke into thousands of sun-filled stars. Evening was approaching with her shadowy songs of joy and sadness—and memories of a recent past . . .

The island is beautiful at twilight, when the sun brushes her clouds with color. But as day takes its rest, the insects of the night awake, hungry from their slumber. And babies whine as they eat, while parents rub their slowly swelling welts and whisper soothing words.

A little girl coughs and cries as her mother tries to comfort her. She mashes taro and tells the girl to eat, but she only cries louder and pushes the food away, choking. The mother holds her daughter's head as she gasps and croaks in an effort to vomit. A long black worm slowly slides out of her daughter's mouth. It falls on the floor and squirms a little until the mother crushes it under her bare feet.

A baby cuts his toes on a rock and screams as medicine is applied and the wound bound. With tears dried, he reaches out for his mother's breast. From the ground a hungry chicken jumps up on the floor and in one accurate peck tears the bandage from the baby's toes. The blood drips again, the baby wails, and his father beats the chicken's head with the back of his hand, sending her flying to the ground with a cry of surprised indignation.

In the early morning, the women leave for the fields. Their bent backs support large rattan baskets, and their strong hands grip iron digging rods. The net bags swinging from their waists hold small tin cans filled with cigarette butts, matches, a few strands of newspaper, and betel nuts.

The babies left behind cry for a little while, then sink sullenly to the ground and gaze at the sea. The women in the fields inspect their sweet potatoes and scare away goats from their patches of millet. And when they see the cows of the soldiers in the distance, they curse them with hot anger, remembering how the thoughtless beasts have trampled their fields and destroyed their crops.

They pull weeds that have grown around their newly planted sweet potatoes and dig up yams for the evening meal. Dirt sticks to their fingers and mingles with morning dew on the leaves. All the while, the powerful sun breathes its heat onto the fields. Drops of sweat soon appear on the women's foreheads and stream down to the necks of their torn work shirts, soaking them to the skin.

Sometimes the older women take off their shirts as they work in the fields, and the breeze wafts around their long sagging breasts. When the wind blows stronger, they sing the ancient songs that echo through the fields and up into the hills, reminding the elements of the strength the women possess. They sing of their youth and their triumphs and their feasts. Their song has an ancient power because it can remember, and remembering gives strength to overcome hardship. And nature, hearing the song, shrinks back in trepidation.

At dawn, the men gather on the shore, carrying oars on their shoulders and fishing equipment in their hands. Using strong ropes, they bind the oars tightly to the sides of the canoes—two-man, six-man, ten-man canoes—and they load a heavy black net and throw in a branch or two of betel nuts. Then they sit on the rocks and watch the sea for a while, smoking and chewing and wondering what the waters will bring today.

The waves lap quietly on the shore, and the sea remains inscrutable and does not tell what it will bring today. With a mighty shove, half on one side and half on the other, the men launch their boats. The sound of the wood scraping on the harsh rocks breaks the morning stillness. Upon hearing the familiar noise, the women in the faraway fields turn their heads to see if they can spot their men in the distance.

When the boats hit the water, the men leap in and swiftly row in unison to their deep-throated chanting: "*Ho, ho, hore hung to heh*!" Far out at sea, lines are let down, the nets are set, and the men wait. The sun pours down its heat, and the sea snugly withholds its treasures.

Then the *Taudoto* from his abode above sees the island of the Yami and stretches forth his hand. The sun covers its eyes, and the sea gives over its riches. The earth opens its arms and surrenders its treasure. The men jump and shout when the fish arrive. They pull up the heavy nets and laugh because they know the One Above loves them more than all the rest.

~

Every Friday after school, I gathered my medicine and cigarettes together and trekked over the mountain to the village of Ivarinu. Sometimes, if I left early enough, I could rest on top of the mountain, where the green and velvet hills lay around me like soft blankets. After the noise of the children all week, such moments were pure joy.

One day, Molung came with me. On our way, he cautioned me to walk slowly because he did not want to get to Ivarinu before dark.

"It is because of the old people," he said. "If they see me in the village, they will start rumors. The Ivarinu boys will become jealous. When I go to Ivarinu to see the girls, I must go at night and return before daybreak. It is safer that way."

We arrived in Ivarinu after the sun had set, and we walked in the shadows to the house of one of Molung's friends. The low workshop-house was filled with teenagers. Evidently, they were all friends of Molung since no one appeared jealous that he had come. The house belonged to a boy named Tamaneng, who was the same age as Molung. Like Molung, he was still searching for a wife because his previous girlfriend had left him.

The house was the size of a large pup tent, but more

elaborate than most workshops. On each wall were carved long rows of fish, painted in brilliant white and red. "The first fish my father ever caught," Tamaneng said, pointing to the walls. "We have a special respect for this fish."

Tamaneng spread thin bamboo mats on the floor and covered them with thick Chinese quilts. A single candle danced in the wind that stole through the cracks in the walls of the workshop. When the candle went out, Tamaneng shuffled in the darkness until he found matches to light it again. The yellow glow illuminated the rows of painted fish covering the walls. Tamaneng adjusted his transistor radio to a low hum as we lay on the mats. Molung rambled on in Yami with snatches of Mandarin, which I understood.

". . . takes medicine, he must," I heard him say. Tamaneng turned and asked me in a whisper if I took medicine.

"What kind?"

"The kind that stops you thinking about girls. Can you give me some?" he joked. They talked on into the night until there was a shuffle of blankets as they crawled out the door.

"Going to catch fish?" I asked.

"No," they said. "Going to catch girls." After an hour they returned. "Any luck?" I asked.

"Caught three, but they got away," Molung laughed. In a few more hours, there was another rustle of blankets and the cry of "Daybreak!"

"Now is the best time to play the guitar," Tamaneng said. I looked around for Molung, but he had already left the village. The other boys raced out of the workshop and up the hill in back to wash in the freshness of the flowing stream. I listened to the guitar music as it kept time to the morning light dancing across the village.

Lazily raising my head just a little from the quilt, I could see people walking around quietly outside in the early morning stillness. The long-nosed black pigs seemed to follow them wherever they went.

An old man squatted near a bush, while a big potbellied pig waited anxiously nearby, hunched on its tiny two-toed feet. It took a few steps forward, staring cross-eyed at the squatting man, its ears folding over its face like large sunglasses. Then it retreated when the man whispered, "Shoo!" The pig circled around the man, scraping its hide against the low leaves of the bush, and crept up once again, waiting patiently for its turn. When the man finished, he picked up a rock to clean himself and walked away. Then the pig dashed forward wildly, as if pursued by an army of hunters, and greedily lapped up the gift the man had left behind.

~

Barigoko scolded me for not going first to his house to eat. "When you are in my village, you come to my house first," he said. "Then you can go to other homes." Barigoko, the church leader in the village of Ivarinu, was the most respected man in his village. In another kind of society, he would have been the chief, but the Yami did not have chiefs. They did have, however, men with the aura of respect, built up through the years by acts of bravery, skill, and kindness. Barigoko was such a man. Emotional, often given to exaggeration, Barigoko would stop at nothing to come to the aid of one of his fellow villagers.

As we ate, a wrinkled old man hobbled to the door. He sat down on Barigoko's floor and dipped into the betel nut basket. The men talked for a while, and then Barigoko asked me, "Do you want to go pig hunting?" He explained that the old man had lost a large pig a year ago. It had escaped to the mountains and turned wild. Recently, several men had spotted the feral pig, only to have it quickly escape into the hillside forest. Barigoko planned to round up a party of hunters and recover the pig for the old man. In addition, he planned to catch several small pigs that had also run away.

Barigoko tied a towel around his forehead, pinning up his long, coal-black hair. He fastened his knife and net bag to the belt of his loincloth, and when he stood up to stretch, his hands almost touched the ceiling of his low dwelling. He was tall and thin, but muscular, and his body rippled with strength. "Let's go," he said, grabbing a coil of rope.

In a field not far from the village, the men gathered one by one until they numbered almost thirty. They squatted on a bluff overlooking a forested area nearby. When Barigoko rose up, holding his head high and proud, the others did likewise. There was just the hint of a smile on the church leader's lips, but as he turned toward me, the smile broadened into a confident grin.

Barigoko began sprinting light-footed down the hill, his bare feet gathering speed as they went. The others followed him at spaced intervals. When they had encircled the forested area, Barigoko let out a high whoop and the men closed in, yelling in shrill voices. Their screams could hardly be distinguished from the frantic squeals of the hogs scrambling out of the bushes. In no time, four of the men were clutching wriggling potbellied pigs that cried in their arms like babies at feeding time.

The second part of the hunt was not as successful. After climbing up into the dense folds of the mountains and spacing ourselves on the paths leading down from their slopes, we waited anxiously as the scouts above searched for the great wild pig.

I crouched with club in hand, ready for the pig to charge

down the hill, whereupon I would smash him in the snout or trip him on the legs and become the new hero of the village. The man in the area above me was more relaxed than I and passed the time by catching colorful insects with his two small sons, who had tagged along with him for the fun. Later, he would sell the insects. It was a growing business on the island.

The pig never appeared, but the man nearby caught quite a few insects. All of the men, in fact, returned home that day with their little tin cigarette cans filled with a number of colorful crawlers. Even though they failed to capture the long-lost hog, nobody seemed to mind much—except perhaps the old man.

Since it was Sunday evening, Barigoko asked me to lead the prayer meeting in Ivarinu so he could conduct a service in a neighboring village. I told him I was not sure how to conduct the meeting. "That makes no difference," Barigoko said. "It is God who leads a prayer meeting."

We sat in a room next to the church and practiced hymns, while the people, mostly teenagers, gathered around.

"Shall we keep singing?" I asked a boy sitting at my side.

"Let's go in and pray first," he said. "You can lead us in prayer."

The others nodded and marched into the church. They pulled the benches up around the kerosene lamp and waited silently. I tried to remember the beginning of the Chinese "Hail Mary." I had forgotten it. Turning to the boy again, I whispered, "Could you, uh . . . start the 'Hail Mary'?"

The boy intoned the prayer and the others answered, followed by silence.

I asked if anyone would like to pray. Silence again. So we sang a hymn. Then the boy next to me spoke.

"Please pray for my uncle who is sick."

"And for my grandmother," a little girl prayed.

"And that when we go up to the mountains, no green snake bites us."

"Thank you for our food."

"And for our clothes . . ." There were some giggles then, and we closed the meeting singing a Chinese version of "This Little Light of Mine".

Everyone left the church with a smile. Barigoko was right: it is God who leads a prayer meeting. I should not have been worried.

~

For over a month, I had watched my young neighbor Funai construct his first Yami canoe. After going to the hills and carefully selecting which trees he would cut, he had hewn twenty-four various-sized planks and used these to put together his boat. Beginning with the keel, he added the prow and stern parts. Gradually, he built up the side planks, fixing them to both sides of the keel with hundreds of wooden pegs rather than steel nails. Between the planks he packed a cotton-like fiber to prevent leakage. When the boat was assembled at last, he smoothed its rough sides with a flat chisel until it curved and shone like his own amber skin.

The boat was now ready for Funai to carve and paint with traditional designs: *mada* (eyes) for the prow and *tau* (Yami figures) and geometric waves for the sides. Every Yami male was expected to make at least one boat, and Funai wanted his to be as good as possible. He made sure every blow of his chisel and every stroke of his paint brush hit the right mark.

When he had finally finished, I watched as Funai rested his eyes affectionately on the canoe. The coat of white paint was still wet, shimmering pale blue in the early evening. The red and black designs were in perfect balance.

"Tomorrow, I will launch it and see if it is a good boat," he said. And as he gazed at the work of his hands, his eyes filled and shone like drops of silent water in the falling darkness.

~

In the large winter house of Nachid, the men of the village had already assembled by the time I arrived. The soft glow of a tiny oil lamp hanging from the ceiling highlighted the faces in the crowded room. Nachid sat on the second level of the terraced floor. There was nothing especially unusual about his appearance. He was short and rather squat and had a kind, simple face. From all outward appearances, in fact, one would not guess that Nachid was a prophet.

No one was sure exactly why he was a prophet. But everyone knew when Nachid had first begun showing shamanistic tendencies.

"It was after his last son died," Funai, the boat builder, told me. "Since three of his sons had passed away, perhaps the *Taudoto* pitied him and gave him this special gift."

Nachid sat on the level above us with downcast eyes and outstretched arms. He spoke softly and rhythmically, and except for his voice the room was very quiet. Although I could not understand his words, I was aware of the presence of Another. I knew it was not Nachid alone who spoke.

"He is speaking in the name of the *Taudoto*," Funai whispered to me. "His soul is with the *Taudoto*, who shines like the rays of the sun. He says in the land of the *Taudoto* all is gold and there are countless pigs and goats."

The shaman spoke for perhaps a half-hour, and when he paused, the men bowed their heads and began to sing.

"He has given us instructions," Funai continued, "on how we must be more diligent in planting our crops and less lazy if we expect to have food. Tomorrow, Nachid will kill a pig, so the *Taudoto* is pleased and has chosen this time to speak to us. He also told us not to change our ways, to remain as we have always been, to work hard, and not to depend on outside help."

While the medium continued speaking in his low voice, Funai told me more about shamanism.

"Every village has a person like this," he said. "They are like priests. The greatest prophet in our village was Syi Lingish. He was born near the Beginning, when the stone fell from heaven. Syi Lingish was like Jesus. He always heard the voice of the *Taudoto* and the *Taudoto* revealed to him how to build boats and how to catch flying fish.

"The prophet helps us in many ways. For instance, if someone's sweet potatoes are missing, he reports that crime to the prophet. If anyone has stolen anything, he confesses his sin to the prophet. If he fails to confess, he will surely meet with misfortune."

Nachid spoke slowly and softly far into the night. When he finished, he fell sideways on the floor, as if the Spirit resting on his shoulders had just left him. His soul had returned from the land of the *Taudoto*.

~

While the full moon was growing pale in the light of breaking dawn, Nachid, back from his heavenly sojourn, was feverishly slicing up a fattened pig. Earlier, he had slit the pig's throat with his long knife and placed its carcass on a pile of straw. The straw was lit and more straw was laid on the pig, until its hair had all been burned off and only the black form remained, stiff as a cast-iron statue. Nachid washed the pig and started cutting it up.

He began by slicing from the snout across the back and then severed the head. Turning the pig over on its back, he cut deeply into its sides and removed the slabs of meat with bloodied hands. Carefully, he brought out the entrails and handed them to his small son, who ran to wash them in the flowing spring water. As he washed the intestines, the boy glided his knife gracefully through the long rubbery tubes until they were free of all waste matter. Nachid swiftly cut the carcass into little pieces, and his relatives divided them into portions, so that all would have their share.

The prophet looked up at me with a wide grin. He held the large dripping pig heart in his hands and asked me if I wanted it since the Yami do not eat the heart. I accepted the gift but later gave it to Principal Chen, who was happy to cook and consume it himself.

When Nachid had finished dividing the pig, he took a few portions of the choicest meat and placed them in a round rattan basket. His wife, who had been boiling millet and yams since dawn, rolled several balls of millet dumplings and placed them in the basket, along with yams and taro and pieces of goat meat given by relatives who had killed goats for the *Paros* Festival. The time for sacrifice had begun.

The men and women of the village gathered along a low bluff above the beach, near Molung's stilt house. The older men wore silver helmets, their most prized possessions. The helmets had been painstakingly molded from the silver of Japanese coins or from silver said to have been brought back from the Batan Islands on voyages to the Philippines centuries earlier. The loincloths and striped vests of the men had been washed and dried in the sun the day before and shone with freshness. Clothed in their red and white dresses and long strands of agate beads, the women stood watching as the sacrifice began.

Solemnly, the headmen of each of the forty houses in the village marched down to the beach. They carried their gift-laden rattan baskets under one arm and placed them in rows facing the surf. Then the men sat quietly and watched the sea. The prophet intoned a chant, and the others began to sing. An old man holding a dagger rose and exhorted the others. He was followed by a few elders, each delivering short orations. After this, the men chanted again, and then walked swiftly away. The prayer meeting on the beach had ended.

As soon as the men left the shore, the youngsters came swooping down on the food offerings like birds. "Do not worry," Funai told me, as we walked away. "They will not eat the food. It has been offered to the *Taudoto* as a sacrifice for our crops and animals. Only the pigs may eat the food now, and the young people will see to that job."

~

Two days before Christmas, I filled my pack with cigarettes and candy and set out for Iraralai, the furthest and most isolated village on the island.

Aegi, the church leader of Iraralai, was highly respected because of his extraordinary skill in fishing, building houses, and concern for others. Aegi had begun the island's first cooperative. Since Iraralai had no store, he had organized twenty members who contributed money each month and shared in the dividends. As a result, the villagers were able to purchase soap, dried noodles, and other products.

I gave Aegi some Christmas cards. His quiet, pregnant wife picked up a card and said, "My husband knows this story." Each time she picked up a new card, she remarked that her husband knew that story. She was very proud of her knowledgeable husband.

At the prayer service that night, Aegi spoke softly but with authority, and the people listened with reverence. As he preached, his two-year-old daughter danced playfully in front of the altar, perhaps sensing that the congregation would notice her just as they did her father. Once, she slipped and fell on her face and cried out in pain, and her mother ran to pick her up and carry her back to their spot on the floor. Otherwise, the people ignored her.

The villagers of Iraralai danced after the prayer service, even though it was still two days before Christmas. It was a benefit performance on my behalf. I shared candy and cigarettes with them, so they could benefit, too.

The next day I went to the village of Ivarinu, where Barigoko had planned a Christmas pageant. His sermon ran a full two hours, interspersed with hymns. I dozed through most of it. Barigoko seemed to be having a contest of sorts with the Protestant church leader to see whose service could last the longest.

Later, the teenagers presented an ingenious Christmas play. They had constructed a rickety manger from bamboo and abaca grass and stuffed a little blond-haired doll beneath the straw. When the boy and girl playing Mary and Joseph reached "Bethlehem" after trudging around the church in circles for a good five minutes, they crawled inside the manger and merrily plucked the little blond doll out of the grass. At the play's climax, once the evil and jealous King Herod had sent soldiers to capture all the newborn boys, the teenagers grabbed twenty or so little children from the audience and threw them onto the middle of the floor, screaming "Kill!" Fortunately, the play ended at this point.

Molung and some of his friends had come over the hill

to Ivarinu to watch the festivities. It was almost midnight when the program finished, and I walked with them back over the mountain to Imurud. The sky was flooded with stars, and we all sensed there would be a boat the next day because the weather was so nice.

Over a month had passed since a boat docked at the island, and planes had long since been grounded. Stores were lacking cigarettes, which was a major tragedy for the island. As we walked up the hill, Molung and his friends scoured the ground for discarded cigarette butts they could recycle.

When we began our descent from the mountainside above Imurud, I saw what looked like little bonfires scattered throughout the village. Drawing closer to the steep cliff overhanging Imurud, I could see it was the light of candles. The children were Christmas-caroling, a tradition brought over by the Presbyterian Church. It was midnight, and the village of Imurud glowed with the warmth of Christmas.

Sometime earlier, the Medical Missionary Sisters in Taitung had sent me a "care package" containing Spam, instant pudding, Jell-O, and other goodies. I had eaten them all, judiciously choosing moments when the children were away. But there was still one tempting package left, which I had not yet opened—a luscious-looking box of Duncan Hines cake mix.

How often I had gazed and drooled at that box's photograph of a fluffy spice cake, only to turn back resolutely to my plate of boiled taro and snails. I would save the cake for a special occasion. Besides, not only did I lack an oven, I had never made a cake before. But Christmas Eve was here, and I could wait no longer.

As Molung and his friends fell asleep on the *tatami*, I stirred milk and water into the cake mix, trying to figure out the simple instructions. I worked until 4 A.M. Then I stood back like a true artist viewing my creation: three large, crumbly cookies, each the size of a skillet. My apologies to Duncan Hines. I placed these marvelous cakes on the table and went to bed. When I awoke the next morning, Molung and his friends had left—and so had the three cookies. All that remained were a few crumbs. Merry Christmas!

~

That night in Imurud, we had a rousing Christmas dance contest. The old women, clad in their traditional costumes, performed a "hair dance", in which they bent back and forth at the waist, sending their long hair flying from the ground to high above their heads. Molung watched the old women dancing and shook his head and said, "We can dance better than that." When the old women had finished their number, Molung led the youth in a pulsing snake line. Not to be outdone, the older men danced with intricate, seemingly impossible foot movements. It is good I was not the judge because each of the dances looked the best to me.

The only village I had not yet visited for Christmas was Yayo, near the harbor. But by now, all our candy and cigarettes had been used up, so no presents were left for the villagers. Then providentially, the long-awaited boat arrived on Christmas Day, and I was told there were two packages waiting for me at the harbor. As expected, they were full of candy and cigarettes: gifts from Father Hans and the Sisters in Taitung. Now Yayo could have a party! In addition, the package contained instant oatmeal and canned food marked, "Do not give to Yami. These are for you!"

During that Christmas evening in Yayo, there were dances and skits, but what I remember most was the last timeless moment on the beach. Everyone had joined arms in a long line that lengthened as it picked up more and more dancers. The human snake curved and swayed beside waters alive with the light of the stars. A young man in a bright red shirt pulled the line with strong arms, and we pushed forward at his command. When he leapt, we leapt, pounding our feet in unison on the hapless earth. Waves of harmony and unity bolted through our entwined arms and captured my heart with a single beat.

It was like some kind of dream—beautiful and unreal and indescribable. At some point during the dance, I felt sure we had become one with the earth and the waters and the stars. Perhaps we had even been born into the land of the *Taudoto*, where everything is made of gold. I wanted to ask somebody if it was real, and I looked out and reached out, but there was no one to ask except those here with me in the dance. And how would they know if it was real?

Chinese New Year. The rhythmic clapping of a dragon dance pierced the morning stillness. The gyrating red beast was slowly making its way down the hill into the village of Imurud, carried on the backs of some thirty weary prisoners. The dragon writhed and fumed in front of Old Ma's store and Principal Chen's home, greedily consuming its victim's money after each performance. Then it headed to the church.

After the dragon had entertained me and my neighbors and relieved us of all our loose change, I escaped to the village of Yayo, where the prisoners had invited me to their New Year's party and banquet.

I was singing my set of songs for the prisoners on a makeshift stage in the prison compound when I noticed a man with a bright red shirt smiling at me from behind the long rows of prisoners. I recognized him as the leader of the snake dance at the Yayo Christmas party. When the show was over, and the prisoners and guards were wishing each other a Happy New Year, I squeezed through the tipsy crowd to where the man was standing. When I approached him, he whispered to me with an air of mystery, "Come over as soon as you can. I will wait for you in the village."

After dinner, while the prisoners and guards were still toasting each other with rice wine, I slipped out of the prison compound and raced to the nearby village. The sun was just setting on the Yayo waters when I spotted the young man with the red shirt waiting for me along the side of the road.

"Hurry!" he said, grabbing my arm. "We'll be late."

"Where are we going?" I asked apprehensively.

"To the police station. *Combat* is on TV tonight."

There were three television sets on the island, but the one in Imurud had no reception and the one in Iraralai had no electricity. The only TV that worked was at the Yayo police station, which boasted a generator. So that night, for the first time on Orchid Island, I watched television.

The atmosphere at the police station was like that of an outdoor movie, with scores of little children squeezed up front and older ones behind. The young man in the red shirt introduced himself as Bamya and explained how TV had helped the children learn more about the outside world.

"They can sing the commercials," he said. "And now they know how to play war games."

After *Combat* ended, a long Taiwanese soap opera began. Finally, late in the evening, the generator went off, and everyone returned home. Bamya invited me to his house, where we talked about our lives until the early hours of morning. I watched as Bamya's expression alternated from a crinkled, carefree smile to a mask of pain and loss. His face, at twenty-four, was lined with sensitivity and sorrow. The candlelight, seemingly in tune with his feelings, painted one half of his face bright yellow and the other half a rusty brown.

"Losing a father is hard, yet you can get by," he said. "But not having a mother is almost unbearable. My mother died when I was still in primary school. There was no one to go to the hills and gather food for us. Sometimes my brothers and sister went to dig for taro when we grew older."

Bamya paused in his story and lit a cigarette. He leaned back against the wall and studied the ceiling. It was very dark in his little workshop.

"My father asked me if I had found a girl yet to marry. He was getting anxious because there was still no one to cook for us and keep house. I told him I did not want to marry a pretty girl because pretty girls are lazy and always have one eye on the soldiers and the prisoners. I wanted a plain-looking girl who was a good worker and could go to the fields to get our food when we were hungry. My father agreed, so I found such a girl and got engaged.

"After our marriage, I built this workshop for us. As soon as I finished it, my wife went to Taiwan to work. I asked her not to go, but she said we needed the money, and since I did not listen to her when she told me not to smoke and eat so many betel nuts, she would not listen to me when I told her not to go to Taiwan.

"Soon, I will also go to Taiwan. My wife and I will work in the mountains on the east coast. We can earn more money in Taiwan than we can here."

When I told Bamya that I wished I could work in the mountains with them, he only laughed and said, "It would be too hard. You are not used to that kind of work."

Bamya told me that at dawn his villagers would hold the annual *Mivanoa* ceremony to call flying fish to their shores. There would also be the launching of a new boat. "The *alibangbang* are swimming from the Philippines to our island," he said. "They are almost here, so they will hear us call them."

The next morning, long before the sun arose, I could hear noise and excitement in the village. Everyone was already heading toward the beach.

The Yami canoes were all lined up pointing to the sea. The men once again wore their large silver hats, bracelets, and gold necklaces as they climbed into the waiting boats and sang loudly, "O you fish in every place, swim here to our fishing grounds!"

After this call to the sea, a chicken was killed alongside each of the boats. The men and boys crowded around to dip their fingertips in the blood. Then they ran to the water and smeared the blood on wet pebbles. Some of the blood was also smeared on small bamboo cylinders that were afterward brought back to the houses as charms.

Ten of the men pulled the newly built canoe to the water's edge, scraping its hull on the coarse pebbles beneath. Together, they began to chant and with a thrust hurled themselves into the boat as it hit the foamy breakers, rowing the oars in rhythmic harmony.

Out a certain distance, the men stood up in the canoe and called again to the flying fish. The endless sea stretched before them, echoing their call in the silence of sun-filled stars sparkling on its early morning waters.

I watched until the boat became a dark silhouette against the glow of the rising sun. In another moment it was gone, and only the stillness and ripples of the waves remained.

Alone on the beach, I prayed the silent sea would answer the call of the fishermen and send plentiful schools of *alibangbang* swimming to their shores.

~

Even with the arrival of flying fish, Orchid Island still had an acute scarcity of staples like rice and tubers. The typhoon of the previous summer had blanketed the hills with salt water, suffocating the island's sweet potato crop. The taro roots had survived the typhoon because of their strong leaves. But taro was not enough. There was no place to buy rice, and Old Ma only sold small sacks of flour, which were not sufficient for the islanders.

Father Hans would periodically send bags of rice over on the boat. But the need grew, and there was never enough rice no matter how much he sent. Each time rice arrived, there was nearly a riot, and moving and distributing the large rice bags was an ordeal. Invariably, many were left out and had to rely solely on taro, and the taro roots grew smaller and smaller each day.

People came daily to the church to beg for rice or to ask when the boat with rice would come or if I would sell them just a little bit. An old man with a withered arm often came to the church. Because he was unable to work, he asked for money. I would give him a few *kwai*. Then he would hand the money back to me and say he wanted to buy a little rice with it. I would shake my head sadly because there was not any rice left. Sometimes, an elderly woman would come to the clinic complaining of stomach pains. I would give her medicine, but what she really needed was food since her problem was hunger.

To add to my worries, I broke a tooth while crunching on a hard betel nut. The cavity was exposed and ached when I ate, so I used the other side of my mouth to chew on. But a cavity developed on that side as well, so I had to munch with my two front teeth, like a rabbit. The pain was becoming intolerable. I heard there was a dentist at the airport military compound and went there for help.

The dentist had gone to Taiwan, but his young teenage assistant offered to help me. In one corner of the barracks was a table with several bottles of medicine covered with dust and cobwebs. The boy placed me in a chair in front of the table and attached a needle to an overhanging drill, which was operated by a foot pedal like a sewing machine. I held my breath as he began drilling a hole in one of the broken teeth "to let out the gas inside". When he was finished, he stuffed some cotton in the hole he had made, and added more cotton into the exposed cavity on the other side. Then he told me to come back the next day.

There was less pain now, except when I ate anything sweet. I returned every day for a week, and each time the boy put a little bit of medicine in the cavity and stuck some fresh cotton in the hole. "I hope the dentist comes back soon," he said at the end of the week, "because I don't know what to do next. This is as far as I have studied." That is when I decided to go back to Taiwan and find a real dentist.

Since the first semester of school had ended, and the children were having their long winter vacation, this would also be a good time to find work in the mountains, if possible.

The plane flew regularly now that business at the new hotel was picking up. I booked the 9 A.M. flight. In the early morning, while I was packing my bag, the usual crowd came to the clinic asking for rice and medicine. The man with the withered arm was there begging for money. The woman with the stomach pains was there asking for medicine.

I wanted to bring my guitar back with me to Taiwan. But a boy from over the mountain had borrowed it the night before and taken it to his village. There were only two hours before the plane was scheduled to arrive—barely enough time to race over the mountain and retrieve my guitar.

But first I needed to eat. Otherwise, I would not have enough strength for the journey. Since there was no food at the church, I ran down to the store to buy some biscuits. But Old Ma had not made them yet. I hurried back up to the church and found some instant oatmeal that I softened up with cold water. Although out of sugar, there was still half a bottle of cherry cough syrup in the clinic. I poured the syrup in the mixture and spooned it down. It tasted so good. Then I bolted out the door, leaving the old man with the withered arm and the woman with the stomach pains still whimpering.

I panted up the hill behind the church until I reached the first level. Then my teeth began aching. The cough syrup—why had I dumped it all in the oatmeal? The throbbing pain was unbearable, and I could go no farther. I stumbled back down the hill to the clinic.

"Oh, you came back!" The old man with the withered arm smiled greedily. The woman with the stomach pains said she had been wondering where I had gone. I gave them a wordless stare and fumbled for some cotton. Dousing the cotton with a strong liquid that tasted like whiskey and burned like hell, I stuffed it into the holes in my teeth.

"Aah . . . ," I groaned as the pain let up. The old man with the withered arm and the woman with the stomach pains looked at each other. How could *he* have pain? Tossing them a final glare, I galloped over the hill.

The boy who had borrowed my guitar had gone fishing. His sister said he had not brought my guitar with him when he came over the mountain the night before. I stumbled back over the hillside in dejection.

Sweaty, dirty, and aching, I lugged my bags down to the hotel and scanned the sky for the 9 A.M. flight. Then I paused outside the hotel door to catch my breath. Through the blur of sweat on my glasses, I spotted the pretty young lady who made plane reservations for the hotel walking toward me, smiling innocently, carrying my guitar on her shoulder.

"Thank you for the guitar," she cooed. "I asked that boy last night if I could borrow it. I knew you wouldn't mind. Oh, and by the way, the plane won't come today. Maybe tomorrow. Bye-bye."

I took the guitar and thanked the girl as politely as I could under the circumstances and collapsed on the ground, waiting for the man with the withered arm and the woman with the stomach pains to find me.

Several months a year, many of Orchid Island's younger generation travel to mainland Taiwan to look for work. Some acquire jobs in factories or on freight trucks, but the majority of them prefer planting trees in the high rugged mountains off the southeastern coast. After arriving back in Taiwan and getting my teeth fixed, I hoped to spend the waning days of winter working there as well.

However, I had several uncertainties. My first fear was that as a foreigner I would not be permitted to do this kind of labor. My second fear was that I would not be capable of it. The Yami, like all tribal people, were used to hard work. The difficulties could prove too much for me. My third fear was that I might get hurt. I could slip down a mountain slope, crash into a tree, and have to be carried down to the hospital. But finally, after putting these worries in God's hands, I looked for a job.

The Yami workers, who were waiting in Taitung to go up to the mountains, were skeptical. "You can't work," one of them told me. When I asked him why, he just shook his head. "It is too hard. They only give you rice to eat." Some of the other men laughed, but there was a new, concerned look in their eyes that I had not seen before.

When the workers realized I was serious about wanting to work in the mountains, they arranged for me to go to the town of Chihpen with them the next day and meet a pick-up truck that would take us partway to the work camp. That night, the men helped me buy the things I needed: rubber boots, gloves, a bamboo hat, a lunch tin, and a scarf. I also packed a warm jacket. Before dawn, we set out for Chihpen. There were seven Yami men with me. About thirty workers had gone up the day before.

Once in the town of Chihpen, we walked up a grassy knoll to an old brick farmhouse, where a waiting truck was being loaded with supplies. The sky was a deep blue and the trees around us shone brightly in the morning sunshine. The mountains loomed far and purple in the distance. It was very quiet except for the sporadic singing of the birds and the soft strumming of a nearby guitar.

By 9:30 in the morning, the truck had been loaded and was ready to leave. We piled in the back and began our ascent to the mountains. As the road became narrow and steep, I sensed a constricted feeling in my stomach, realizing there was no turning back now. After an hour, we came to a checkpoint where I was required to present a mountain pass in order to travel to the restricted area of the higher mountains. I had thought of this beforehand and applied for one. An officer looked at my pass, opened a book especially for foreigners, which only had one other name written in it, and asked how long I planned to stay.

"A week."

"A week! What are you planning to do up there?"

"Work."

"Work! Did you come by yourself?"

"No. Those are my friends on the truck."

"Send them in here!" the officer ordered. I was worried now. Mountain areas are often difficult to enter, either for security reasons or because they are too dangerous. When the seven Yami had assembled before him, the officer warned them: "Take good care of this foreigner. If anything happens to him, I could lose my job!"

The workers nodded, and we went back to the truck. One of them politely helped me climb on as the officer watched. When we were out of sight of the checkpoint, they asked me if I was comfortable or needed anything, and we all burst out laughing.

We traveled for another hour and a half before finally reaching the end of the road. The blue sky had long since given way to mist and clouds, and the air was chilly. There was a little wooden shack perched at the road's end, and my fellow travelers told me the farmers there usually gave rice to the workers who passed by at mealtime. However, because no one had told them we were coming, no rice had been prepared. We still had five hours of walking before reaching the campsite, so we set off quickly in order to arrive there before dark.

We forded five or more mountain streams until the path began to get steeper. In single file, we pushed upward through the dense foliage. The squawks of wild chickens and the scolding of monkeys as we invaded their privacy blended into the music of the forest.

We were getting hungry. Most of us had not eaten all day. But as we were resting, one boy proudly pulled a large loaf of Chinese New Year's glutinous rice cake from his bag. He divided it evenly among us and that was enough to keep us going. Later, when we were thirsty, the workers found some thick grass stems with water in them that we could drink.

The only person in our group who had worked in these mountains before was a young man named Jyalikning. He became our leader and set a fast pace. During the most difficult climbs, he managed to whistle or sing a few bars of the latest Mandarin hit. The others caught his song like a rope, and the song lifted them up and gave them energy. Jyalikning was cheerful and self-confident, and his long straight hair blew in the wind. When we were nearing the camp, he whispered to me with a mischievous grin, "We will be there in a few minutes, but I will tell the others we still have another hour's climb."

Just before dark, through the drizzle and the mist, we saw the camp. It consisted of two buildings, a long and a short one. Jyalikning whistled loudly, we heard voices, and the thirty Yami workers who had come earlier rushed out to meet us. To my surprise, Bamya and his wife were among the workers who had arrived the previous day. Bamya looked at me with disbelief and exclaimed, "You are not going to work here, are you?" I answered that I had not come all the way up this mountain just for the fun of it.

Inside, the work camp was hardly what I had expected.

At least three cassette players were blasting the latest pop songs. Guitars were everywhere. In one corner a noisy card game was in full swing. It looked like a party! Everyone was clean and well-dressed except for the newcomers. As soon as we arrived, the workers hustled us into the washroom.

After bathing, we ate rice and talked. The workers told me about the work, the boss, the pay, everything I should know. There were three types of work: cutting grass, which meant clearing an area in order to plant trees; preparing the ground, which meant hoeing out spaces for the trees; and the actual planting of the trees. They said the boss and the foremen were nice to them, although they only gave them rice to eat. The workers could buy cans of tuna, brown sugar, or a few vegetables, but most did not want to spend their money on food.

"Patience" was the word I kept hearing over and over. The pay was eighty *kwai* a day (two U.S. dollars) with five *kwai* deducted for rice. The working hours were from 6 A.M. to 3:30 P.M. with a half-hour off for lunch.

The barracks we stayed in consisted of long, raised wooden floors on each side of a dirt alley that ran through the center of the floors. The wooden platforms were used for sleeping, eating, and anything else one might do with his shoes off. There were two large wood-burning furnaces spaced a distance apart in the alley. The workers' damp clothes were draped on clotheslines near these furnaces. Everyone lived together on the wooden floors. There was no separate area for the women. They stayed with their husbands or boyfriends.

The camp issued fluffy white quilts to us newcomers. Normally, two persons would share one quilt, but because there were relatively few workers, I received a full one. The workers arranged an empty space for me on the wooden floor next to a furnace, so it was very warm. At 8 P.M., the last of the candles went out, and voices and music faded into dreams.

~

At five in the morning a voice shouted, "*Chi chuang, chi chuang*—Get up! Hit the deck!" Nobody made the slightest movement. All blackness and stillness. A few minutes later the voice came again, "*Chi chuang, chi chuang.*" Still no movement, although I suspected everyone was awake. Gradually, a few creaks were heard, and some shadowy forms emerged from their quilts. A candle was lit, and a cassette began playing the Mandarin pop song, "*Wode Ai Tsung Nali Lai*?—From Where Does My Love Come?" The day had begun.

After washing, all rushed to get their rice. Bamya called for me to come and eat with him and his wife. Later, they filled my lunch tin with rice, and Bamya showed me how to wrap the tin in my scarf and tie it around my waist. The lunch tin rested on my back just above the hips so that it was hardly noticeable. Then we put on our boots, bamboo hats, and gloves and went outside to plant trees. On the way, we picked up clusters of *shu miao*—tree seedlings, and stuffed them into cloth bags. We hung the bags on our hoes and slung them over our shoulders. It was still dark when we set out along the path to the work site.

As we walked in single file, the sun rose lazily over the distant mountains and suffused the morning mist with a golden hue. The forests around us took on an enchanting atmosphere. Our foreman was a young Taiwanese man with a yellow jacket and a thin, serious face. He assigned each of us *hang*—rows leading up the steep slopes. We were to check if a tree seedling had died or if a suitable spot had no tree. Then we were to hoe the earth and plant a seedling. The seedlings were to be spaced about three or four feet apart.

This sounded very easy, but it was hard for me to distinguish the rows, and often there was a tangled mass of brush blocking the *hang*. I seemed to spend most of my time trying to climb over the barricades of bushes and find the way back to my row, if there was any row at all.

After I had planted several seedlings, the foreman came over and watched me. When I stuck the little tree in the ground and covered its root with dirt, he reached down and pulled it out. "That's not right," he told me, and demonstrated the correct planting technique. The earth followed his every movement. I tried again as he watched, and when I finished, he reached down and pulled the seedling out again. "Still not right," he said. "Take your time and plant the tree firmly. You shouldn't be able to pull it up afterward." I tried again as the foreman went away, attempting to catch up with the other workers. But I lagged hopelessly behind.

The bag of seedlings on my back was heavy and cumbersome, and I was continually slipping on the wet earth. After what seemed like a long time, I dared to look at my watch, hoping it would be lunchtime. It was only 8 A.M. I kept trudging up the slopes and hoeing and planting. Each time the foreman came by, I gave him an awkward grin and hoped he would not be able to pull the seedling out.

When 11 A.M. finally arrived, I sat with the other workers, opened my lunch tin, and stared at the white rice gleaming up at me in the sun. I started eating, trying to make the rice go down. But it all seemed to linger at the bottom of my throat. Then Jyalikning reached over and put a lump of brown sugar in my rice. He had taken it from his tin. I mixed the sugar into the rice, hoping to get a crumb or two of it with each mouthful. It was delicious. But I ran out of sugar with still a third of my rice left.

"If you cannot finish the rice, throw it out," Jyalikning told me. "But bury the rice because if the foreman sees it, he will scold us." Then he pulled a small canteen from his waist and smiled, "Here." I drank a little of the fresh water and felt the rice slowly slide from my chest to my stomach.

"That was so good," I told Jyalikning. He laughed and said, "You are not used to it yet. This is just the first day."

While working, I tried to focus on the meaning of my work. I was participating in the process of regeneration—planting seedlings that would one day become mighty trees, helping the earth to be born again and grow. These were lofty thoughts. But soon I found myself dreaming of orange juice and fudge sundaes and turkey dinners—or even a good hamburger. I imagined myself relaxing at a coffeehouse, watching a movie, playing the guitar by a warm fireplace, or talking with friends. Time passed quickly.

At exactly 3:30, we stopped working and headed back to the camp. We cleaned our boots and washed our feet in the icy water of the river below the bunkhouse. When the others went to bathe and change into clean clothes, I realized that I had forgotten to bring an extra pair of pants with me. As soon as I mentioned my predicament, two pairs were promptly tossed in my direction. Community life. I hung my jacket to dry near one of the furnaces and began eating.

Although all of us stayed in one room, each group of two or three had their particular floor area that they rarely left, even though it was only a few feet from the next area. These private spaces became like rooms without walls, so much so that I felt I should knock before crawling a few feet over to the next group!

In the evening, someone shouted, "Too bad! Whose jacket

was that?" I turned to see my coat smoldering, with all but the sleeves and zipper burned off. I had not realized the jacket was flammable nylon when I placed it next to the furnace. Consequently, for the next week I had to wear only my sleeves and zipper to work each day. But it was not a bad work outfit—not too hot and not too cold—with a built-in ventilator.

After supper (rice and watery soup), I returned to my floor space and played the guitar. Bamya's wife came over and handed me a bowl of hot brown sugar soup. "I heard you like brown sugar," she said smiling. The sugar drink tasted like the best of French wines, and I passed it around to the other boys sitting near me. It seemed to flood my tired body with energy. We strummed the guitar and sang and almost drowned out the sound of the three cassette players.

The head foreman came over to my "room" and talked for a while. He gave me a bag of brown sugar (word travels fast) and a Chinese novel "in case you get bored". He was a Taiwanese named Lim and had a kind, lonely face. When he talked, he held his hand over his mouth so I would not smell the rice wine on his breath. Lim was thirty-seven, unmarried, and said he enjoyed living in the mountains. I asked him, "Do many foreigners come up here to work?"

"No, no, not many foreigners. Not to work, that is. Not many. Very few. In fact, you are the first one," he stammered, adding that he was "moved" that a foreigner would want to work in the mountains.

"He wants to be your friend," Jyalikning whispered to me when the head foreman had left. "Be sure to ask for his address so you can keep in touch." Jyalikning seemed proud that the foreman had wanted to be my friend. Maybe my being friends with the foreman gave "face" to the Yami workers, as if I represented them.

"They will probably want to make *you* a foreman next," Bamya kidded me.

"I could never do that," I said. "I can barely find my own *hang*. How would I direct others to theirs?"

Around 8 P.M., the voices and music and candles dimmed into soft whispers and night talk. I was very tired and closed my eyes, but I could still hear the conversation around me. A young Taiwanese worker had crawled up next to Jyalikning, and they were talking about the various jobs they had held. Their common language was Mandarin, so I could understand everything they said. As they discussed their adventures and plans, I learned what they thought of the different freight truck routes, the bosses in the factories and lumberyards, and the girls in the cheap hotels of the south and east coast.

The next day, we planted pine seedlings that smelled like Christmas trees. The fog was thick throughout the day and erased from view all but the nearest trees. The effect was eerie, as if to slip would be like falling into nothingness. I felt my back and legs getting accustomed to the work, and the time passed quickly now. In the morning, no one talked; they just worked silently. After lunch, there was more conversation, which changed into singing around 2 P.M. The singing increased in volume as quitting time drew near and the workers grew wearier.

As we were finishing up the day's work, Jyalikning asked me, "Are you going to be a priest?" When I nodded, he said, "That is good. Priests make lots of money. I would like to be a priest, too." I did not know how to reply to that. Then he asked, "Can priests marry?"

I was a little surer of this one. "No," I answered.

"Since you are not a priest yet, can you marry?"

"No."

"Can you have a girlfriend?"

"No."

"Well, don't you ever *think*, I mean, have desires?"

"Yes. But God helps me."

Jyalikning did not say anything, but after a while he whispered to the boy next to him, "He must take medicine."

That evening the head foreman came again, and this time he gave me a big pot of steaming pork and two cans of tuna. He remarked how "pitiful" I must be because I had nothing to eat with my rice. Then he quickly went away.

"Be sure and ask him for his address next time," Jyalikning reminded me, eyeing the pork lovingly. Maybe that was why he was happy I was making friends with the head foreman. I split the pork with Jyalikning and the workers around me. Then I took the two cans of tuna and gave them to Bamya and his wife. The next day there would be a little chunk of tuna in my lunch alongside the rice and brown sugar.

~

The morning was cold and rainy as we sloshed again to our work site. Everything was muddy and slippery, and the rain seeped through my backless jacket like melting ice. It looked like a hard, slow day, but after lunch the foreman called it quits, and we headed home. We jogged the half-hour back to camp, laughing, slipping, and bumping into each other. Our carefree racing seemed to brighten the darkness and shield us from the hostile elements of nature.

When the sun came out in the afternoon, I offered to take some photos, being the only one in the camp with a camera. I might as well have announced the president was coming to see us. Everyone leaped for their backpacks and struggled into clean clothes, combing their hair and giggling with excitement. I spent the rest of the afternoon writing down names and addresses so I could send them the photos.

The workers appeared happy about dressing up, although they seldom lay around in the barracks wearing their dirty work clothes. Everyone bathed daily, even when there was no hot water. I also made it a point to shave every day or two and comb my hair and try to appear neat, although my natural tendencies were in the opposite direction.

The following days took on a rhythm: the morning's work and the long wait until lunch, the afternoon with its expectation of going back to the camp, and the evening with its fun and relaxation. The barracks was a little world in itself. Once inside, no one left except to wash or go to the bathroom. There were those who always listened to music, memorizing the new songs; those who quietly practiced the guitar; those who sang and those who talked and those who listened; those who played cards; those who read; and those who made love. In that one room there was something for everyone.

One afternoon, Lim came over to watch me work. He told me I should rest more and not work so hard. Then he took my hoe and planted several trees for me. I asked him what kinds of trees we were planting.

"Two types," he answered. "One is a cheap pine that will be used for making telephone poles. The other is a very expensive wood. It is too expensive for Taiwan since no one here uses such nice wood for their houses. It will be exported to . . . to . . . to America . . . for their—for your—houses." I looked down, kind of embarrassed. We both felt the incongruity of the situation.

That evening when I went into the barracks, it was quieter than usual. There was no music playing, and no one was singing. Everyone spoke in whispers. In one corner,

Jyalikning lay crumpled in his quilt. He had been chopping logs with some of the others, fallen on a piece of sharp wood, and sliced his leg to the bone. His relatives and fellow villagers were huddled around him. I stared at his leg, which was bandaged with gauze and soaked in blood.

"Bad luck," Lim said. "It could happen to anyone. They will have to carry him down to the hospital tomorrow. The boss will pay the medical expenses. Will you go with them?"

Nodding, I packed my bags since we would leave early the next morning. Then I exchanged addresses with Lim and the thin, serious Taiwanese foreman, who gave me a small wooden carving he had made. They both invited me to come back some day when I would not have to work. Later, I spoke with Bamya and his wife and the other Yami workers. By then I was beginning to feel sad about leaving. When we talked, the workers seemed to have that new look again in their eyes. I think it was the look of brotherhood.

That night I lay awake. The rain was falling hard, and I knew the steep road down the hill would be slippery the next morning. Jyalikning would have to be carried piggyback style since the path was too narrow for more than one person, and he was one of the heavier workers. I thought of the work, the workers, and the misty atmosphere of these rugged mountains that made it so hard to leave.

In the morning as we prepared our descent, Bamya put his arm on my shoulder and told me to be careful. His wife pressed a little packet of brown sugar into my hand, then ran quickly back to the barracks.

Jyalikning had three relatives with him in the camp, and they took turns carrying him on their backs. Every ten minutes or so, they would stop and alternate their load. I watched the blood trickle down Jyalikning's foot. It fell in big red drops on the ground, mingling with the rainwater and the mossy brown earth. In time it would be drunk by the yellow-brown soil beneath in its own strange kind of communion.

It seemed to take forever to get down from the mountain. The boys walked quickly. Jyalikning's cousin kicked off his muddy tennis shoes so he could have a better grip with his bare feet. The cousin he bore on his back was much heavier than he was. We stopped only once on our downward journey, and that was to watch a family of curious monkeys swing down from their trees to watch us. They again scolded us for invading their domain.

We reached the road at last and lay Jyalikning on a bed in a wooden shack. He was cold and white. We covered him with a thick quilt, and I held his hand while he moaned. Three old Hakka men lived in the shack. They looked at us indifferently. We asked if there would be a truck soon. They complained about how bad it was living in the mountains and said they did not know when a truck would come. The foreman had phoned earlier that we had an injury, but he did not know if the call went through. We waited.

One of the old men, whose ashen face looked like death itself, poured some cold tea from a pitcher into a greasy glass with a dead mosquito on the rim and said, "*He cha*—drink some tea." We were very thirsty, but none of us drank the tea. I went outside to a nearby creek and mixed the brown sugar that Bamya's wife had given me with fresh mountain water and brought the mixture to Jyalikning, who managed a weak smile after finishing the nourishing drink.

In the early afternoon the truck came, and we sped down the mountain. We stopped again at the police station so I could check out. The same policeman said, "You stayed up there a long time. What did you do there?"

"I worked."

"Well, come again sometime for another vacation." He still did not believe me.

We took Jyalikning to the home of the boss and then to the hospital. He was released a week later, and the boss paid for all his expenses. Jyalikning was as carefree as ever and was already making plans to go up the mountains to work again.

I threw away my sleeves-and-zipper jacket, although I had thought of saving it as a souvenir. After we received our salaries, we went to a Chinese kung-fu movie together. While I watched the film, I thought of my friends working in the mountains—Bamya and his wife, happy-go-lucky Jyalikning, kind and lonely Lim. They were like faces appearing through a morning mist and then fading ever so slowly away.

The voyage from Taiwan had been sunny and smooth until we reached Orchid Island, where a black cumulus mass hung over the island like a water balloon. With us on the boat were sixty bags of rice and peanuts donated to the people by the government because of the increasing shortage of sweet potatoes. The sixty bags were to be divided equally among each family on the island—enough for one extra meal.

Waiting for us at the harbor in his three-wheeler was Old Ma, eager to make an extra buck. Just as we started loading the rice bags on his vehicle, the water balloon above began pelting us with a downpour. We covered the bags with a tarp, and Old Ma drove off to the village of Imurud. As the wind blew and the rain fell and the day wore on, Old Ma made four more trips, each time picking up a nice price for his services. Finally, we loaded the last of the rice and peanuts and climbed up on the back of the three-wheeler together with Old Ma's store supplies.

It was dark by now. Old Ma was cursing at the rain as his car sputtered over the bumpy road. Halfway to the village, the front wheel came off its axle, the three-wheeler turned, and Old Ma's shipment of fragile "century eggs", a Chinese delicacy, went pummeling into the mud like depth charges.

Old Ma scolded us for overloading the vehicle, then stalked down the road to the airport for help. I sat on the ground with the teenagers who had helped load the rice, and, after carefully removing their broken and muddy shells, we began eating gooey century eggs. Dripping wet, we laughed at the rain. It was good to be back.

~

The principal of the school in the village of Iraralai asked me if I could teach in their village on the other side of the island. He said they needed help since there were only two teachers for three classrooms. So, I decided to move to the village of Iraralai and teach there for the following semester.

Iraralai was Orchid Island's most remote village, unlike any of the others, consisting entirely of traditional homes. To me, it had a timeless, mysterious rhythm of life that was almost seductive. The changes and wars and discoveries of man had scarcely affected its people. They appeared content with who they were and what they had.

When they heard I would be moving, the children of Imurud objected. If I left, who would teach them to sing and draw pictures? But Principal Chen had promised to recruit another music and art teacher to replace me.

Little Jayud sat watching me pack and asked with a frown, "Are you leaving Orchid Island again?"

"No," I answered, "I'm just moving to another village. Why?"

Jayud lowered his head, smiled shyly through rotten teeth, and said, "Because we love you."

Such a short phrase. But it made it all worthwhile.

The church in Iraralai had a small attached room that served as the village co-op as well as my new living quarters. Half of the room consisted of a raised wooden platform with shelves containing canned goods, soap, toothpaste, candy, and other household items. This was where I would sleep.

As soon as I arrived, the tiny room filled up with inquisitive parents and children. It seemed visitors rarely came to Iraralai, and no foreigner had lived there before, so I was a curiosity.

How can I forget my first day in Iraralai?

Not far up from the shore was a deep coral hole. The top of the crevice was wide and had steps leading down to a dark cavern below, where an underground stream of fresh water flowed into a large shallow pool. This was the village water supply.

At daybreak the water hole was a pool of activity. As soon as the villagers awoke, they went there to draw water from the mouth of the stream, bathe, and brush their teeth. My first morning in the village, I stood ankle deep in the tingling, soapy water, surrounded by scores of sleepy villagers splashing water on themselves. I kept trying to find a place to spit out my toothpaste so it would not mistakenly land on someone's head.

There was a rhythm in the apparent chaos of bodies. People flowed in and out of the cavern like the river itself, aware somehow of each other's movements. I alone seemed in the way of everyone.

Twice that day the rhythm of the village was disturbed. In the morning, I heard a commotion from a nearby home and went there to see a woman and her small daughter lying on the floor sobbing. Rocks had fallen on them from the stone ledge above their underground dwelling. The woman was pregnant and afraid she would lose her child. An old man rubbed the woman and her daughter with pork oil and sang quietly beside her.

That afternoon, a pale, sweaty wisp of a boy appeared at my door and said he had hurt his wrist. I asked him if he thought it was broken. He shook his head and soon after collapsed on the floor. While I was bandaging the boy's arm, his cousin came in and told me the boy had been caught by a spirit.

In this faraway village, it would take hours to notify the doctor at the health clinic on the other side of island, and it would take even longer to persuade him to come over.

Evening fell in Iraralai with haunting swiftness. The bright powder moon highlighted all the colors of the night. On one side of the village loomed the sharp black outline of a mountain. On the other side, the dark blue waters breathed softly. But in front of me, on the jagged rocks above the beach, stood scores of white figures, still as statues. Careful not to disturb them, I stepped lightly over the coral on my way to the water hole.

When I entered the ghostly stage, the shaggy white figures moved not an inch from their prayerful stance—as if such a displacement would disturb the rhythm of it all. The mountain goats of Iraralai were inviting me to be with them in their worship of the night.

~

That evening, several parents wandered into my room carrying their children. They sat on the floor, quietly chewing betel nuts. Teenagers also dropped by, climbing up on the wooden platform to inspect my few belongings. They smelled my tube of hair oil and asked if they could use some. When my room became completely full of people, I wondered why they were there. Did they need anything?

"We just want to be with you," one of the young men told me, "because we are afraid you will be lonely."

My candlelit room was a sea of silent, glowing faces. Soon, a man next to me began a soft chant, and the others picked it up. They sang of the *alibangbang*—the flying fish that had heard their call and were now swimming in droves to their shores. When the fish arrived, the men would use torches to attract them to their boats and catch them with long-handled scoop nets.

"The *alibangbang* are our friends," a man beside me explained. "They *want* us to catch them, so they come near to our boats to dance and play. We respect them as friends, even though we do not talk to them, nor they to us. We always speak naturally, never raising our voices. If anyone on the boats uses bad language or loses his temper or has evil thoughts in his heart, the *alibangbang* will turn away. The quieter we are, the more they enjoy our company."

Some other men came to the door of my room and said it was time to go. I followed the men down to the shore. They spoke softly as they carried bundles of abaca branches to be used as torches to the large boat. Even the launching seemed quiet, as though the pebbles beneath the hull also revered the great flying fish. There was a hushed silence as the oars swept through the churning waters. Then the shiny bodies of the men in the boat disappeared into the black and silent sea.

~

The villagers who had not gone fishing went back to their homes, where they continued their ancient songs. As I listened to the music that filled the night, a tall thin man opened the door to my room and held out a coin. Because my room was also the co-op, I was the proprietor after closing hours.

"I want to buy candy for my boy," the man said. "Since we do not have enough food, I buy candy for my children so they will feel full. Then they will sleep."

The little boy was covering his swollen mouth with his hand. "What is wrong with your son's mouth?" I asked.

"The roof leaked last night during the rain," the man replied. "When my son heard water coming in, he got up. There was no candle so he stumbled and broke a tooth."

The thin man then told me about his family. "My wife died after our last baby. I remarried an older woman who already had three children. Now we have seven. There is never enough food." The man spoke slowly and matter-of-factly, implying that was the way things were. Then he smiled weakly and said, "My child is tired. Good night."

I sat alone in the room and thought of the men who had been singing. They were not singing of freedom because their life was already free like the wind and the sea. They were not singing of love because love was all around them—in the little one nestled in their arms, and the woman next to the fire, and the friend who laughed like the summer breeze.

They had been singing about food—of the times when there was plenty, of the great fish they had caught in the past, and of the abundance the flying fish would bring them again. It was the song of the fisherman.

Wandering outside into the hot, full-blown night, I tossed my sleeping bag onto a nearby stilt house and climbed up its stairs. I prayed to the *Taudoto*, who watches over us with ten thousand eyes in the starry night and cools our faces with his loving breath, who is always there giving us light as we reach out in the night and will never leave us.

Surely the *Taudoto* heard the song—the One Above, whose love is as vast as the sky and concern as deep as the sea. Yet, the typhoon had ruined the sweet potatoes. And the men had sung to forget their hunger. The children ate roots, and candy sometimes. The babies danced in the sand, then cried, not knowing why. And the people waited patiently. The song of the fisherman was the song of life.

~

Dragnet fishing was considered more of a sport than work. In the early morning, a party of some sixty Iraralai men hauled their long, thirty-meter net to the shore and flung it atop a six-man canoe. They lobbed the rest of their gear in another boat: fish line fastened onto chunks of Styrofoam, long strips of white cactus plants, chunks of odd-shaped iron weights, and a large stash of fat cucumber melons. As the two boats set out along the coast to the day's fishing site, their oars softly caressing the awakening waters, the remainder of the Iraralai men began walking to the same area. I went with them.

We strode in single file across the village inlet to the road heading to the next village of Iranumiruk. On the side of the road, there were three weathered, wide-branched trees bearing octangular fruits. I picked up one of the dried fruits from the ground and held it out to the man in front of me. But when I started to ask him the name of the fruit, he drew back in alarm and told me to throw it away. As I tossed it back on the ground, he hurried up ahead.

For several minutes, we marched in complete silence. Since it seemed to be a silence that was meant to be, I was careful to walk quietly, trying to keep my slippers from flapping noisily on the ground. After a while the atmosphere became more relaxed, and the men broke up into groups and began talking. I asked Aegi, the church leader, for an explanation.

"The fruit you picked up comes from the *toba* tree, which is taboo. If you touch either the tree or its fruit, your arms or legs will swell into the shape of the fruit. The *toba* is a disgusting thing. When we curse someone, we use that term. We walked quietly in single file because we were passing burial grounds. If the spirits heard us passing, they would join us and spoil our fishing."

After an hour, we arrived at Ipanatosan, a monstrous coral rock shaped in the form of two fighting lions, which jutted up from the shore. We stopped there a few moments.

"Are you really going fishing with us?" one of the men asked me.

"Yes," I replied.

"You should stay here and rest."

"Why?"

"You will get tired. It can be dangerous." Were the men just being polite, or did they really think it would be too much for me? I hoped they did not feel I would be in their way.

We secured our goggles and plunged into the cool waters, swimming far out to a distant islet. It was the island the Americans had bombed after mistaking it for a Japanese ship. Just short of the island was a small pyramidal rock, and there, climbing up its bony surface, we paused. The sixty men of Iraralai spread out over the rock, covering almost the entire stone with their bodies so that it must have looked like a human rock to the Taudoto, who watched from above. When the two boats carrying fishing equipment arrived, the men dove with graceful, sun-splashed arches from the peak of the rock into the cool ocean below.

The men let out the massive net, pulling one edge down to the ocean floor and securing it to the coral sand with stones. Each man dove down to arrange the net and to check it afterward.

We swam to the nearby boats, where we were given a long coil of rope festooned with strips of white cactus plants and heavy iron weights. When I reached for mine, the coil slipped from my hands and plunged deep into the waters below, carried down by the weights. I looked helplessly at Aegi.

"I dropped mine," I told him.

"Next time do not drop it," Aegi replied tersely and dove to the bottom to retrieve the coil.

The men began swimming out in a long line until they formed a wide semi-circle with the boats on both sides and the net in front. Then the game began. It was similar to a football match. When someone spotted a school of fish, he shouted, and the men jerked their ropes up and down. The fish heard the clanging of the iron weights and saw the eel-like strands of white cactus and fled quickly away.

Following them in pursuit, the men relayed the hapless school of fish to one another like an amorphous soccer ball spiraling down a field. With shrill shouts and keen eyes, the skillful swimmers effortlessly funneled the fish into the waiting net. Then all sixty men bunched together and pulled their ropes up and down while screaming in high voices at the frightened fish. The net was drawn up, and the men pressed against each other to view the writhing mass of marine life they had caught. After they had poured their quarry into a hollow space in the hull of the boat, we swam to the ship-shaped island in the distance to rest.

It was a long and difficult swim for me. The rest of the group was already reclining on the shore by the time I arrived. I pulled myself onto the coral beach, tired from the swim and exhausted by the excitement.

Aegi walked over to me as I collapsed on the fine pebbles and said, "I scolded you when you dropped the weights because it is our custom to scold a person when he is careless. If we do not scold, then the men will not take heed. They will let the fish pass by. But scolding does not mean we are angry. You must be tired. Rest here on the sand and have some betel nuts while we go out for another catch."

The men rose up and ran lightly over the sharp coral shore and disappeared into the waters. I wanted to go with them but rested as Aegi had told me to do. Besides, it was so comfortable on the small islet . . .

In my dreamlike state, I saw the main island across the channel float farther away. Or were the blue waters coming closer? Soft and cool, like crystal snowflakes, the gentle waves lapped around me. I would let the ocean carry me back to the other side. I was too tired to resist, and why should I? The waters would not harm me. We were friends. We were one.

It was very silent below, peaceful and quiet. The cool waters ran beside me, and together we rose and dipped and rose again.

I felt myself lengthening, as if I had grown a long, finned tail. I followed the fish wherever the waters led them, swimming in single file, flowing with the pulse of the ocean. Around me all was a deep blue with soft sunlight shimmering through the patchwork ceiling above my head.

Floating freely, I merged with the welcoming sea and its kindly creatures. Everything was good in the watery depths and nothing bad—except for a cluster of odd-looking white objects bobbing up and down in the distance.

Whatever it was, the white menace was coming closer. Aware of a foreign presence, the fish became restless. So did the waters, churning relentlessly. As the fish broke from their single file and swam away in all directions, I was turned this way and that by all the commotion.

The white shapes screamed out in metallic voices, and the waters around me turned into a whirlpool of frenzied fish swimming in haste to escape the danger.

But where could we go? The dangling white shapes brushed by us with long silky arms and grasped at us with thin metallic fingers.

I could feel my body swelling until it became a large octangular fruit. The white shapes began scolding me.

"Why did you pick up the *toba*?" they yelled. "Now you look like a *toba . . . toba . . . toba*!"

I quickly dropped the fruit. It fell down to the ocean floor.

"Next time do not drop it," Aegi snapped.

"I'm sorry. I won't do it again."

"Now eat the melon," Aegi told me.

"The melon?"

"Eat the melon," he repeated.

His hand was on my shoulder. I awoke and saw that Aegi was bending over me, holding out a fat cucumber melon.

"Did you rest?" he asked me.

I looked at the men around me. They had already returned from the second catch. I glanced quickly at my arms and legs to make sure I had not turned into a *toba*.

"Yes," I replied. "I rested well!" Then I took the melon and bit into it hungrily.

The melon filled me and quenched my thirst as well. That was all we ate before returning to the village in the late afternoon. The fish were then scaled on the shore and divided among the fishermen.

Women hurried over with baskets and wooden plates to the division area, where they scoured the catch for "women fish". These were soon divided, and the women left with their portions. A few "men fish" were given to the children on separate plates to take home. In this way the women could begin cooking while the men divided the rest of the catch.

Division was very exact. Large fish were divided into sections, with each fisherman receiving the same number. Small fish were divided according to their worth. This was done by first giving ten fish to each man, then five, and then one— until there were no more fish. The fisheyes were grabbed by the red-mouthed children. The mangy dogs and potbellied pigs lurched on the side, waiting for the guts to be tossed to them. I received my share of fish, although I felt I had been of little help in the expedition.

"It does not matter," Aegi said kindly. "Even if a person fishes only for a short time, he is still entitled to the same number of fish. Only those who row the boats on the way home receive extra portions. You fished, so you must share in the catch."

~

Old Yen, a plump and bald Taiwan Mainlander, who had lived on Orchid Island for many years, was everybody's friend. His job had something to do with guarding the island in case of attack (which was unlikely). Since he lived only a mile from Iraralai, Old Yen would often visit the village. One evening he came bounding over, greeted all the teenagers, and invited them to his house. The boys urged me to go with them because, they said, "Old Yen is a nice man."

It was a peaceful, quiet night. But as we walked along the shore, Old Yen took out his transistor radio and held it close to his ear as it screamed out Peking Opera. The shrill reception of the radio almost drowned out the charm of the night's own music.

Old Yen lived in a small, thatched hut. Inside, there was a gallery of pin-ups pasted on the walls. Apologizing that he had nothing to give his guests, Old Yen packed his small table with biscuits, cookies, and candy and prepared a large cup of milk for me. To the boys who were inspecting his gallery, he poured rice wine and handed out cigarettes.

"All the young people come here," Old Yen said excitedly. "My house is always crowded with young people. I am their best friend. They all know me. They all love me."

"It is true," a boy told me as he reached for another cigarette. "You might say Old Yen is the 'Father of Iraralai'."

Old Yen was delighted when he heard this. He poured more wine for the teenagers and talked happily with them. Finally, he accompanied us back to the village.

"I am the best friend of the young people," he shouted periodically. "They all love me. They all come to my house. My house is always crowded with young people."

The boys began singing as we walked along the beach. Their voices were thick and powerful in the wine-filled night. They sang Mandarin songs and then their traditional Yami songs, and the songs welled up from their hearts like the waves of the sea.

"They all like me. Everyone likes me," Old Yen screamed above the thunder of the music. The boys sang louder, and the night became their song. But still Old Yen's voice could be heard. "I know all the young people. They always come to my house!"

When we reached the village, Old Yen left us, and there was silence once again. We watched him disappear into the darkness as he made his way back home. The boy next to me leaned against the post of a stilt house and closed his eyes.

"Old Yen is a nice man," he said in a voice thick with wine. "He gives us many things." The boy pulled out a bottle Old Yen had given him. He took a long drink, dribbling most of its contents onto the ground, and passed the rest of it to the boy next to him.

And I wondered . . . would the richness of the Yami culture someday vanish like the spilled rice wine even now seeping into a thirsty earth? It had happened to other indigenous cultures. Would theirs be next?

~

The skinny old man came into my room just as I was eating breakfast and climbed onto the wooden platform that served as my bed and table. I wondered how the man's pencil legs could support even such a slight weight as his.

The old man asked me if I had any matches. I offered him a cigarette. He looked appalled and refused my offer. I was "too pitiful", and my cigarettes were "too few". I insisted. The old man shrugged, fluttered his eyelids a bit, and accepted the cigarette.

After lighting up and puffing for a while, the old man crossed his ankles and leaned comfortably against the wall, chatting on and on. I could understand nothing—less because of my little knowledge of Yami than from the man's total lack of teeth. After some time, he bent closer to me. Using very precise Mandarin, he asked, "Biscuit?" And his eyelids began fluttering again.

Before the old man left, he had received an extra biscuit, along with peanut butter and jelly and a cup of instant milk, which he simply could not refuse.

A little two-year-old girl stood alone in the doorway, staring at me with almond eyes. She walked over to my platform and tossed her hands out, making insistent sounds for me to pick her up and put her on my floor. Seated there, she once again stared at me with hypnotic eyes, never hinting at a smile. Slowly and carefully, her hands reached up to my glasses. She removed them and put them on her head, but they slipped down around her neck. When this game failed, she fingered my cross, removed the chain from my neck, and placed it on her own.

After a while, my little friend had no interest in things at all and simply stared at me with something of a scowl. Neither my bottle of vitamins nor my plastic peanut butter jar could satisfy her.

Then she eyed my air pillow. I inflated it, and she began to bounce on it. Soon the corners of her mouth turned up, her almond eyes crinkled in playfulness, and she squealed happily, clapping her little hands. This was so thrilling for her that she urinated on my pillow.

~

The eighty students of the Iraralai primary school were very well behaved. They were at their desks long before the bell rang, and I never had to raise my voice to discipline them. They listened attentively and did their work diligently.

But as good as the students in Iraralai were, they could not express themselves with originality. Every day, no matter what I taught them to draw, the little girls drew the same pictures of houses and flowers. The little boys always drew the same boats, although some were learning to draw planes.

The students of Iraralai were part of their environment, and change and originality were not characteristics of Arcadia. Yet the children were expressing the only world they knew. It was a beautiful world, and the more I understood it, the more I knew why they were content with that world.

In the end, the children did not change. But I did. My houses and flowers were always the same. My boats, however, were getting better. And I was learning to draw planes.

The weeks in Iraralai passed slowly. I especially enjoyed the afternoons when the men returned from fishing, singing in their boats. It was then that the children would race to the beach to meet their fathers and help scale the fish and bring home the gear. The sky would turn into a canopy of pink flowers while time stood still to let the sun have its rest. Night would then arrive with its music, dances, soft whispers, and the croaking of the frogs to lull us to sleep.

Spring was a special time for frogs. While the warm south wind beckoned the men to the sea for flying fish, the symphony of the night lured the children to the fields for frogs. Any child who could manage a flashlight was eligible for the exciting late-night frog hunts, returning sleepy-eyed to school the next morning. The older boys had developed a science out of it, employing a gas lantern as their weapon. They spread out into the taro fields like commandos on a night raid and descended on the frogs singing dismally in the darkness.

"If you catch them when they are on top of each other, it is even faster," a little boy told me. Although this sounded a bit unfair to the frogs, the children could make a small fortune out of their efforts. The frogs were sold cheaply to Old Ma, who then sent them to Taiwan for a profit. On a good night, frogs were big business. This delighted the young people but not their parents, who wanted nothing to do with the miserable pests.

"In the morning, we find our taro plants uprooted," the tall thin man complained. "I guard my fields when I am not fishing, but I cannot be there every night. Last night my wife went out to keep away the children, but some boys pretended they were soldiers and scared her away. When it comes to ruining our taro fields, children are almost as bad as cows."

~

When school ended in June, I went to the village of Imurud to attend the graduation of my former students. With great emotion, Principal Chen exhorted the graduates to lead good lives, which moved the students to tears. Even Big Lee, usually so stern, brushed away a tear or two.

The big change for Imurud in the year since I arrived was the influx of Taiwanese tourists. When the weather was favorable, large tour groups would take the ferry from Taiwan and stay at the new hotel. Some of the tourists viewed the scenery, while others inspected the people.

Molung's mother did not look up when the two tourists passed her house. She and her husband were sitting on their small stilt house peeling sweet potatoes. A few little children sat naked on the ground nearby, shelling and eating peanuts. Molung had gone fishing.

"Aren't they pitiful?" one tourist remarked to the other. "Look at that dirty food. We would never eat food like that. And see the children. Nothing to wear or eat. What a pity. Someone should really help them."

Molung's mother looked down, smiled, and even laughed in embarrassment as if she had not understood.

The two tourists continued up the path, arm in arm, peeking into the Yami workshops and underground homes. Molung's mother asked me if I had eaten and handed me a peeled sweet potato and some dried fish.

After a while, the tourists came back down the path and stared at me as I squatted on the ground eating a yam.

"Do you eat their food?" one tourist asked me. "We would never eat such food."

"Their food is delicious!" I said, adding mischievously, "It is probably better than yours."

The tourists were shocked. Molung's mother tossed her head back and cackled hoarsely, "Yes! Yes, it probably is!" And she and her husband laughed and laughed, with red betel nut juice streaming down their chins. Surely the *Taudoto*, who watches from above, was laughing, too.

~

For the prayer service in Imurud, I prepared a sermon in the Yami language. It was a local version of Jesus' parable about the Sower and the Seed. But instead of sowing seeds, a man went out to plant taro. Rather than birds eating the seeds, cows trampled over the taro. If the taro survived the rocks and weeds and cows, there would be a rich harvest.

It would be the same for us if we accepted the teachings of the *Taudoto* into our hearts amid the difficulties of daily life.

I practiced the sermon repeatedly, going through every word of it. I even painted large pictures to accompany the story. The evening before, I went to ask Jayud if I should change anything. After carefully listening to my sermon, he said it sounded fine. Then we feasted on a dinner of delicious crab and mashed taro Jayud's wife had prepared for us.

The next morning, my heart beat with excitement as a sizeable group of parishioners arrived at the church. After several hymns and a rousing introduction by the church leader, I began delivering my well-prepared homily. The congregation listened with silent respect as I read from my notes and pointed to the colorful illustrations. Jayud smiled knowingly at me from the front pew, giving me confidence.

But just as my sermon was reaching its climax, and the wicked cows were getting ready to trample over the unfortunate taro plants, my stomach felt as if someone had shoved a basketball into it. Nausea began to take hold of me as the "basketball" began its rapid descent into my bowels.

I needed to make a run for it—as soon as possible. Sweating profusely, I shoved my notes and illustrations into the hands of the bewildered church leader and dashed outside and into the bushes. Grimly, I reflected on the generous helping of crab and mashed taro I had consumed at Jayud's home the night before and regretted eating so much.

After some time, I crept back to the church. The people had already gone home, and my illustrations were stacked neatly on a bench. I sat down beside them and thought, well, so much for the man who went out to sow his seed.

The door behind me opened, and Molung came into the church. Little Jayud trailed behind him.

"Am I too late?" Molung asked.

I was surprised because Molung rarely came to church services.

"No, you are not too late," I replied, somewhat glumly.

"I have something to tell you," Molung said, his thick eyebrows drawing together and his oversized eyes appearing even wider than usual. "Did you know I used to be very bad? I only began to change when I met you and read your books about Jesus. I used to fight with knives and rocks. See my scars." Molung pointed to the scars on his legs.

"I have a bad temper. When I was young and my father told me to go and gather wood, I threw rocks at him. I never cared about anything. Not even dying. Once I climbed a tree and fell off and almost died, and I did not even care."

Molung paused, and his bushy eyebrows relaxed. "But now I care."

From the door of the church, I could see the fantasy of waves playing upon the seashore. I am not sure how long it was before Molung's mother came by and told us to come and eat. People were already going to the taro fields.

~

Molung's grandfather sat cross-legged on the floor of his house, singing the ancient stories. When he was young, he caught many fish, and everyone in the village admired him. Now he was old and could no longer fish, but his heart was at peace because he had known good days. His grandchildren sat beside him, listening to him sing of the boats and the flying fish. Molung translated the old man's Yami song for me:

"When our ancestors built their first boats, they went to the mountains and found the best trees, cutting them into slabs that were joined together with wooden nails. They stuffed fibers of the cotton root around the nails to prevent leakage, and they altered their boat many times before they settled on a style that could slide smoothly through the rocks to the sea. After they had carved and painted the boat, they held a ceremony to purify the boat of evil spirits, and they decreed this ceremony be repeated each time a *chinurikuran* canoe was built."

It was a long song, and the old man's eyes closed as he sang. The children fell asleep on the floor, and the night grew still. The day of the boat launch would soon be upon us.

In the morning, Molung and I sat on his stilt house and watched the sun rise over a hill, spreading its light like a silver carpet over the awakening village. Behind the house, twelve potbellied pigs grunted in a deep pit, awaiting their fate. Beside the pit, a small herd of goats stood quietly in a bamboo enclosure.

Directly in front of us was the great *chinurikuran* ten-man canoe, sunlight glistening off its stern. It seemed to command the village. Freshly carved and painted in white, red, and black, and larger than the homes around it, the elegant boat loomed like a large gull waiting to fly to the sea.

Molung reached for his betel nut basket, selecting a nice yellowing one. He chewed intently for a few moments, spit out the blood-red juice, and leaned back under the shade of the stilt house's straw roof. "Tomorrow morning, everyone will come to our village to eat," he announced proudly.

Below us, a line of men trudged up from the road, backs bent under heavy loads of taro. "They are returning from the fields," Molung said. "Today, they will bury the boat in taro. Tomorrow, they will distribute it to the guests."

The men walked back and forth from the fields, each

time pouring more baskets of taro onto the boat. Soon a pyramid of brown taro roots rose over the boat, burying it completely from view.

When they had finished preparing the boat, the men dressed in their bright silver helmets and traditional ornaments. Grouping around the taro pyramid, they began to sing. They sang throughout the day and into the evening and were still chanting when guests from the other villages began to arrive.

The brightness of the full moon flooded the village with light. The normally empty paths in the village were now crowded. Young men and women danced in a large circle on the beach, while older women grouped together for hair dances. Old men sang in small clusters around their homes. They would sing until dawn.

The night was flooded with the soft chanting of men, the gentle laughter of youth dancing in the moonlight, and the shuffling of soldiers playing mahjong in a house across the road. Since it was a warm, clear night, I chose to sleep on Molung's stilt house. Its grass roof hung low over my head.

But sleep was out of the question—there was too much excitement. As the rich sounds of the night harmonized into background music, the memories of my past year on Orchid Island—and what it meant for me—floated in and out of my consciousness like a recurring chorus.

I could identify with the great *chinurikuran* canoe lying silently in the middle of the village, buried under the taro.

Many hands had formed this boat and fashioned it into something that could benefit others. The men had brought their gifts of taro to the canoe—mounds of taro piled up and overflowing. But the boat could break free of its burden and sail to the distant sea only if it shared its riches with others. So it was with me.

At the first glimmer of dawn the men stopped singing. The soldiers across the road finished their mahjong game and went back to their posts. The villagers on the stilt houses hurried down their ladders to wash and eat. The day of the boat had begun. "We have to hurry," Molung told me. "Otherwise, there will be no taro left for us."

There was a flurry of arms and legs as villagers and guests alike scrambled for their share. In a matter of minutes, the taro was gone and the boat stood shining and empty in the morning sun. The village elder stood up on the boat and scolded his relatives for taking too much taro and not leaving enough for the guests. Then, pigs and goats were slaughtered, and the hair burned from their carcasses in a dozen scattered straw fires. The meat was distributed and cooked in each home, and we feasted on it.

In the late morning, a crowd again began gathering around the boat. The men of the village, one hundred strong, wore only their loincloths and a look of fierce determination.

"Now it begins!" Molung exclaimed. Twenty men climbed in the boat and started chanting in low voices as if in worship. "The men are asking the *Taudoto* to bless the boat," Molung said, "and for our ancestors to protect it at sea."

The men poured water with grains of millet onto the stern of the boat, then dipped their knives into the mixture, rubbing them on the sides of the boat for protection.

Molung suddenly jumped up and clambered down the ladder of his stilt house. "I have to go now. It is time to drive away the evil spirits!" And he ran to join a group of teenagers crouching in the distance.

The village elder began the exorcism by leaping in the air and emitting a ferocious battle cry, screaming and rotating his fist. In response, four columns of shrieking men slowly advanced toward the canoe from different directions, violently shaking their heads and fists at unseen spirits that could potentially harm their new boat.

A tall man wearing a silver helmet and brandishing a long dagger steadied himself in the canoe as groups divided by age encircled the boat, stomping their feet and turning their fists. At last, with a thunderous roar of voices, they lifted the canoe on their shoulders and tossed it into the air like a toy.

The men retreated and then attacked again, heaving the boat high above their heads. Their bodies streamed with sweat and shone like the giant white canoe that shimmered in the morning sun. Majestically, they carried the purified boat to the beach, as if for sacrifice, where it was lifted high again, this time to the *Taudoto* above. From nearby rocks the women leaped and shouted, "If we were men, we would be there with you!" And then the great boat was launched.

The fishermen flung themselves into the sea, splashing and churning the waters to frighten away any remaining spirits. Only when the boat was safely streaming through the waves did they relax in the foamy shallows of the inlet. The children farther out on the coral reef shouted and clapped as the *chinurikuran* canoe raced toward the open sea.

The boat was home at last. I saw it surging through the waters and knew it was truly alive—at one with the sea and the earth and the heavens. I watched the canoe growing smaller and smaller until it became just a speck in the distance. And when the ocean sparkled and flashed its smile, in a moment, I could see it no more.

3

THEOLOGY

As soon as I arrived for classes at Fu Jen University's theologate, Jerry insisted on taking me to town to buy new clothes. When I asked him what was wrong with the ones I had on, my big brother replied that I had worn them for a year on Orchid Island, and it was time for a change.

"Besides," he added, "your pants are too baggy. They make you look like a rhinoceros. Haven't you ever heard of bell-bottoms?"

Jerry should have known that if I had a habit of wearing baggy pants, it was because I had always been given his hand-me-downs, which were usually several sizes too big. All I wanted were pants that were not so tight that they would rip at the crotch, which had happened to me once before, when I hopped on the back of a motorcycle.

It was autumn of 1972 in Taipei. The Beatles, with their flamboyant hair styles and colorful outfits, were all the rage. Although strict "hair laws" prevented Taiwan's youth from imitating the famous band's mop tops, every student on campus appeared to be decked out in flashy bell-bottoms and beads. And folk music, in addition to the Beatles songs, was sweeping across college campuses.

Jerry and I were together at Fu Jen for my first year and his third year of theological studies. Naturally, the most important thing we did after I moved in was to start singing again. My solo year on Orchid Island had left me a bit rusty when it came to harmonizing, but in no time, we were back to our old routine—and learning new songs as well.

Since Jerry lived just down the hall from me, I felt almost spoiled to be able to talk with him at any opportunity. It was six years ago at the Los Gatos novitiate that we last lived together in the same Jesuit residence, and we had "grades" then, meaning we couldn't speak to each other except on special occasions. This would be a welcome change!

~

There are ten Taiwanese and ten foreign scholastics studying here at the theologate. One of the Taiwanese students is very frail and has been in the hospital for over two months. He tries to keep up with his studies but doesn't have much stamina. We hope he will be back with us soon.

During our classes, most of the teachers talk so fast I miss a lot. In addition, if they were originally from Shanghai, they still have very strong and almost (to me) unintelligible accents. But in some ways, I am more fortunate than the local Taiwanese students because I can supplement class notes with reference books in English. There is little theology that is written in Chinese. This semester, we are taking courses in revelation, the Church, the prophets, Mariology, the sacrament of marriage, and the theological virtues.

Last year, I was challenged to love God with all my heart and soul and strength. Now I am being asked to love Him with my mind—which may be more difficult than the other three. However, I am confident God will help me.

Our first-year theology classes are open to anyone studying at the university, so some of my classmates are Taiwanese Sisters or seminarians from the major seminary. Two of the seminarians are aborigines, friendly and fun to be with. We sit together in the back of the classroom, and they help me decipher what the teacher says, if possible.

We had elections at the theologate, and I was voted to be the officer in charge of "joy". That means I have to introduce guests and lead everyone in singing Happy Birthday at meals whenever someone has a birthday. That may sound like an easy job, but I have to keep track of everyone's birthday, and last week I was reprimanded for forgetting one of them. Not much joy when that happened.

Being here at the theologate, surrounded by scholastics, Sisters, and priests, is such a change from last year when I lived with the Yami people on Orchid Island. But maybe it is not such a huge change after all, because the people, not the place, are most important. When Jerry noticed how I was struggling to fit into my new community, he tried to console me with the observation that "everyone is just a Yami at heart." In other words, all people are poor in some way (even though they usually try to hide the fact), and they need to be loved for themselves, as God loves them, just as they are.

~

After a month or so, I am not improving much in class, even with the help of a generous Taiwanese Sister, who translates the teachers' main ideas into English for me. A lot depends on my own private reading in the library since I do not get much out of the classes. Listening to Chinese lectures that I can hardly understand for five hours a day is very tiring, so my "hobby" of writing a "book" about last year's experiences on Orchid Island is a good diversion.

Writing this book has not been a distraction. On the contrary, it helps me to reflect on my experiences. And reflection is, or should be, an integral part of theology. Discussing theological issues with Jerry and other Jesuits is also beneficial. Less helpful for me are classes. But even though I do not understand many of the Chinese lectures, I already know more theology than many of my Taiwanese classmates. Recently, I have been teaching catechism at a nearby primary school, which helps me simplify theology for the children.

~

Last week, Father Minister (the priest in charge of house finances and maintenance) summoned me to his office to inquire about a bill for NT 300 (U.S. $10) which he had received in my name from the Jesuit residence in Hsinchu. I told him I had asked for the money to buy a boat ticket to Orchid Island in order to bring my belongings to the theologate. The minister said he could not pay the bill because it was for the previous year.

"Where were you working last year?" the minister asked me.

"On Orchid Island," I replied.

"Then you must ask the Orchid Island Jesuit residence to pay the bill."

"There is no Jesuit residence on Orchid Island," I replied.

"Then where were you before you went to Orchid Island?" the minister persisted.

"At the language school in Hsinchu."

"Ah!" the minister exclaimed, "Then I will send the bill to the minister of the language school."

A few weeks later, the minister called me to his office once again and told me that the language school refused to pay the bill because I had already left the school at the time the bill was incurred. Fortunately, by then I had already scraped together $10 to pay the bill and gave it to Father Minister, to which he smiled in relief. And that was the end of the story.

But not quite. During my entire year on Orchid Island, I had miraculously survived with no money except for $30 given to me by the Medical Missionary Sisters for hygienic drawings they wanted for their hospital. My food (six biscuits and a cup of milk daily) was provided by the schools where I taught, but I was given no salary. At one point, when I had no money left at all, the Orchid Island post office notified me that they had a registered letter for me. I went to the post office and found a ten-dollar bill from my Aunt Julia enclosed in the letter. She had sent the money as a birthday gift three months previously, and it had only then arrived.

When I returned to the church, there was a worried mother with her sick child waiting for me. She needed to take a boat to Saint Mary's Hospital on mainland Taiwan as soon as possible for her child's operation, but she had no money for boat fare. After a few moments of prayer to decide what to do, I gave her half of Aunt Julia's donation and kept the remainder to pay for my own voyage, which I took shortly afterward.

Ten dollars here and ten dollars there. "The Lord gives and the Lord takes away." Although we do not study about this aspect of God's personality in theology, He certainly must have a sense of humor!

~

The first semester here at the theologate has turned out to be one of the most difficult periods of my life. The change from living on the paradise of Orchid Island to the dry desert of the theologate was harder than I had thought it would be. So many things have bothered me—the headache-inducing air pollution, an environment encased in concrete, my inability to understand the classes, and, worst of all, not having much interest in the classes even if I could understand them.

I told Bihan, one of my aborigine classmates from Saint Thomas seminary, that I was not learning anything in class. He said, "Well, maybe you should pray more. Remember, the greatest theologian of all was Saint Thomas Aquinas, and he received most of his inspirations through prayer."

But sometimes after five hours of classes a day, I am so exhausted I cannot even think, much less pray. Jerry has helped me a lot in this, since I am able to laugh together with him during the hard times. In fact, it seems that the more difficult something is, and the more pain it causes, the funnier it becomes when I look back on it in perspective. Jerry certainly has the gift of a sense of humor, which includes the ability to laugh at oneself. He taught me not just to carry my cross—but to carry it with a smile.

And Jerry is not the only one. Our late-night reveries in the first-floor coffee room are full of good cheer as we recount the tribulations of our latest horrible day in class. One of the French-Canadian theologians, Michel Marcil, is a multi-talented mimic and does wicked imitations of all our teachers. Sometimes he appears in the coffee room dressed as one of the professors, and after the initial shock, we end up roaring with laughter. So, there are good times as well.

~

Father Chin, who teaches a course in moral theology, is the most demanding of our teachers. He often throws out a question to some unsuspecting student—usually one of the seminarians who is falling asleep in the back of the classroom. Indeed, the rear section is taken up by seminarians (including myself), while the more studious Sisters occupy the front rows. I often while away class hours by sketching in my notebook or writing poetry. Unintelligible lectures provide inspiration for this. But in Father Chin's classes, I must be careful not to be caught off guard by an impromptu question.

A few days ago, Father Chin held oral exams for his students. He sat like a high magistrate on a raised platform in his classroom as we filed in one by one for our tortuous exam on morality. Actually, the exam material was easy. It was Father Chin's severe demeanor that was so frightening. With his hair slicked back and his piercing eyes that already had "fail" written all over them, he had a formidable "Last Judgment" presence. And we were the lost souls cringing before him.

I crept into the room and sat down at a single desk, piled with books, that had been placed about five feet lower than Father Chin's dais. Bihan was nervously waiting next in line by the door and gave me a "thumbs up".

"Open up the volume on the Second Vatican Council," Father Chin intoned.

"The Second what?" I asked.

"The Second Vatican Council. It's the red book."

"This one?" I fumbled through the book pile.

"Yes. Now open the book to page 211, number 13."

"Let's see, page 13, number 211."

"No!" A column of smoke appeared to be rising from the top of Father Chin's shiny hair. "The other way around!"

"Oh, right. I have it."

"Now read."

"Read what?"

"Read what it says!" The smoke turned into a fire.

I read the passage.

"Now explain it."

"Explain what?"

"What you just read!" The fire was now blazing.

The rest of the exam was just as bad. I was so nervous I could not think straight. If Father Chin had asked me my own name, I would have gotten it wrong. However, it seems many other students had the same disquieting experience during their oral exam, so I was not alone.

After the exam was over, Bihan wanted to celebrate. He invited me and Andrew, a short and stocky seminarian from the southern Paiwan tribe, to see a movie at Hsimending, which is in the heart of Taipei's glittering entertainment zone. The massive cinemas there have oversized, hand-painted billboards three stories high advertising the current shows.

The movie was called *Fist of Fury* and starred a new kung-fu actor I had never heard of before named Bruce Lee. There were so many kicks and punches in the film that I was practically worn out afterward. But this was no ordinary kung-fu film. With his capacity for empathy, sense of humor, and athletic ability, Bruce Lee stood far and above any other Chinese performer I had ever seen.

Immediately after the movie, Bihan suggested we go to an adjoining theater to watch a sequel to the movie, called *The Way of the Dragon*. Needless to say, after the second bone-crunching film, I was a die-hard Bruce Lee fan, although my friends practically had to carry me out of the theater. This incredible actor encompassed in his very person a long-ago suppressed Chinese identity. Moreover, since the theme of self-sacrifice was so apparent in the films, he came across as somewhat of a "Christ-figure". It was not long before

I learned Bruce Lee had become the most famous actor in the Chinese-speaking world.

~

Since the people on Orchid Island would not have a priest for Christmas Mass, I asked Father Bill Klement, an elderly Father in his seventies, if he could accompany me to the island during Christmas break. During the short flight from Taitung to Orchid Island, we sat with a young Taiwanese Army doctor who was stationed at the island's airport. After the plane landed, I joked with the doctor that if I got sick, I would be sure to let him know.

It felt wonderful to be back "home". We had no sooner landed than we started hiking around to the six different villages for Masses and Christmas parties. Everything went smoothly with crowds at each church and Yami dances afterward. Then on Christmas night, as we were sleeping at a friend's house, I began getting a severe pain on one side of my lower abdomen, which grew progressively worse.

There was no doctor in the village where we were staying, and I had not brought medicine for whatever type of illness I had. When Father Klement saw me groaning in pain, he did not know what to do. So, the poor Father decided to borrow a motorcycle at two in the morning and find our doctor friend at the airport. Although he had never driven a motorcycle before, Father Klement figured out how to start it, but since he did not know how to use the clutch, he had to putter all the way to the airport in first gear.

The rocky cliffside road that lined the seashore was perilous, especially at night, but God must have been with him, and, fortunately, so was a full moon. He found the doctor, woke him up, and the two of them rode back together on the motorcycle. The doctor tested me for appendicitis, which I did not have, and finally decided the pain was caused by a stone caught somewhere in my urinary tract. He gave me some morphine, which I promptly threw up each time he administered it.

When dawn came, Father Klement rode with the doctor to a public health clinic in another village. Meanwhile, I decided to take some Dramamine pills and see what they would do. The Dramamine put me to sleep and evidently relaxed my abdominal muscles, allowing the stone to pass through and the pain to subside.

By that time, Father Klement was so worried he had already bought us plane tickets to go back to Taiwan. My friends flagged down a three-wheeler going to the airport and hoisted me onto the back of it. Before I got on the vehicle, the doctor gave me an injection, but by then the pain was almost gone. My last view, as I was leaving the village on the back of the truck, was of the faces of the catechist and his wife, filled with fear and concern for me, and my friends standing sad and forlorn by the roadside. They must have thought I was done for.

After arriving back in mainland Taiwan, I went to see Sister Maureen at Saint Mary's Hospital, who patiently listened to my tale of woe and told me there was a much easier and more enjoyable way of eliminating a urinary stone.

"Just relax, drink some beer, and jump up and down. The stone will pass through in no time." If only I had known that beforehand.

I felt not only exhausted but also frustrated because there were still two villages that we had not had a chance to visit for Christmas Mass. I had not been able to complete our mission, and, even worse, my health issue had brought unhappiness to others instead of Christmas joy. This hurt much more than the physical pain.

Later, I began to see there was a lesson for me in that unforeseen experience, in the sense of how little I have really suffered and how petty I have been in accepting the small, everyday trials at the theologate. Most of all, the pain I underwent helped me to realize my true weakness and total dependence upon God. I thought I was helping Him, but it was I who needed His help.

Before returning to the theologate, I traveled to the Hsinchu mountains for a visit with my Tayal friends. The children I taught two years before had grown so tall I could hardly recognize them. Some of the families now had their own TV sets, and the villagers were earning more money. But many of the young men still struggled with drinking problems, while the girls often left for work at bars in the city. It was the mystery of beauty in poverty and joy in suffering—with God watching over us and knowing much more than we ever will and wanting our happiness more than we ever could.

~

This semester, I decided to cut back considerably on my classes in order to study on my own. The turning point for this decision came from a harrowing psychological incident at the end of last semester. It happened to me late on a Friday afternoon during my last period, when I was exhausted after attending five straight days of five Chinese lectures per day.

I was sitting at my usual spot in the back row of the classroom, as far away from the instructor as possible, flanked on one side by my friend Bihan and on the other by Andrew, who was struggling even more with his studies than I was with mine. Father Aloysius Chang, the rector of the theologate, was lecturing about the "fundamental option" all mankind faces—whether to say "yes" or "no" to God. It was a fascinating topic, and I was trying as hard as I could to catch every word he said.

Father Chang, a well-known theologian, had a loud, high-pitched voice and an extremely strong Shanghai accent. He was scribbling Chinese characters on the blackboard as he talked, and on this particular day he delivered his lecture louder and higher and with even more passion than usual.

As I focused my eyes intently on Father Chang's mouth, straining to decipher his thick accent, it seemed that his round head slowly became detached from his neck. The head began floating down the room in my direction like a balloon, with high, ear-splitting screams spewing at me from its red mouth at an ever-increasing volume. When the shrieking head reached me and was bobbing and shouting in front of my eyes, I reared up in shock and banged my head against the back wall of the classroom.

Bihan and Andrew turned to me in surprise. I did not say anything to them before racing out the nearby door as quickly as possible. I do not think any of the other students besides Bihan and Andrew noticed I had left. Shortly after that traumatic experience, I asked to take reading courses as much as possible rather than go to classes.

~

Not long ago, Andrew, my aborigine classmate from Taitung, told me he did not think he could become a priest. Although I tried to persuade him to continue his studies, he decided to leave anyway and go back home. I missed him very much, as did Bihan, the only other indigenous seminarian now studying theology. Then one day Andrew called and asked me to come to Saint Mary's Hospital in Taitung as soon as possible. When I asked him why, he said he could not tell me over the phone, but his cousin had a serious "emergency".

I had known Andrew's cousin well from the frequent visits Andrew made to her home when she was working in a factory near the theologate. Sometimes Andrew took me with him to visit her.

Since the next day was Saturday, I caught a night train to southern Taiwan and then traveled over the mountain by bus, arriving in Taitung in the morning. I raced over to see the Sisters at Saint Mary's Hospital to find out what had happened to Andrew's cousin.

"Thank God you are here!" Sister Maureen cried out when she saw me. Lively and excitable Sister Maureen was not only a good friend of mine but of Andrew's as well. "Hurry," she added. "There is no time to lose."

Sister Maureen ushered me into a quiet hospital room. Andrew and a priest stood solemnly over a young woman moaning in pain.

"What happened to Andrew's cousin?" I asked in alarm.

"She is not his cousin. She is his *girlfriend*. And she is having a baby—Andrew's baby!" Sister Maureen replied breathlessly. "We want to get them married before the baby comes out. I'm the maid of honor—and Andrew wants you to be the best man!"

So that was the "emergency". Andrew glanced at me shyly as he and his wife pronounced their vows between contractions. When the service ended, as if on cue, the little baby popped out to join in the festivities.

~

During the past few months, Jerry and I have sung at several folk concerts around town, and we keep receiving more invitations. Each time we go to a university for a concert, students sign us up for some future event at another college. I enjoy these occasions and am pleased folk music is getting so popular over here, at least on college campuses.

For our performances, Jerry and I devised a gimmick that seems to resonate with the audience. While most of the Taiwanese performers at student concerts sing English songs by folk singers like Bob Dylan, Jerry and I incorporate local Taiwan songs into our repertoire. Jerry sings Taiwanese favorites the students have known since childhood, and I belt out aborigine songs or Mandarin pop hits I have heard on my transistor radio. These songs always get a rousing ovation, probably less because of our musical talents than from the shock of hearing two foreigners singing in Chinese.

Recently, Jerry gave a lecture on folk music for some one hundred students here at the university. He told jokes, played recorded music, and even had me sing along with him at times during the presentation. He is a charismatic teacher and uses every trick he can think of to keep his audience not only informed but entertained.

Jerry and I sometimes sing at the Colombia Coffee House in Taipei, where Kimbo, an aborigine friend of ours, is a popular entertainer. I had met Kimbo not long after coming to Taiwan and was struck by his powerful voice. The coffee house is packed with college students on weekends. When all the seats are taken, the students squeeze together on the floor in front of the tiny stage. Kimbo likes to invite guests to sing also, and several well-known folk singers often appear with him. Each time we go there, Kimbo asks us to entertain the audience for a half hour or so. The atmosphere is electric, and the Columbia Coffee House is fast becoming the most popular musical hangout for college youth in the city.

Tonight, we watched ourselves perform on TV. It was a program on San Francisco that we had taped last week at Kuangchi, the Jesuit-run TV and radio studio. The show's director needed some "guests", who were supposedly from San Francisco, to introduce the program and sing a song. First, we went to the studio to record "This Land Is Your Land". The next day, we went through the motions (lip-syncing the lyrics) and had an interview with the star of the show, Louise Tswei. The interview was in Chinese with no rehearsal, so we had to figure out what to say on the spot. Since Jerry already knew Louise, a popular singer on TV, and had no trouble ad-libbing, he did most of the talking.

It was fascinating to watch the director put the show together from beginning to end. The technicians worked for days just to produce the half-hour program. The show comes on once a week and introduces well-known cities, their music and culture. The director tries to find people who actually come from the city they are introducing, but usually they just pretend to be from there—as we did.

Since Jerry and I were worried the show would not come out very well, we did not tell anyone at the theologate about it. Then someone spilled the news, and the whole community crowded into the TV room to watch us. I was more nervous viewing the show than making it. As it turned out, the program was fine, much better than we had expected, and the engineers in Kuangchi's recording studio made sure we sounded good. They even corrected our mistakes.

~

I am reaching the end of my first year of theology. In many ways, it has been a hard year—but hard with the constant, gentle assurance that it was meant to be this way. The most difficult part was obviously the "return" to a life away from the people I most wanted to be with and serve. Not to say that my classmates here at the theologate or the university students are not interesting and fun to be with—they are, but it is not the same as living and being with the poor every day.

The experience of being away from those I most wanted to be with on Orchid Island or in the mountains has been very difficult. But Christ seems to be calling me now "to come apart to a desert place" for greater reflection and prayer. My Jesuit brothers here have facilitated this slow, almost imperceptible growth to a deeper life.

Writing about my experiences on Orchid Island has also helped me to understand my life in relation to the poor. After finishing that manuscript, I started working on an illustrated mythological tale that was handed down verbally many years ago by elders on the island. If I could find a way to have this story published, it would be a good present for the children of Orchid Island. This is because more than any other gift, the young people need the gift of themselves. Being able to read stories about their own culture might help them appreciate themselves more—help them know their identity and be proud of it. My story book could enable me to teach them what they have taught me.

The members of our community are an outstanding, dedicated group of Jesuits. But in my experience of living with them (including Jerry) every day, they often seem to be the most ordinary and dull collection of men God could possibly have brought together. However, that is evidently not the way others view us. A student recently remarked that each time he saw Jerry and me sing together he knew "what love was all about".

When I am with Jerry, everything seems so natural—nothing out of the ordinary. I do not see this love. What others notice, I am likely to take for granted. I think it is the same with each of those in our community. Others appreciate us much more than we appreciate ourselves.

The intellectual highlight of the semester was an opportunity to present a joint seminar with Jerry on the theology of non-violence. We used the life of Gandhi as an example and incorporated some peaceful protest songs into our talk. This turned out to be more controversial than we had expected and provoked a heated discussion from some of the faculty. Strange, when a call for world peace can be more problematic than one for self-defense. But the Vietnam War is still raging in a neighboring country, and Taiwan continues to be wary of its big brother across a narrow strip of sea. So I understand the concern.

Our exams are over, and I did well in all of them thanks to Ricardo Gonzales, a kind and gentle Jesuit classmate from Spain, who summarized the main ideas of each of our courses into easily digestible portions. With Ricardo's helpful summaries in my pocket, I went across campus to Saint Thomas Seminary and reviewed the lessons with Bihan and the other diocesan seminarians. After that, they insisted I join them for a game of bridge, which went on for hours and left me more exhausted than my preparation for the exams.

~

Jerry became a deacon shortly before the school year ended and was ordained a priest at Holy Family Church in Taipei a few months later, along with seven of his classmates. What made the ordination ceremony an especially memorable occasion—at least for Jerry and me—was the arrival in Taiwan of our mother and younger brother Glenn for a lengthy two-month visit. During this time, an American couple residing at the foot of Taipei's scenic Yang Ming Mountain generously let our family use their comfortable home while they were away for the summer.

Before his ordination, Jerry was anxious to be fully prepared, so every night he would practice saying Mass. Since we shared the same room, I would watch him. He used saintly Father Francis Rouleau's fiftieth Jesuit anniversary remembrance card as a "paten" while practicing Mass. I would not have thought Jerry needed to practice how to say Mass because he had attended liturgies all his life. But my older brother prepares well for everything. And this was his big day.

The ordination ceremony was spectacular. Over a hundred priests concelebrated the Mass on a long altar going down the center aisle of the church, with a chalice for every two priests. An orchestra of brightly clad musicians playing traditional Chinese instruments accompanied the hymns. Everyone Jerry knew in Taiwan was there.

After the ceremony, a huge reception was held under an awning on the church patio, where the centerpiece was a tall, ornately decorated ice cream cake. But Jerry and the other newly ordained priests were unable to get to the reception area because of the dense crowds surrounding them and the blessings they were asked to bestow on each of the attendees.

Meanwhile, the July heat steamed down on the hapless ice cream cake. Ricardo Gonzalez, who was in charge of the reception delicacies, kept pleading with the ordinands to cut the slowly disintegrating cake so the others could start eating it. But his supplications came to no avail. Eventually, Ricardo and I sliced the cake ourselves and distributed it before the ice cream had completely melted.

The next few days, we traveled around with the other ordinands for their first Masses. Even though Mother and Glenn could not understand the Mandarin Chinese that was used at all these Masses, they both looked happy to be there. Everyone loved them.

But living together as a family for the first time in thirteen years was not completely trouble-free. We had our scuffles, and I am afraid that I, for one, sometimes reverted to patterns of behavior not seen since childhood. Reconciliation always came during our daily Mass, especially when there were just the four of us. We were aware of each other's feelings as well as our failings. The difficulties and joys of living together—sometimes hurting one another but always asking for forgiveness—enabled our familial love to grow deeper and more intense in its expression. To be sure, we have all grown closer because of this time with one another.

We stayed in Taipei for a month, often making short forays to outlying areas to visit Jerry's friends. Then we set out for a trip around the island. Our first stop was Hualien on the East Coast, where the family of my classmate Bihan lived. Bihan picked us up at the airport and shuttled us to his indigenous village, which was nestled at the foot of Taroko Gorge's marble-laced cliffs. Despite its proximity to Taiwan's most famous national park, Bihan's village was poor and underdeveloped. His parents, whose faces were adorned with traditional aboriginal tattoos, warmly welcomed us.

Mother slept in the only house in the village that had a bed. Although Glenn found dozing on a stiff *tatami* floor to be a challenge, he immediately took a liking to the family motorcycle. One drizzly evening, Bihan wanted to bring us to an aboriginal dance show fifteen miles away in Hualien City. He placed Mother on the back of his motorcycle and borrowed another one for Glenn and me. Jerry stayed behind to entertain the village children, who had put on a show for us the previous night.

Halfway to the city, the misty rain turned into a heavy downpour. When Bihan momentarily parked his motorcycle under a leafy tree, Mother—always prepared for anything—whipped out a thin, collapsible raincoat from her purse and put it on without missing a beat. Then they started off again for the dance performance. Afterward, I asked Mother what she thought about the aboriginal cultural show, and she said it was okay, but what she liked most of all was the motorcycle ride!

A few days later, we took a train to Taitung, where Mother stayed with the Sisters at the hospital and the rest of us boarded at the priests' residence. Since a large number of tourists were trying to get to Orchid Island, the five-passenger Cessna was booked solid for most of its flights. I managed to fly over to the island first, and the others came the next day. Unfortunately, an aerosol canister that had been packed alongside our bag of rice exploded during the flight and drenched the rice and other food items with insect repellent, rendering them inedible. But since we only planned to stay on the island for a few days, that mishap did not worry us.

By chance, we had arrived in time for the island's yearly boat festival. The Yami were having their celebration in the village of Ivarinu on the other side of the mountain from where we were staying. With no vehicular transportation, we needed to hike up a steep cliff to get there. Although Mother is a good walker on level ground, she found it difficult to climb the mountain's nearly vertical incline. When we finally reached the summit, she burst out laughing and said she could not think of anyone her age who could have made that strenuous climb and lived to talk about it.

The boat festival was every bit as exciting as I remembered it from the previous year. But Mother and Glenn were a bit nervous when the men in their traditional loincloths began screaming and shouting and rolling their fists to drive away the evil spirits. And Mother was understandably taken aback by the flow of blood from scores of slaughtered pigs and goats that streamed down the village paths.

Since it was late when the festival ended, we decided to spend the night in the small village church, sleeping on pews pushed together to make beds. There was no electricity, so I lit a candle to look for a bed covering to put over the pews where Mother would sleep. After finding some material the perfect size, I arranged it so she would be more comfortable. The next morning, I realized it was an altar cloth.

Later that day, we hitched a ride on a three-wheeler for the journey back to the village on the other side of the mountain. Once we got there, some neighbors brought us taro roots, fish, and wild vegetables since they knew our food supply had been ruined. Jerry scouted for canned goods at Old Ma's half-empty store. Glenn built the fire, I cooked, and Mother washed the dishes. It was just like being at home. We stayed at the church for three days and then made a crucial decision. Instead of going back on the plane the next morning, we decided to postpone our flight for an extra day in order for Jerry to say Mass in Iraralai, the island's most remote village. When we hopped on a three-wheeler for a day trip around the island, little did we know there would not be another boat or plane for at least a week.

The weather changed abruptly, and a small typhoon arrived with wind and rain every day, causing us to be stranded on the island with little or no food. One of the convicts I had known from singing in the prison band a year before came to our rescue, hauling over a big wheelbarrow of dry wood and finding us rice and peanuts (I did not ask where he got them). The prisoner was called Buffalo, and with his great strength and burly figure, he lived up to his name. He often joined us for meals and in his broken English told us exciting tales about his life in one of Taiwan's most notorious gangs before being sent to prison.

But even with Buffalo's help, food was scarce, and before long, we were even rationing our peanuts. When the weather finally cleared up enough for a plane to come, there was a panicky struggle among other stranded visitors, anxious to get back. Despite our efforts, we were relegated to the fourth flight of the day. However, it turned out that the pilot of the third flight had engine trouble and had to circle back three times, unloading his nauseous passengers for a rest each time before he tried again. Good thing we did not take that flight.

The pilot came back for us on the fourth flight, which we later found out was the last time that plane would fly for the next three months. When we arrived at the hospital in Taitung and the Sisters saw Mother, now several shades darker, they ran over to embrace her and care for her poor mosquito-bitten skin—all the while scolding me for putting her through such an ordeal. I apologized even though I knew Mother loved the trip and would not have traded our adventures on the island for anything.

We rested for several days before continuing our travels around Taiwan. First, we stopped at Andrew's indigenous village, where his family had prepared a feast for us, including wild boar, snails, and Formosan barking deer. Glenn said his favorite dish was the plate of snails. I think he mentioned that just to aggravate Mother, who would not go near them.

Then we traveled on to Hsinchu for a visit of several days with the American Jesuits, which was more comfortable and had more palatable meals than any of our previous stays.

By the time we arrived back in Taipei, it was almost time for Mother and Glenn to leave. Before going to the airport, Glenn gave me $100 of his hard-earned money to help the sick of Orchid Island. I knew that was not easy for him to do since it was the last of his funds, but he made up his mind himself and did not even tell Mother about it.

I felt sad to see my mother and little brother go back home, but I am so grateful for the time we had together. It was an experience none of us will forget, and it caused us to grow closer together as a family than ever before.

In coming to Taiwan, Mother and Glenn were more like missionaries than tourists since they were willing to give as well as to receive from another culture. In sharing their lives as much as possible with each person they met, they gave the greatest gift of all—love and acceptance—the gift of themselves.

The new school year began, and our first activity was the annual Fu Jen University fair. I was chosen to draw portraits of the students to raise money for school charities. I had no trouble getting customers to sit for a ten-minute sketch, but after a while, this grew tiresome, and I realized all my portraits looked practically identical. That did not seem to bother the students, though, who ran off waving their pictures in the air and attracting more customers.

My classes are all reading courses, the same as last semester.

The advantage of this is that I do not need to struggle through Chinese lectures. But the drawback is that I miss seeing classmates like Bihan and the other friends I have made. Studying dry theology texts alone in my room or in the library can be pretty boring, especially after a stimulating summer traveling around Taiwan with my family.

Singing with Jerry at college folk concerts and school functions whenever we are invited lessens the tedium. But Jerry is much busier now than last year. In addition to studying his fourth year of theology, he is involved in teaching philosophy, counseling, instructing students who want to become Catholics, and acting as assistant chaplain on the Fu Jen campus, so I do not see him that much, even though he still lives just down the hall from me.

On Friday afternoons, I often take a bus to Chutung, which is the nearest town to the village of Chingchuan, where I worked the summer before last. After staying at the Chutung church for the night, I catch an early morning lumber truck heading to the village and spend the weekend there, hitching a ride back down the mountains on Sunday afternoon. These are the best moments of the week for me. To be able to relax with the tribal people in the clean and pure air of their pristine natural environment always gives me energy and motivation for the much drearier life of studies.

Sometimes in the evenings, I bump into Jerry at the theologate's makeshift coffee room, where we congregate for bedtime snacks. On one particular evening, Jerry mentioned that he found it hard to understand why I did not spend more time at school, ministering to the students as he did.

"Why do you go to the mountains each weekend?" Jerry asked me. "It doesn't make sense—unless you plan to spend the rest of your life working with aborigines."

I had not thought that my frequent visits to the habitat of Taiwan's indigenous people could look unusual to others. But on reflection, it might seem as strange as a Taiwanese seminarian going to work with Native Americans in the States. Nor had I considered that ministering to the aborigines could be my life's vocation—a kind of vocation within a vocation. But at that moment, it seemed clear that it was.

"Maybe I will," I said to Jerry. "Maybe I will spend the rest of my life with the aborigines."

Jerry was silent for a moment before remarking, "Then I guess it does make sense after all. I understand you now."

This was quite a statement coming from Jerry because his ambitions were much higher than mine. He wanted to change the world—and he had the personality and talents to do so. It was a different story with me.

A young Taiwanese priest, who was drinking tea across the table from Jerry and me, cut into our conversation with a cautionary note.

"Living in the mountains is a dead end," he said to me with a frown. "If you work with the aborigines, you will never amount to anything. You will never become somebody."

"I don't want to become somebody", I replied, staring blankly at the young priest. "I just want to be me."

~

For Christmas vacation, which was very short since it was not a public holiday in Taiwan, Bihan invited me to his village in the mountains of Hualien, where I stayed for three days. The weather was so cold that we spent each evening sitting outside beside a campfire, chewing betel nuts and sipping rice wine to keep warm. But that is what all the villagers did there in wintertime, and it was a relaxing time to get to know each other and share stories.

Lodging in Hualien for those days was just what I needed to give my mind a complete rest. It was good for me not to have to *think*, but only to live in a timeless present, immersed in the ethereal environment of a hilltop village and its friendly inhabitants. I returned to the theologate refreshed.

On New Year's Day, the American Jesuits invited Jerry and me to join them for their annual get-together in Hsinchu. After a sumptuous meal, we watched an old Elvis Presley movie on TV. This was followed by the debut of a much more interesting musical production, starring our aborigine friend Kimbo as host. His new weekly music show is called *The Garden of Eden*. And the sponsor is "Adam's Chewing Gum"! Kimbo has promised Jerry and me a spot on his show. With a name and sponsor like that, it would fit right in with our theology course.

I have started taking a private class on reading the Bible in Chinese. The teacher is also correcting some of the bad habits I have picked up (from associating so much with "common folk") in pronunciation and grammar. This is probably the most practical course I have taken so far at the theologate.

~

I am back on Orchid Island for the lengthy Chinese New Year vacation. Purchasing a bus ticket to go south from Taipei at the start of the holiday season was challenging. After waiting in line three hours for a ticket on a night bus, what I finally wound up with was a fold-out seat with its back broken, placed in the middle of the aisle, that squeaked all the way to Kaohsiung. It was a happy time of year, though, and the other passengers seemed content to endure the discomfort of the long ride. I did not mind it, either. When you really want to go someplace, it does not matter how you get there.

Going back to Orchid Island was like going home. Several times, I was invited to go fishing with the men. Some of them even asked me if I wanted to help them plant sweet potatoes and peanuts or chop wood with them. Before, when I asked if I could work with them, they didn't seem too keen on it. Now, they ask *me* if I would like go with them. There has been a change. Maybe this means we have grown closer and there is a greater sense of equality.

After spending several days hiking around the island to visit each village, I returned to the church in Imurud just before a heavy downpour began. I did not mind the rain. It gave me a chance to stay inside and write. Also, there was a deliriously aromatic scent that accompanied the raindrops as they fell, washing the greenery with freshness. Each time I have come over here, I have been swept away by that seductive scent. It is one of the reasons I like this place so much.

I arrived back at the theologate only two days late for the new semester. Because of the inclement weather, there were no planes from Orchid Island, and I had to wait some time for a boat. After getting to Taitung, I quickly boarded a bus and traveled over the mountain to Kaohsiung. But since I still had several hours before departing on the train to Taipei, I decided to go see Bruce Lee's final, spectacular film, *Enter the Dragon*. The theater was packed, and there was standing room only. Ever since the kung-fu artist's sudden death last summer, Taiwan and the Chinese-speaking world have been in mourning for him. Theaters continuously show Bruce Lee movies, and he is becoming a cult personality.

I am seriously thinking of continuing my theology course in the Philippines once school ends in June. Although I have gotten used to studying at the Fu Jen Theologate, I am not getting the most out of theology here—all that would be needed if I were to serve the aboriginal people as their priest—because of my unresolvable difficulties in comprehending the course in Chinese.

Not long ago, Alex Tan, a young Filipino Jesuit studying theology in Manila, was here for a meeting and told me all about Loyola House of Studies, which is the theologate for Jesuits in the Philippines. He indicated that it would be a good place for me to study theology and that the Filipino theologians would be happy for me to join their community. He concluded what almost sounded like a recruitment pitch by assuring me, "You would love it there!"

To transfer to another theologate would be a big change, and I have mixed feelings about moving from the community here, which I have grown to love. The benefits of what could be gained by going to the Philippines—such as studying theology in English in a new environment—are offset by what could be lost by such a move—namely, my proficiency in the Chinese language (such as it is).

Also, schools in the Philippines schedule their classes differently from those in Taiwan because of an earlier summer vacation, which lasts from April to June. Our classes in June would end two weeks after theirs started. So, if I chose to transfer to the Philippines, not only would I have no vacation, but I would be late for the beginning of classes there. However, this seems like a minor point that could be worked out later.

Meanwhile, I spent Easter vacation hiking with Brother

Lee, a Tayal aborigine brother who studies theology with us in Taipei. We trekked close to six hours a day, climbing steep slopes and mashing through muddy trails in the Jianshi mountain district of Hsinchu, where Brother Lee grew up.

Some of the remote little villages consisted only of a few homes, and there was rarely anyone at home. A few of the villages had run-down bamboo churches. We held a makeshift Easter service in one of them, together with a few families who lived nearby. The homes where we spent the night were poorly constructed shacks, and most of the people who lived in them were either sick or drunk. Despite the lush mountain scenery, our three-day trek was cold, rainy, and depressing.

The only enjoyable part of the hike was running down the other side of the mountain for the final leg of the journey. We were high above the river below on a winding trail that seemed to go on forever. When we finally reached a town with a bus stop, I felt the joy of Easter in being able to take a ride back to the theologate, dry off, and rest my weary feet.

After discussing with my superior the pros and cons of studying theology next year in the Philippines, we concluded that it would be more profitable for me to transfer there for the remainder of my studies. Although I'm relatively satisfied here doing reading courses, my superiors agreed that attending classes in English, which I could actually understand, would be a better preparation for the priesthood than staying here.

Since Taiwan is my adopted home, I feel a certain sense of responsibility to my family and friends here. But even my Jesuit classmates have told me I should take this opportunity to go to the Philippines. The four Taiwanese scholastics at the theologate will also study abroad, leaving only a few foreign-born scholastics in the community. When I pray about my transition to studying in Manila, I hear a small Voice within me say: "This is my gift to you. I want you to be happy."

From what I know of the Filipinos, I will not have any problem adapting to them. In fact, some say that the main danger could be that after being in that country, I would not want to come back to Taiwan. But while the Philippines may be the "Rome" of Asia and in constant need of apostolic workers, Taiwan is where I want to spend my life as a priest—to give back to its people what they have given to me.

I would not say Taiwan is a particularly rewarding place to see apostolic results since many of the Church's projects here do not succeed very well. It is not a Catholic country, and there are great forces like materialism working against the Church. But this is what makes Taiwan such a challenging place to live and work. Even Taipei, which did not charm me at all when I first arrived here, with its traffic, congestion, and air pollution, has grown to become a city I know and love more than any other city in the world—in spite of the numerous times I have gotten lost in its labyrinth of dense, convoluted streets.

I often wonder what God has in store for me in the future. There has never been the slightest doubt about my priestly vocation, but I am not sure how that will be expressed in my future ministry. How will I be able to share the lives of the poor in a society that is growing richer and more materialistic every day? Would it be better to go "where the need is greater", as Saint Ignatius advised us, or where I can function better as a servant of the people? I am sure the answers to these questions will become clearer when the time is at hand, so God probably does not want me to worry about them now.

I will certainly miss Jerry and our singing group when I go to the Philippines, although that very musical country should also provide plenty of opportunities to sing for others. Speaking of Jerry, he is into music and performing arts even more than I am, and the provincial seems to have him earmarked for a future ministry in mass communications at Kuangchi Studio. This change will not be easy for Jerry since he has immersed himself in his work with the students for the past year and enjoys being with them as much as he can.

Although I have not attended many of our theology lectures in Chinese, there is one class that I would not miss for the world, and that is Father Diaz de Rabago's course on the priesthood. It is also the most popular class at the theologate. What Father Rabago teaches is really his own love of the priesthood, and he communicates this beautifully to a receptive class with humor and sincerity. Despite his poor Chinese, we understand everything he says. He has us look at Jesus, and keep looking, and from there draw our concept of the priesthood. This kind of course—in any language—is something I look forward to and need.

After frantically finishing up term papers and final exams, I struggled through the seemingly never-ending red tape of getting a student visa for the Philippines. Since classes had begun in Manila before ours had ended, I wanted to get to my new theologate as soon as possible. That left only one day to pack my meager belongings before it was time to leave for Manila. The community gave me a warm send-off, and Jerry and Bihan rushed me to the airport. It only took an hour and forty-five minutes for the plane to arrive in Manila.

Flying over Manila Harbor, I could see thousands of tin-roofed houses glittering in the brilliant sunlight. Beyond the harbor, tropical greenery stretched to lavender mountains in the distance. A loud band was playing when I reached the arrival area, and a crowd of people shouted and waved little flags. Although the welcome party was for a government official, I could not help but laugh and imagine it was for me. An elderly Jesuit Brother brought me to the theologate in Marikina City, an hour's drive from the airport. It was June 12, 1974—Philippine Independence Day—a good omen.

Loyola House of Studies lies near a precipice on the prestigious Ateneo de Manila campus, overlooking a lush valley of banana and coconut trees. What strikes me most about the theologate is the abundance of windows, which enables light and fresh air to circulate without the aid of air-conditioning. Since a typhoon had recently drenched Manila, flowers are blossoming everywhere, and the air is very fragrant. There is no hint of dreaded air pollution here!

Alex Tan, whom I had previously met in Taiwan, showed me around the theologate. One wing of the building is for theology students, while another section across the garden houses philosophers and theology professors. Everyone I met was so friendly that Alex warned me just to say "I'm tired" if I did not want to accept all their hospitality and invitations, and they would understand.

Only three minutes away, down a steep path below the theologate, is a crowded barrio called Barangka, where several theologians minister to the poor. Shortly after I arrived, I was hustled down to this barrio for the dedication of a new basketball court, followed by a match between the Jesuit scholastics and local youth. As I sat on the sidelines, several little children came up to me and asked me my name and where I came from. I was disarmed by their friendliness and simplicity, and by their respect for me, even though I was still a seminarian. They spoke to me in English, but also taught me my first Tagalog phrase: "What is your name?" What a personal touch to my arrival in a new country!

~

I have already started classes. Although I arrived two weeks late, my classmates have brought me up to date on the subject matter. It is fascinating for me to hear professors teaching in English—and to understand every word for a change! Since I have already finished most of the required courses, this semester I will only have twelve hours of classes each week—in contrast to the twenty hours a week I had at Fu Jen. We are not allowed to take more classes than that, which is nice.

I have interesting courses on the Trinity, the priesthood, Saint Paul, and spiritual direction. In addition to classes, we also have small group seminars where we can discuss questions that are relevant not only for society but for ourselves as well. In one seminar, simply called "God", we share how our experience of God relates to ministering to those in need.

I was pleasantly surprised to find that other students had feelings much like my own because most of them had also worked with the poor. The teachers speak about the problems of the people, and the students talk about theology even outside of class, so our conversations are packed with practical insights rather than speculative theories unrelated to the human condition.

The theologate has delicious food choices, a nearby swimming pool on the college campus, and even classes in karate. I am making use of all of these. But even with such material comforts, the students here do not seem to forget the less fortunate who are living almost at their doorstep. As a rule, each student must have some personal involvement with the poor, either in the barrios or outlying resettlement areas.

I think that if the Philippines only consisted of our Jesuit community, I would still be happy to be here. Everyone in the community is Filipino except one student from Hong Kong, one from Australia, and me. To be in such a large, friendly, and lively community again makes me understand even better the words I heard from God before I came here: "This is my gift to you." Being here is like an ordination-year "present". But in this outgoing group of friendly Jesuits, something spiritual is also happening at a deeper level.

For instance, in each wing of the theologate, a group of six or more students holds a prayer meeting for forty-five minutes each evening before gathering in the coffee room for late night snacks. Each student shares his day prayerfully with the others, highlighting moments that have drawn him closer to God and thanking Him for them. Then there are prayers for different intentions, songs, and readings from Scripture.

Some of these gatherings are more stimulating than others, but the emphasis is put on fidelity, so we keep on meeting every night. Since my classmates rotate the prayer meetings in one another's rooms, it is also a timely reminder to clean up our quarters. I especially enjoy the songs, and sometimes all we do at a meeting is sing. Tagalog hymns are so melodious that it is comforting for me to sing them even without knowing their meaning.

Although I am in awe of all the aspects of life here—spiritual, communal, and apostolic—I am still reticent to give myself over completely to joy because I expect the "Cross" will surface at any moment. I wait for it and expect it. It is almost as if I will not feel completely at home until it arrives. My experience has shown that Jesus calls me to share in a life that only comes to fulfillment on the Cross. All my joy must be in preparation for that. I do not know how or in what way that Cross will come, but I want to be ready for it.

~

Over the weekend, I went with ten Jesuit novices to a far-away resettlement area that was formerly vacant land but is now crowded with poor people who were removed from their shanty towns in Manila. The arid, dusty resettlement project we visited (one of many in outlying areas of Manila) has over 7,000 families living in tiny wooden shacks.

Many families we met in the resettlement area appeared to have practically nothing, yet they still retained a noticeable dignity beneath their crushed spirit. They had not wanted to move, but since there was no choice, they had to make the best of the situation. As I watched long lines of hapless people lining up for necessities such as water and food, I realized I had never witnessed poverty on such a vast scale before. And yet, God's presence was surely there even amid such misery.

I could not help but feel sad when we jumped onto the jeepney for the ride back. The novices seemed gloomy, too, even though they had been visiting that desolate area each week for months. But as soon as the jeepney rolled on to the main road, two of the novices pulled out guitars, and we all started singing, and we sang all the way home. After a while, the songs turned into prayers for the people we had just visited. Some of the songs were for acceptance and some were for change, but all were sung with peace and love. And there, too, was God's presence.

~

All the theology students have been encouraged to find ways to serve the poor. I chose to work in Barangka, the barrio closest to the theologate, so I could go there as often as possible. Father Bobby Nery, the popular newly ordained pastor of Barangka's small church, invited me, along with three of my classmates to assist him. He has introduced us to his friends in the barrio, which seem to include almost everyone.

It is a joy to work with other like-minded companions for the people we love and who love us, too. Although most Barangka residents are poor and their living conditions far from ideal, the barrio is like a big family. Most people readily help each other with good humor. When I visited the living room of one family who lived in a ramshackle complex of wooden shacks haphazardly joined together, I saw a sign on the wall that read, "God bless this lousy apartment."

Since some of the youth in Barangka are taking karate lessons, and Father Nery is the teacher, I decided to join the class also. This was not easy for me. I am a slow learner and do not exactly have a "fighting spirit". But because I am from Taiwan, where Bruce Lee's kung-fu exploits still reign supreme, I was readily accepted into the karate club. Karate is an art form. I look at it as a kind of dance more than something related to violence. For the youth here, it is also a safe and useful outlet for their often unruly feelings of aggression.

Speaking of dancing, Barangka held a barrio dance last Saturday on its new outdoor basketball court. I was chosen to be a chaperone. Restlessly watching the youth salsa around the court to the tune of "Tie a Yellow Ribbon Round the

Ole Oak Tree'' and other American pop favorites, I wanted to dance so much I could hardly keep my feet still. Afterward, there was a beauty contest, and my Jesuit companions and I were designated as judges. It was difficult to choose a winner since all the contestants looked as if they belonged in the Miss Universe Pageant, which was being held in Manila that same weekend. Beauty always takes first place in the Philippines.

~

For ten days in August, it rained so heavily that the Philippines' entire island of Luzon seemed to be underwater. Because the Ateneo campus sits on a hill, the floods did not affect us. But from a nearby cliff, we had a clear view of the river of mud that inundated most of Barangka. I went down with some of my classmates to help Father Nery shovel mud out of his church and neighboring homes.

President Marcos called off school throughout the northern Philippines to allow for students to participate in flood recovery efforts. A group of ''reconnaissance'' Jesuits scouted out areas with the worst flooding, gathering reports on what they had seen. Armed with that information, my classmates and I fanned out across Manila to solicit funds for medicines and donations.

Within two days, the recreation room at the theologate was packed to the rafters with food, medicine, and rescue equipment, giving the appearance we were preparing for war! Every last person at the theologate was involved in organizing the vast number of items that had been collected. We worked until dawn, preparing emergency supplies for ten different medical teams, each with its own doctor. After a few hours' break, we were divided into ''rescue teams'' and boarded jeeps or amphibious vehicles to ply through the water-logged roads as far north as we could. Then we transferred to *bangkas*, or narrow canoes, and paddled over miles of rice fields that had been turned into mammoth lakes.

I joined a rescue team that consisted of Cris, a short but muscular first-year theologian, who has become a close friend, four Sisters of Charity in their immaculate white habits, and three student doctors from the university medical school. When our flotilla of *bangkas* reached a village in the low-lying province of Pampanga and began drifting through neck-high waterways between the homes, the villagers huddled on the top floors of their tall stilt houses called out to us. We tossed up packages of *nutribuns* to those near enough to catch them and then headed for the main church in town.

The towering, centuries-old church of Saint Augustine was constructed entirely out of wood and had survived wars and revolutions and doubtless its share of floods. The fact that the church was now half underwater probably would not do it much more damage. Saint Augustine's was to be our center of operations. Fortunately, it had a spacious second-floor living quarters that could serve as our makeshift clinic.

Entering the massive church entrance, we were greeted by the surreal sight of pews floating down the aisles or bunched up together like logs stuck in a lake. Upstairs, the church had become a refugee center, with families sprawled out wherever they could find room. As I wiped the mud from my clothes, the Sisters, without a trace of dirt staining their spotless white habits, went to comfort the villagers.

Then we set up the clinic. My job was "pharmacist". While Cris channeled patients over to me and deciphered the doctor's prescriptions, I searched for the correct medicines among the carefully labeled bottles we had prepared the night before. For the next few days, we spent mornings at the church and afternoons doing house calls.

One "house call" was particularly interesting. An elegantly dressed old man was waving frantically to us as we paddled by his home. "We are Christians!" he yelled from a balcony. Tying our *bangka* to a conveniently positioned coconut tree, Cris and I splashed into the filthy water and swam over to his huge Spanish-style mansion, where over a hundred villagers had gathered for refuge. However, neither the man nor the people there needed help. They only wanted us to pray with them. Instead of asking for aid, they gave us *nutribuns* and coffee.

The mansion's ornate second-story parlor had a dusty antique piano and elaborate mirrors bordered by thick purple curtains. It looked like the ballroom of a grand eighteenth-century hotel. Only after the man had entertained us with a repertoire of traditional Tagalog love songs, accompanied on the piano by his equally well-groomed wife, did we manage to escape the kindness of these strangers and get on with our business.

In the evening, we relaxed with the other medical crews. One baby was being watched closely by several of the doctors, but his infection was too serious, and he died in the morning. We baptized him Norming, which was the name of the typhoon that had started the flooding. I'm not sure how they were able to bury the child since the cemetery was still underwater.

The medical students in the rescue crew I had joined worked tirelessly throughout the day. Finally, when we could hardly keep our eyes open any longer, we made the arduous trip back to the theologate. None of the team members complained about the difficulties of the past few days. They were happy for the opportunity to help others in need.

~

Then another crisis happened—not to us, but to our brothers at the Jesuit novitiate.

The Philippine military conducted a surprise raid on the novitiate in Novaliches, which is a subdivision of Manila. Some three hundred soldiers, backed up by Army jeeps and helicopters, surrounded the peaceful grounds of the Jesuit house of formation and retreat center, having heard reports that the head of the Communist Party was hiding there. The hard-line Marcos government appears to have an uneasy relationship with the Society of Jesus, even though Imelda Marcos, the president's wife, regularly seeks out Jesuits for spiritual counseling.

During the raid, one priest, who was holding a seminar for forty students, was arrested. Everyone at the novitiate was searched, even a group of Sisters who were there on retreat. The Jesuit provincial, who was making a visit to the novitiate, was also briefly arrested, evidently by mistake. Needless to say, all the Church officials in Manila were in an uproar when they received news of the raid and arrests. The archbishop called for a prayer vigil at the cathedral to make reparation, not only for the injustice of the raid, but also because of other wrongs attributed to the increasingly aggressive military. President Marcos asked for the prayer service to be called off, but the archbishop refused, and we all attended it.

As a result, the Jesuit who was arrested was offered immediate release. When he refused to leave unless all the others who were detained with him were also freed, he was kicked out of prison. Similar situations have been happening regularly in the Philippines ever since Martial Law was recently declared. There is no longer any freedom of speech or of the press and media. The officially stated purpose of Martial Law is to prevent the spread of Communism and eliminate corruption. But the general consensus is that it was implemented to keep the present government officials in power. Many people are not happy about the side effects of Martial Law, such as this raid. We are praying the novices can get back to their peaceful routine as soon as possible.

It is only the beginning of October, and the first semester has already ended. I was surprised to have done so well in my studies and especially in my written reports. But maybe it is not so surprising considering that I can write much better in English than in Chinese. I actually spent more time helping some of my classmates polish their essays than doing my own. Since writing has always been easy for me, I was happy to be of help to others.

For a community break between semesters, around sixteen of us spent a three-day vacation at a beach in nearby Batangas, a quiet town by the sea—and probably what most people imagine when they think of the Philippines. We stayed at a large tumbledown villa, constructed almost entirely of bamboo and banana leaves. There were no walls—only a cone-shaped roof to draw out the heat. The floor was a raised platform made of thin bamboo slats, seemingly fragile, but durable enough for my rambunctious classmates to sing and dance upon whenever the urge came to them. Each day, we swam in the sea, played ball on the sand, or rowed *bangkas* until the evening sun settled serenely into the South China Sea.

But that short vacation in Batangas was not enough for me. It only whetted my appetite for further adventure. I had come to the culturally rich Philippines not only to study but also to explore the country whenever there was a chance to do so. I wanted to go where few had traveled before—somewhere tribal and primitive and remote. Cris suggested I journey to the hills of northern Luzon, where the rarely encountered Dumagat people dwelled. They are among the poorest and most reclusive minority tribes in the Philippines.

My solo journey began with a grueling ten-hour trip to the foothills of the Sierra Madre Mountains in the northern province of Nueva Ecija, near Cabanatuan City. Five of those hours were spent walking since there had just been a rainstorm and the roads were washed out. Wherever a bit of asphalt remained, I took a jeepney. Otherwise, I either sloshed through the mud or straddled a slow-moving tractor, which plowed through everything in sight.

Father Joe Campana, a tall and affable American Jesuit, was pastor of the rural church near the mountains where the Dumagats lived. When I finally arrived there that evening, muddied from my journey, I found him quietly playing dominoes with some of his parishioners. He was surprised but obviously delighted by my visit. One of his assistants spotted my muddy shoes and offered to clean them for me.

Father Joe told me that although he had never gone up to the nearby mountains to visit the Dumagat tribe, he would accompany me to look for them the next morning. He told me that the Dumagats sometimes came down from their high villages to trade with the people. They were a nomadic tribe known for their hunting skills, Father Joe added, and they only needed one arrow to hit their prey on the first try.

We set out the next morning after breakfast. Since my shoes were not yet dry from washing, I left them at the church and only wore flip flops, along with jeans and a T-shirt. I also left my backpack at the church, with the little money I had brought with me, since I only planned to be gone a day.

The narrow, seldom-trod mountain path we climbed was overgrown with branches and tall grass. Father Joe's local assistant, who was walking in front of us, used his machete to slash away the foliage that blocked our way. After a while, we came to a plateau with a wide, slow-moving river.

To cross to the other side, the three of us grasped our hands tightly together—and I held my breath. The water came up almost to my neck in places. One false move and we could be swept off by the strong current to who knows where. But we made it safely to dry land.

The path to the higher mountains took another three hours. It was a gradual incline, though, that did not require much effort. Finally, we arrived at a broad clearing, where we found a small village of settlers originally from the lowlands. Simple bamboo huts had been constructed on each side of a muddy stream that flowed through the middle of the village.

Father Joe greeted the settlers in Tagalog. They were overjoyed at seeing him and brought their young children to be blessed. Most of the villagers were Ilocano people, who had come to the mountains to do farming. They had even started a small school for the dozen or so village children.

"It's starting to rain," Father Joe reminded me. "I wouldn't want to get stuck up here. It's too dangerous. You can remain here if you like, but I'm going back."

"I'll just stay for tonight," I reassured him. "Another day won't make much difference."

"Then I'll see you tomorrow," Father Joe said. After quickly saying goodbye to the settlers, he headed back down the path with his assistant.

A young man with a wide smile named Jun, who said he knew where the Dumagat chieftain lived, offered to lead me there. He told me it was not far.

After climbing farther up the hill, we reached the home of the chieftain in half an hour. He was huddled in his house with his wife and family when we arrived. But his "house" was only a few boards propped up at an angle to keep off the rain. It was the smallest home I had ever seen.

"The Dumagats carry their houses with them wherever they go," Jun whispered to me, "like snails."

Short and stocky, the young chieftain emerged from his home carrying a beautiful, smiling child in his arms. His thin and obviously shy wife remained inside, beneath the roof covering. As Jun translated for us, the chieftain pointed to his bow and arrows and other belongings, which were very few. Proudly, he explained the significance of the colorful beads and arm bands he and his small son wore. The tasseled arm bands and loincloths were their only coverings.

Jun told me it would soon be dark, and he had no flashlight, so we said goodbye to the chieftain and his family and walked back down to the village by the stream.

"I will take you to visit more Dumagats tomorrow morning before you leave," Jun assured me, smiling broadly.

That night, as I lay on the floor of Jun's bamboo hut, I could hear the rain pouring down even heavier than before. In the morning, I noticed that the little stream that separated the two parts of the small village had begun to swell.

"You cannot go back today," Jun warned me, poking his head inside the bamboo hut. "The river is already too high. My brother Felix went down earlier and had to return because there is no way to cross the river. You will have to stay here for a few more days until the water goes down."

Nevertheless, Jun kept his promise to bring me to more Dumagat dwellings. He tossed me a clean dry shirt and a floppy hat, and we set off through the drizzle into the higher mountains. During the frequent downpours, we took refuge beneath some thick forest trees until the sky was clear again.

The Dumagats we met lived with their families in low, angled homes, much the same as that of their chieftain, but situated quite far from one another, perhaps so they would not infringe on one another's hunting area. Their appearance was extraordinary, each one with individual characteristics.

The men seemed fierce at first sight, clasping their bows and arrows, but they were really gentle and welcoming. Some were thin and dark with wild, wiry hair, others light and full-faced, looking like they would be as comfortable in a coat and tie as in a loincloth. The women were dressed in tattered dresses, and most appeared fearful or timid.

One tribesman, with a toothy grin and long, tangled hair, invited Jun and me to sit down with him and his companions beside a large vase in front of his dwelling. Then he reached into the vase with his dirt-caked hand and pulled out a handful of fermented rice wine, sloshing it into a stone bowl, and put the bowl in front of me. After doing the same for Jun, he motioned for us to drink.

The other men also dipped their hands into the vase, drinking from their bowls and urging me to do the same. I stared at the cup of fermented rice for a few moments as it bubbled darkly in the aromatic liquor and then slowly raised the cup to my mouth. But it was no use—my lips pulled back uncontrollably as soon as the pungent cup neared them. The tribesmen laughed when they saw my expression. Eventually, I managed a few sips. But I was less concerned about the taste of the questionable wine than about the consequences it might have on my health. The rain was bad enough, but diarrhea would be disastrous.

I lay awake that night, listening to the rain pouring heavily on the flimsy roof of Jun's hut and echoing throughout the forest. Soon, the thunder of the rain merged with the roar of the stream creeping closer to our hut. At dawn, I awoke in alarm when I felt water flowing over my feet.

"We have to move—now!" Jun shouted as he rushed in the doorway and saw the encroaching river. "Either we climb the trees or swim across the river to higher ground."

I quickly scrambled off the floor and out the door, where I was surrounded on all sides by raging water. After snatching two squawking chickens by the neck with one hand, Jun grabbed me with the other and pulled me into the former stream—which was now an angry river—and we began wading to the other side. Although the stream was not wide, the water was so turbulent I was afraid my feet would slip and I would be washed downstream.

Halfway across the river, I was startled to catch sight of Jun's little brother, Felix, struggling frantically in the frothing water beside a large protruding rock.

"Look what I caught!" Felix gleefully yelled to us. "A crocodile!" With one hand grasping the boulder, his other hand held up a bright green iguana that he clutched by its tail.

"Bring it along," Jun shouted back. "We will cook it for breakfast."

I was worried about how little Felix would get out of the surging waterway with a giant iguana writhing in his hands. But a few bangs on the rock stunned the lizard long enough for Felix to put it under his arm and swim to dry land.

After setting up camp at a spot much higher in the mountains, Jun and Felix, together with me and some of the Dumagat youth, feasted on the unfortunate iguana. It did not taste bad—kind of soft and mushy, if I remember right.

Another tribe, called the Ilongots, had huts in that area, where they engaged in farming. They welcomed Jun and the villagers who had fled the river and said we could stay in their homes until the rain subsided. The Dumagat youth also invited us to live with them, but their houses were hardly big enough for their own families, much less guests.

The rain continued to fall that day—and all the next. On the evening of the third day, as we gathered around a campfire outside one of the bamboo huts, I finally saw the moon breaking through some scattered clouds. When the rain began to slow to just a drizzle, I began thinking about how to get back to school, which by then had already started.

"Is there any other way to the city besides crossing the river?" I asked the Ilongot man next to me, who wore a faded red headband and loincloth. "I have to get back to school."

"The only other way is through the mountains, but you could get lost by yourself," the man replied. "My son will go with you. His godmother lives in a village near the city."

In the morning I met my guide, a short, fragile, and taciturn Ilongot youth with a slight build and confused look, who was nicknamed Angel. Hopefully, his name rather than his ungainly stature would be a good omen. One of the Dumagat youth shyly pulled a plastic bag of fermented rice from his back pocket and handed it to me. Jun also gave us some food. At least we would not starve on the journey.

"It's good you know how to get to the city," I casually remarked to Angel, as we set off on the long hike. "I would definitely get lost by myself."

Angel fingered his wide headband hesitantly and then glanced at me, whispering in a timid voice, "But I do *not* know how to get there. I have never gone this way before."

It struck me then that I might have been chosen to be Angel's angel, rather than the other way around.

After only walking a short distance, the thong on one of my rubber sandals broke off. Since hiking with only one sandal was impossible, I discarded the other as well, glumly resigned to walking the rest of the way barefoot. But bare feet cling better to wet rocks than sandals. Whenever we crossed streams, we held on to each other, and neither of us slipped.

After a few hours, we rested and shared the rice and small dried fish Jun had given us. When I saw Angel eyeing the bag of fermented rice in my pocket, I gave it to him. After consuming its content in a few gulps, his spirits picked up, and he began to sing some Ilongot songs. Despite his fragile build, Angel turned out to be strong and agile, keeping a steady footing while fording the streams. I hoped that would continue after drinking such potent rice wine.

Our trek up and down the hills and across the countless streams took over six hours in all. During that time, I kept praying that neither of us would cut our feet on a sharp rock along the way. But we both made it through the journey unscathed and eventually spotted a village in the distance. As we drew near, I brushed the mud off my shirt, rolled down my pant legs, and tried to tidy myself up as best as I could.

Although we had reached a village, the main town of Cabanatuan was still much farther down the road. My backpack was at Father Joe's church on the other side of the city, separated by an impassable river, so it could not be retrieved. And I had no money and no shoes. Manila—and the theologate—were still far away.

Angel found the way to the home of his godmother, Almida, who lent me enough money to get back home. She also gave me some used flip flops and helped me find a motorcycle taxi to Cabanatuan. From there I could take a bus to Manila.

I wrote a note to Father Joe explaining my situation and asking that he pay back Almida with the money I had left with him and give my shoes and backpack to Angel. Then I drew a picture of my swollen feet on the envelope and added the Bible verse: "How beautiful on the mountains are the feet of those who bring good news."

Damp and dirty, I arrived at the Manila bus station later that night. From there, I took a jeepney to the theologate. But I felt uneasy appearing at the front door of our school at such an hour in my disheveled appearance. So, I went around to the back of the theologate, where there was a low wall near my room, and quietly climbed over it. Once in my room, I collapsed on the bed and did not awake until morning.

When I strolled into the refectory for breakfast, my classmates broke into a thundering ovation. School had already started, and they had evidently given me up for dead.

Now, as I reflect back on that rugged adventure, the strangest thing about it was that when I was in the mountains with the tribal people, I was anxious to get back to the city. But once in school for a few days, I wished I were back in the mountains. I missed my newfound friends.

After returning from my experience in the wilderness, I decided to take formal classes in Tagalog. One of the reasons for this was that when I was staying with the local villagers, Jun had told me, "Many of the people here want to talk with you and get to know you, but they don't know how because you can't speak Tagalog." Another reason was that I wanted to understand what my Filipino classmates were saying when we conversed in a group. Most of them spoke Tagalog, even though they also knew English. Unfortunately, when my classmates found out I was taking Tagalog classes, they mischievously made it a point to speak English when I was with them. So, you can't win . . .

Armed with a basic background in Tagalog, I was invited to help give a retreat for high school students from the Tondo slum area of Manila. I drew pictures on the blackboard to help the students better understand what I was saying and had them dramatize stories from the Gospel according to their own interpretations. One of the stories was of the woman caught in adultery. When the mob of students started to stone the condemned woman, the boy playing Jesus cried out, "Don't kill her—she's pretty!"

The retreat was held in the covered basketball courts on the beautifully manicured campus of Saint Francis Xavier School, which mostly serves wealthier students of Chinese descent. A young teacher at the school gave the Tondo students a tour of the campus and proudly showed off their new Olympic-sized swimming pool. As our retreatants filed quietly by the pool's edge, one of them commented with a shrug, "We have a swimming pool in Tondo, too . . . when it rains."

A few weeks ago, the Ali-Foreman battle for the world heavyweight boxing championship was held in Manila. Traffic came to a standstill, and businesses closed during the event, which was entitled, "The Thrilla in Manila". All my classmates were glued to the TV set during the fight, and when Muhammad Ali won, the Philippines stock market almost crashed.

Then there were the festivities for All Souls' Day, when everyone went to the cemetery to clean graves. Loudspeakers blared music throughout the day as families brought candles and even tents to spend the night with their departed loved ones. In the evening, I went to the crowded hillside cemetery nearby to pray with families from Barangka. We strummed guitars and quietly sang hymns while a couple next to us played chess on one of the tombstones.

~

My main joy since arriving in the Philippines has been the opportunity to converse at a deep level with fellow Jesuits. I have learned so much from them, been in awe of their simple yet profound faith, and enjoyed participating in religious devotions that remind me of those of my youth. However, mixed in with the heady exultation of such companionship comes a heartbreaking sadness when one of the brothers chooses to leave the Jesuits—especially if he has become a friend. Then the Cross I had been expecting finally makes its appearance.

Cris, the scholastic with whom I have spent so much time conversing, giving retreats, and serving the poor in Barangka, has decided to leave us and begin a new life in his hometown of Davao in the southern Philippines. Of course, I prayed for him and tried to talk him out of it, but to no avail. Cris is a few years behind me in theology and has experienced many of the same problems I did with studies. Although I eventually grew out of these difficulties, it was not the same with Cris. He was overcome by them.

Although I am very close to Cris, I did not want our friendship to be the only reason I felt he should stay with us. I also wished the best for him. Even God never forces us to follow a certain path. He only invites us—and if a different route is preferable, He gently allows us to follow our desires.

In the melancholy aftermath of Cris' departure, I reflected on my own experience in the Philippines. Although I really enjoy serving the Filipino people, especially the poor, joining in their laughter and familial atmosphere, I still think my main vocation will play out in Taiwan. Even the poor here seem rich to me because they have such a strong faith and God means so much to them. They are materially poor but spiritually rich—probably more so than I. The location of my future mission might transcend national and emotional boundaries. It could simply be that place where God whispers me to go. And when I follow, He gives me peace.

~

At the beginning of December, the four of us Jesuits in third-year theology were ordained deacons by Cardinal Sin, the Archbishop of Manila. A simple but beautiful ceremony was held at the theologate chapel with an overflowing crowd. The diaconate is the final stage on our long journey to the priesthood—with ordination only months away. During the ceremony, I felt both humbled and astounded that God would choose to put His confidence in me as His servant.

The choir sang the powerful and moving "Suscipe", a hymn reserved for those moments when a Jesuit gives himself wholly to God. In union with that hymn, I offered my *intellect*, with all its limitations, my *memories* that mean so much to me, my often-confused *understanding*, and a *will* that cannot depend on itself—but only on God.

My three fellow deacons were all from rather wealthy families, so most of those in the congregation were dressed in their finest. But not all of them. Since I had no relatives in the Philippines, my Barangka "family" attended the ceremony in raggedy clothes and noisy flip flops. Besides the children, the boys and girls in our karate club and members of the toughest gang in the barrio were also there as my guests.

At one point in the diaconate liturgy, the archbishop intoned our duties as deacons, and one of them was "to give bread to the hungry". On hearing that, I could not help but chuckle because I knew my guests were looking forward to the mouth-watering buffet refreshments to be served after the ceremony. At first, the children were shy about helping themselves to the food. But in the end, they stayed longer than anyone else and emptied the table of cookies, putting leftovers into their pockets for their hungry little brothers and sisters at home.

Soon after becoming a deacon, I was privileged to have another opportunity "to give bread to the hungry". When the government decreed that 30,000 squatter families in the slum area of Tondo should be evicted, a peaceful protest was held, preceded by prayers to God for strength. Together with my classmates, I joined the squatter families in their march for justice. As the procession drew near to the Presidential Palace of Malacañang, armed police began breaking up the crowd, but there was no violence. Later, the president decreed that there would be no eviction. A Mass of Thanksgiving was held, during which a large stone monument was unveiled with the promises of the president inscribed on it.

But my most significant moment of "giving bread to the hungry" came in a more spiritual way during Christmas Mass at the Barangka chapel. For the first time, I was able to distribute Holy Communion—the Bread of Life—to the faithful. Afterward, I began baptizing children singly and in groups, which took all morning. Reading from a Tagalog version of Baptism in one hand, I held the English version in the other to make sure what I was saying and doing was correct. After that, Barangka held a barrio fiesta, which lasted the rest of the day and well into the night.

~

"Don't travel third class!" my classmates warned me as I prepared to take a ship to Cebu and then on to Mindanao.

"Why not?" I asked. "It's so much cheaper."

"Because third class is full of robbers and riffraff, and you will have all your belongings stolen," one of the older, more experienced Jesuits patiently explained.

Of course, I did not listen to them. It was the day after Christmas, and I was setting off for Cagayan de Oro on the island of Mindanao. Miguel, a warm and friendly student whom I had met on the Ateneo campus, had invited me to spend Christmas vacation there with his family.

My classmates also knew Miguel, who was from a wealthy Cagayan de Oro clan, and they mischievously joked about me pandering to the "the rich" instead of serving the poor as I usually did. But Miguel was the only non-Jesuit friend I had on campus, and he really wanted to show me around his hometown. I was grateful for the opportunity.

Arriving at densely crowded Manila Harbor, I stood in line to buy a third-class ticket on a massive luxury ship, complete with a theater, rock band, lounges, and gambling casinos, that was departing for Cebu. But my cheap-class ticket only allowed me to use a fold-up cot on the very lowest level of the ship. I looked around warily to see if there were any robbers or riffraff who might steal my belongings. To my surprise, almost the entire third-class level was filled with harmless Filipino nuns and seminarians, joyfully returning to their native provinces for Christmas vacation.

I placed my cot next to a lively group of Salesian seminarians, and we talked, sang, played, and prayed throughout most of the twenty-five-hour voyage—except when we were seasick or asleep. I never felt safer in my life.

After disembarking the ship on the island of Cebu, one of the Salesian seminarians who lived there gave me a quick tour of the main city and brought me to his seminary for lunch. Then he guided me to the boat that would leave that evening for Cagayan de Oro.

Again, everyone was so friendly and welcoming aboard ship that it seemed like a party. The Christmas spirit was still in the air. But after a good night's sleep on a lilting deck cot, I was awakened at early light by a rag-tag gang of brawny men, who boarded the ship with loud shouts, racing menacingly across the slippery deck. I grabbed my backpack, wondering if these pirate-like attackers were the forewarned "riffraff" coming to dispossess the passengers of their belongings. Fortunately, they were only porters from the port of Cagayan de Oro sent to collect the ship's baggage and supplies.

My friend Miguel lived with his parents and eight younger brothers and sisters in a well-to-do neighborhood, surrounded by shady trees and flowery gardens. Although it was a far cry from hot and crowded Barangka, the people I met there were just as hospitable as my friends in the slums. And the food! Miguel's mother did the cooking, even though they had plenty of money to hire someone to cook if they had wished. For the first time, I tasted some of the most famous dishes in the Philippines. Even with nine children crowded around the table, there was still plenty for everyone.

Miguel's father was the manager of Del Monte, which is one of the largest exporters of pineapples in the world. One afternoon, he invited Miguel and me for lunch on the balcony of the elegant Del Monte Country Club, overlooking an enormous pineapple plantation. After the meal, when his father left to talk to some associates, Miguel spoke to me about what it was like being from one of the wealthiest families in Mindanao.

"You might think it is easy being rich," he said. "But in this society, I have very little freedom to choose my own way of life. I am expected to continue in my father's footsteps, even though that is not my preference. To make matters worse, my girlfriend is a Muslim princess and if we get married, I would have to become a Muslim. Since my family are devout Catholics, they would never accept this."

I learned a lot in my few days with Miguel, and not only from him but also from his brothers and sisters. My general impression was that every family has its problems, and money is not always the answer.

From Cagayan de Oro, I flew to the sprawling city of Davao on the other side of Mindanao. I had wanted to take a bus, but the only road there had recently been destroyed in a battle between the Philippine Army and Muslim rebels. I met up with Cris in Davao, and, after a quick look at the city, we boarded a *bangka* for the tiny, undeveloped island of Samal. Cris and his family were trying to start a seaweed farm there. But so far, they only had a small plot of sand near the beach, where they had built a temporary nipa hut.

It was almost evening when we arrived. The few other villagers along the beach insisted we go to their huts for dinner, which mainly consisted of fermented coconut milk (*tuba*), Tanduay whiskey, and nuts. It was tricky trying to combine such a warm reception with the resolve not to drink too much. Although I was not entirely successful in this and was rewarded with a blistering headache the next morning, a quick dip in the refreshing seawater more or less cured me.

When Cris and I returned to the city of Davao, we boarded a boat for the port of Zamboanga, a three-day journey across the tail end of Mindanao. Cris wanted to go there to retrieve seaweed clippings for his future farm on Samal Island. We slept on deck cots, which provided a magnificent view of Mindanao's coastline, along which the ship hugged through most of the voyage.

Zamboanga was almost like another country, with a bright, South Seas atmosphere. The Muslim fishermen at the harbor wore sarongs and sported hair bleached gold from sun and sea. Cris and I stayed at the local Jesuit high school in town, where we were warned not to go out at night because of the nearby battles. When I heard a steady stream of machine-gun fire that evening, I understood the precaution.

In the morning, one of the Jesuits at the school brought us to a seaweed farm he had set up for Muslim refugees who had escaped fighting in other areas. On the way to the seaweed farm, our *bangka* passed by a village that had been entirely destroyed by fire. The Muslim guide said the Philippine Navy had looted the village first, then burned it—another senseless tragedy in the endless conflict between the military and the Muslims. Otherwise, the islands were indescribably beautiful and idyllic.

After two days in Zamboanga, I said goodbye to Cris and boarded a plane for Manila, arriving there within an hour. I would have liked to stay longer in that fascinating southern area of the Philippines, but I did not want to make a habit of always arriving late for school.

~

I received notice from our provincial that I have been approved for ordination this coming spring. Accompanying this welcome news was permission for me to be ordained in San Diego at the little parish church where I grew up. Originally, my ordination was slated for Taiwan, where ordinations in our province are usually held. But I asked for an exception since otherwise my mother would not be able to attend. And I felt the ordination ceremony should be mainly a gift for the family. Although Mother was able to go to Taiwan for my brother Jerry's ordination, she would not be able to do the same for mine because of her job at school.

Meanwhile, there are several application forms and letters that must be sent to the bishop of San Diego and other diocesan offices. Mother will assist the church officials in choosing a suitable date for the ordination. Since she works as secretary at the elementary school attached to the church where I will be ordained, she can complete most of the formalities without my presence there. Our academic year ends in March, so I plan to go to the States sometime after Easter to prepare for the ordination. I will pass through Taiwan to see Jerry on the way there. It is 1975 now, almost six years since I left my home country as a missionary to Asia, and I have not been back since. But what a way to go back!

After ordination, it will still be necessary for me to complete my fourth year of theology here in the Philippines. This is called the "pastoral year", and it will entail juggling my newly active priestly ministry with preparations for final oral comprehensive exams covering all four years of theology. Some students also write and defend a thesis during this year in order to earn a Master's degree in Theology. I might do that, too, although I do not see any practical reason for it. But knowledge is knowledge, and writing a thesis could help me go deeper into some specific area of theology.

~

For a break before final exams, our community traveled to the mountain resort town of Baguio, several hours north of Manila, to Mirador Retreat House. This was where Jesuit theologians who had been studying in Mainland China relocated after the Communists took over their theologate in Shanghai and before they arrived in Taiwan. Mirador must hold bittersweet memories for Jesuits like Father Rouleau, my spiritual father, who taught for many years in that theologate. From what I have heard, the Jesuits spent equally long hours playing mahjong games there.

Although Baguio is a lovely town, I was in search of more exotic adventures, as usual, and wanted to visit the remote Ifugao tribe that lived in the hills far above Baguio. So, when our short vacation ended and the rest of the community returned to Manila, I hopped on a rickety bus heading toward the famous rice terraces of Banaue, which many consider to be the seventh wonder of the world.

But the old bus came to a standstill far short of my destination because there was no longer any traversable road. At that point, it was necessary for me to hike up a long and steep trail, which eventually led to a small Ifugao tribal village perilously perched on a misty cliffside and surrounded by the remarkable emerald green rice terraces. It was an otherworldly sight.

I stayed for five days in a nipa hut attached to the village's bamboo church. Most of the Ifugao tribespeople were Catholics and treated me as though I were already a priest. If I had been ordained at that time, I could have done more for them because they were rarely visited by a priest. Nonetheless, every night they asked me to lead them in a prayer service, and I was happy to do so.

Clare, a fair-haired and very thin American nurse, was the only foreign resident in the village. She had been staying in the village for the past two years and had fallen in love with a handsome Ifugao villager. But they were not permitted to get married since in the Ifugao custom, the women go to the fields to work while the men stay at home to care for the children and manage the housework. Clare, with her frail constitution, was obviously not suitable for fieldwork in such a harsh mountain environment. The famed rice terraces were tended primarily by women, a formidable task regardless of gender.

Clare introduced me to the Ifugao chief and other villagers, who regaled me with stories and tribal lore throughout my stay in the village. Incredibly, their English was better than that of Filipinos in the lowlands. They explained to me that this was due to the American teachers who had been sent to their mountain village some fifty years previously. They must have been gifted teachers to have left such a long-lasting linguistic legacy with the Ifugao people.

The Ifugao still kept their ancient customs and wore traditional garments throughout the day. Seeing the men in their bright red loincloths and the women in colorful tribal dresses made me feel I was back on Orchid Island. But there was one custom I found somewhat disturbing.

While walking around the village one day, I chanced upon a small stilt hut with a cluster of Ifugao women gathered around it, appearing as though they were having a party. They invited me to join them for food and drink, and when I asked the reason for the celebration, they pointed to an old woman sitting peacefully in a chair under the stilt house. Evidently, the party was for her. But on closer inspection, I realized the poor lady was dead. She had a scarf tied around her chin that was fastened to a rafter above in order to keep her head from drooping.

"She is the guest of honor," one of the women told me. "Will you say a funeral prayer for her?" Of course, I complied, thinking to myself that this was the strangest burial custom I had ever encountered.

Before I left Banaue, the people asked me to return after my ordination to say Mass in their village. I told them I would try to do so, but that their faith was already strong, and they were managing well even without a priest. Like the impressive rice terraces their ancestors had carved into the mountainside centuries ago, and the English language that had been handed down to them so carefully throughout the years, the seeds of faith sown by a few missionaries in an almost forgotten past had blossomed into the vibrant faith I witnessed in my short visit with the indomitable Ifugao people.

~

During Holy Week services before Easter, I was able to make use of my newly attained powers as a deacon to the fullest. Father Nery welcomed me to be in charge of all the ministries in the main church of Barangka, while he went to other more distant chapels in his far-flung parish. Between services, I watched a brutal three-hour reenactment of the Stations of the Cross, including a mock crucifixion of the church's unfortunate youth leader, and listened throughout the day as prayer groups lining the main road chanted, without interruption, the Pasyón, an epic seventeenth-century poem sung in Tagalog detailing Jesus' suffering and death. It was an interesting but exhausting Holy Week leading up to a joyful Easter.

And now it is time to go to the States for my long-awaited ordination. Along the way, I will stop off in Taipei to see Jerry, who was recently assigned to work at the Jesuit-run Kuangchi Program Service. I am very grateful for my year of theology in the Philippines. My only regret is that because of such a full schedule I was not able to take more courses that could have been profitable. Looking back, I am sure the reason I studied so well and had such a successful year was due to my almost constant contact with the poor families in Barangka and the equally invigorating conversations with Jesuits in my community.

The problems and needs of the families I have grown close to in the barrio are intrinsically related to the issues we discuss each day in theology class. This experience of theory and practice has given me the energy and enthusiasm to study, knowing that the subject matter of my classes will help me to become a better priest for the people. Unlike before, I can safely say that now I am interested in theology.

4

ORDINATION

On April 5, 1975, Chiang Kai-shek, the president of Taiwan, died, plunging the nation into gloom. Jerry and I waited in line for hours to view the Generalissimo's body at the Presidential Palace in Taipei, but we eventually gave up since there were far too many people ahead of us. Taipei came to a virtual standstill, which was a shame because I was looking forward to seeing Jerry's debut acting role in a popular new Chinese movie. As it was, we could only view the movie posters outside the dark and empty theater.

Yes, my brother Jerry is becoming a star! In the short time after being assigned to Kuangchi Program Service, Jerry has captivated audiences throughout Taiwan by appearances on numerous television dramas and music shows. The same smiling charisma that previously delighted his philosophy students at Fu Jen University apparently works equally well, if not better, in front of a camera. Oddly enough, though, his TV appearances are only a part-time job.

"My main duty at Kuangchi is translating Mickey Mouse cartoons into Chinese," Jerry told me with a sardonic laugh. "So it's not as thrilling as it sounds."

Begun twenty years ago by the visionary Jesuit Father Philip Bourret, Kuangchi was making TV programs before most of the people in Taiwan even had TV sets. Father Bourret saw the future of mass communications as a way to "pre-evangelize" the non-Christian population of Taiwan, using music and drama in subtle ways that would promote the growth of individual goodness as well as benefit the nation's development—and ultimately make the Catholic faith more accessible to non-believers.

I stayed two days with Jerry and his small community of Jesuits on the top floor of the Kuangchi building in one of Taipei's teeming commercial districts. Jerry had already made friends with the vendors, migrant workers, and beggars in his neighborhood, and he introduced me to all of them. In our conversations, he told me about his ideas for new projects and programs that could influence his "parish", which is the way he referred to the whole of Taiwan. His own visionary mind sounded like it was going at high speed, and working at Kuangchi fitted him like a glove. For sure, he was doing a lot more there than just translating cartoons.

It was sad saying goodbye to Jerry after so short a visit. But after my ordination, I will pass by again and stay for a longer time. Right now, I am anxious to get to the States and start planning for my ordination ceremony. With less than a month to go, there is still a lot I need to do. In a way, it is like getting married—except without a wife.

~

Mother and my brother Glenn were waiting for me at the San Diego Airport when the plane arrived. After many hugs and a few tears of joy, they drove me to their new home not far from our former neighborhood. The beloved old house where I had grown up had been leveled two years before to make room for the playground of a nearby school. When we passed by the playground, there was nothing but an empty baseball field where that beautiful old house with all its memories had once stood.

In a momentary wave of wistful nostalgia, I recalled the moment twelve years previously, when I left home at the age of eighteen, in the freshness of my youth, to join the Society of Jesus. Since that time, I have followed Christ on the long journey of studies and mission work in preparation for ordination. And now my life is filled with anticipation for that long-awaited day to arrive. The ordination is scheduled for May 10 at my hometown parish of Saint Vincent de Paul Church.

Being "home" again is so restful that I can hardly rouse myself to make out invitation cards and prepare for the ordination ceremony. But much of the preparation has already been done. Sister Loretto, an artistic fourth-grade teacher at Saint Vincent's School, has drawn the cover for the ordination booklet and helped me choose the hymns that will be sung. She also leads the children's choir, which is enthusiastically practicing for the big event.

Most days at home are very quiet since Mother works days and Glenn has a night shift. I enjoy talking to Glenn when he wakes up and to Mother when she returns from school. It was a blessing to see old Monsignor Mimnaugh, who told me he was bursting with pride to have the ordination of a "hometown kid" in his parish. I also visited with the students and teachers at the school and expressed my gratitude for all their work in planning the celebration.

There is one person, however, who deserves a longer visit—Father Francis Rouleau, who is, and always will be, my spiritual father. Ever since I met saintly Father Rouleau during my first year of training as a Jesuit novice, he inspired me both by his words and example, ultimately encouraging me to follow his path as a missionary to the Far East. Father Rouleau had spent his younger years in China, where he taught theology and became an authority on Chinese Jesuit history. Only after he was old and crippled by rheumatoid arthritis, had he returned to the novitiate infirmary to spend what he thought were his last days on earth. But after being "discovered" by the novices and renowned for his wisdom and holiness, Father Rouleau took on the role of spiritual "guru" to a new generation of young Jesuits looking for someone who embodied their spiritual aspirations to the fullest. This gave a second life both to Father Rouleau and his spiritual sons. And I was the foremost among them.

Before my ordination, I plan to make an eight-day retreat with Father Rouleau at our former novitiate in Los Gatos. In return, he has promised to attend my ordination ceremony even if he is not able to walk. Although he is now partially confined to a wheelchair because of crippling arthritis, he said this would pose no problem. Our family friend at Los Gatos, Father "Pop" Silva, will give him a lift.

~

On the way to make my retreat, I stopped at the Jesuit theologate at Berkeley to see some of my former classmates who were studying there. They will not be able to take time off to attend my ordination, so it was a chance to be with them again, even for a short visit. Although they spoke highly of their classes at Berkeley, they joked that theology might make more sense in Chinese than English. I assured them that was not true in my case.

Father Rouleau was so elated to see me that he made me feel my upcoming ordination would be the culmination of *his* Jesuit life as well as my own. Having a retreat with this holy Father was like sitting at the feet of Christ for eight days to receive his blessings and teachings. I was open with Father Rouleau about my successes as well as my failures—

and also my regrets about things I wished I had done differently. But this kind and caring spiritual Father urged me to look forward to a rewarding future rather than fret over missteps in the past.

"Never say, 'if only I had done this or that'," he said adamantly. "With God, there are no 'ifs'. Everything is a part of His plan, and He can fulfill His plan with your weakness and mistakes as well as with your triumphs."

Father Rouleau helped me realize that as long as I was trying to do God's will, everything that I had done was good even though it may not have appeared to be so at the time. What a consolation this simple teaching gave me! It was as if God had taken my life till now, wrapped it up and tied it with a ribbon—and given it back to me as an ordination gift.

I was pleased that three of my mother's sisters traveled all the way from Mississippi to be with me during the days leading up to my ordination. Being conservative Catholics by nature, my aunts reminded me I needed to dress in "clerical black" for the event. Because of my hasty departure from the Philippines, I had forgotten to bring along a pair of black pants, so I rushed to Sears, where there was a sale in men's clothing. But the pants I bought were a foot too long. After thoroughly scolding me, my three aunts squatted on the floor below me like fairy godmothers trying to outdo each other in altering the pant legs. Mother just sat on her easy chair and smiled. It really was like getting ready for a wedding.

Father Rouleau came down a day earlier, accompanied by Father Silva, his solicitous chauffeur. Since Father Rouleau had a niece who worked at Mercy Hospital—by coincidence the same hospital where I was born—he wanted to stay there for the night. This would also be a safeguard so that if anything happened to him, a nurse would be close by. I decided to spend the night before my ordination in a hospital room adjoining his, not only to keep him company but also to receive a few final words of wisdom before making my priestly vows. In a sense, this would be the second time I would be "born" at Mercy Hospital.

What can I say about my ordination except that it was the best day of my life? Of course, the celebration was on a much smaller scale than Jerry's spectacular ceremony in Taipei two years before. But that was fine. What was most important to me was having my family there, especially Mother and her friends from the school and parish.

Some welcome figures from my past also appeared at the ordination—including Father Neely, my high school Latin teacher, a few of my former Jesuit superiors, and Father Fox, the parish priest at Saint Vincent's Church when I was growing up. It was Father Fox who had said the funeral Mass for my father when he died. Seeing this beloved pastor once again made me realize my father was there, too, spiritually by my side, smiling with pride.

But it was Father Rouleau who "stole the show". He sat in his wheelchair at the side of the altar, enraptured with joy throughout the ceremony. When it came time for me to impart my newly acquired priestly blessing to each priest at the altar, I first walked over to where Father Rouleau was sitting and placed my hands on his forehead. There was an almost audible gasp from the congregation when I did that, as if some kind of visible electric current jolted between Father's white-haired brow and my hands. After the ceremony, many guests told me that moment had moved them the most.

The schoolchildren sang beautifully at the ordination

Mass, and their mothers prepared a hearty reception that was held on the playground where I used to play ball as a kid. Two of the little Mass servers told me they would like to be priests now, too.

After an exciting and exhausting day, we headed back home for the dinner Mother had lovingly cooked for our family and special guests. When Father Rouleau jubilantly arrived at our house that evening, Glenn seated him comfortably in a plush "grandfather chair" at the head of the table. Throughout the festivities, Glenn had carefully watched over Father Rouleau, who referred to my younger brother as his "bodyguard".

Two of our dinner guests held special memories for me: Sister Patricia, my friend and former classmate at the Hsinchu language school, and Mike Carey, my wise-cracking Jesuit companion in the Oregon strawberry fields where I worked shortly before leaving for Taiwan. They were both "lay people" now, having found other vocations outside of religious life. But for me, they would always remain a sister and a brother who had helped me along the long road to priesthood.

~

On the day following my ordination, I said my first "solo" Mass for Mother and the other parishioners of Saint Vincent's Church. It happened to be Mother's Day—no better time than then to offer the gift of my Mass for the person I love most in the world. Father Rouleau stayed in San Diego for three days, allowing us to concelebrate Mass around Mother's dining room table the next day.

The following weeks were both busy and enjoyable, and my appointment book was filling up fast. While my aunts were with us, we had Mass every day at home. Later, I was invited to say Mass for other families or in nearby churches. Each Mass was different, each so *new*, whether celebrating at a church with a choir and incense or at home on the dining room table. I always felt God was using me to the fullest during my Masses.

One day, rather than partaking of the wafer-thin hosts normally used for Mass, I asked my aunts if they could make unleavened bread that was common in the time of Jesus. Since my aunts are of Lebanese descent, and flatbread is a common Middle Eastern food, I figured they would know how to do this. But they could not agree on the recipe and argued among themselves for hours about the best way to prepare the mix and bake it. However, by the time we were ready for our home Mass around the dining room table, my three solicitous aunts had produced an attractive, circular, flat unleavened bread that could be shared among us.

All went well until it was time for Communion. Then, when I tried to divide the now-consecrated Host so it could be distributed to others at the table, the flatbread was so stiff it could hardly be broken. After much effort, and under the tremulous eyes of my three bakers who had obviously over-cooked the bread, I eventually managed to break it into small pieces, with each division causing a loud cracking noise that startled everyone. Alas, that sound was minimal compared to what happened when we began consuming the Host. There was a thunderous choir of chomping, chewing, and crunching as each communicant desperately attempted to consume the rigid bread without breaking into laughter.

But when Mass was over, we did indeed laugh. I had never seen my conservative aunts giggle so irreverently before. The only redeeming quality of the bread was that it was much tastier than the usual wafers. When I quoted the

Bible verse, "Taste and see how good is the Lord", there were more peals of laughter. This was definitely one of the most delightful moments in my newly ordained ministry. I am sure God must have enjoyed it, too, since our sense of humor comes from Him. But I am glad this happened with my non-judgmental family. When my aunts offered to make another host for the next Mass, I politely declined.

~

Jim, my best friend from high school, visited me with his wife, Elaine, and stayed for several days. I had not seen Jim for twelve years—ever since he left for Boston after our high school graduation. Jim had wanted to be an Augustinian priest but only spent a few years in the seminary, later finding his vocation elsewhere. When he arrived in San Diego, one of the first things we did was to visit our former high school and meet some of the Augustinian Fathers there who had taught us in our youth. Chief among these was Father Neely, who invited us to attend one of his current Latin classes. My impression was that his students were much smarter than I was at that age. But they were not smarter than Jim. He was the top student in every class and also outstanding in sports. Moreover, he was a highly spiritual person.

The visit to my alma mater was like returning to an "age of innocence" that was both privileged and challenging. It was during high school that I had answered an interior call to become a Jesuit, which meant not only dedicating myself to a new way of life, but also giving up the family and friends that meant so much to me. Other than my immediate family, the hardest separation at that time had been from my best friend, Jim. And now here he was again, after all these years. "The Lord gives and the Lord takes away," as the Bible says. "Blessed be the name of the Lord."

I have said Mass in a number of places, some very unusual. When I took Jim and Elaine to neighboring Tijuana, I was asked to concelebrate Mass in Spanish at the Cathedral there. The next day, after admiring the flora and fauna of Balboa Park, we found a secluded spot on the grass to have Mass in the open air. I also said Mass for Catholic Vietnamese refugees, who have been streaming into Camp Pendleton near San Diego ever since the Vietnam War ended last month. And then there were a series of Masses followed by my guitar songs in each classroom at Saint Vincent's School. The teachers remarked it was the first time they had heard a priest singing "Love Potion Number 9".

A few weeks after my ordination, the Soto family drove down from their home in Fresno to spend a few days with me at Mother's house. Seven years ago, during a summer break from studying philosophy, I worked as a migrant field laborer with this large, devoutly religious Mexican Pentecostal family, who taught me not only how to pick strawberries more efficiently but how to pray more enthusiastically.

Mother cordially welcomed the Sotos to stay at her home and made sure each of the ten children had a comfortable place to sleep. I was relegated to the floor. On Sunday, the family accompanied us to Saint Vincent's Church for my Mass. But being good Pentecostals, they had a second religious service with us that evening in Mother's living room—praying together in a circle, hands held together—just as we had done in the dust of the migrant camp so many years before.

The most awe-inspiring Mass I participated in was during a Catholic Charismatic conference held in San Diego. Since I had been attending prayer meetings at Saint Vincent's, the prayer group invited me to concelebrate with the bishop and forty other priests at a huge Mass held at the convention center. A few hours before Mass, some of us were asked to hear Confessions for the many attendees. This would be my first experience as a "confessor", and my biggest surprise was how many people wanted to go to Confession.

As the hours passed and the Confession lines grew longer instead of shorter, I wondered how I was ever going to hear all the Confessions before Mass began. When I realized this would be unlikely, I hoped at least to finish before Mass ended. But eventually I became so absorbed in the problems and sins and often utter despair of the penitents that I forgot about time altogether. What astounded me was how some people could come into the confessional in tears and only moments later walk out of it in smiles after their sins were forgiven. To my joyful relief, I finished hearing Confessions in time for everyone to receive Holy Communion and for me to join in at the tail end of Mass as well.

~

Father Rouleau suggested I stay a few extra months in the States to gain greater pastoral experience. My Jesuit superiors in Manila and Taiwan also thought I should spend a longer time with "my own people", especially since I could help those who may be materially well-off but whose hearts have grown spiritually poor without God. This is so different from what it is like in the Philippines, where even the poor have a rich personal faith that fills their hearts. Since Jesus once said "The poor you will always have with you", I decided to wait a little longer before I returned to them.

But now the time has almost come for me to go back to the Philippines and complete my fourth year of theology.

Before leaving, I wanted to visit my older cousin Rosa Lee, who had recently returned to college in order to work on her Master's degree. When she asked me if I planned to get my Master's in theology, I told her probably not since I would not need it for my future work. Rosa Lee was horrified.

"Here I am, a wife and mother, trying my hardest to achieve a Master's degree—and you don't even care about getting one when the opportunity is right in front of you!"

"I guess I'm not very ambitious when it comes to studies," I explained. "Besides, I'd like to spend more time serving the people than writing a thesis."

"You can serve the people for the rest of your life!" Rosa Lee cried out in frustration. "Now is the time for you to get the most out of your studies. And there is no better way to do that than to get a Master's—whether you will ever use it or not. You owe it to yourself to write that thesis!"

There was no denying that Rosa Lee had a point. And the more I thought about it, the more getting a Master's degree during my remaining year in the Philippines seemed the natural thing to do.

Soon afterward, the theme of a possible thesis began to come into focus. I could write about my pastoral experiences in Taiwan, the Philippines, and the States in light of what I had learned in theology. Not only would a thesis like that enable me to reflect on my own life, it could also help me understand how God works in the lives of the people I have come across in these three locales—and how He wants to save each of them in his or her own way.

These thoughts filled my mind during the long flight back to Asia. As usual, it was a tearful goodbye when Mother and Glenn saw me off at the airport. And just like many years previously, they were left behind while I was starting off on a new adventure. Living so closely together for the past few months made the separation doubly hard for all of us—and even more gut-wrenching for me this time than the last. But that is the Cross, which I must continue to embrace—just as in the past, just as in the future—just as always.

Stopping over in Taiwan for a few days before traveling on to the Philippines, I stayed with Jerry on the top floor of Kuangchi Studio, where he works. He is now the superior of his small Jesuit community and seems to relish this new responsibility. No longer translating Mickey Mouse cartoons, he now has more important duties, including the writing of a daily religious program that is broadcast to Mainland China.

"Producing these programs gives me a chance to preach directly to the Chinese people," Jerry enthused. "This takes a lot of faith because it may be years before we know if anyone has actually responded to the broadcasts."

The evening I arrived at Kuangchi, Jerry took me to a Taipei coffee house called the Wooden Door, where he sings twice a week. The manager there told me they have more customers on those days than any other.

"They must really like your singing," I said to Jerry.

"It's just because I'm different," he replied with his customary self-deprecation.

But Jerry sang well. The audience even stopped talking during his songs, which was more than they did for the other performers. Jerry said his opening number was always the same—a modern version of the "Our Father" set to guitar music.

"Hearing that song might be the closest anyone in this crowd ever gets to a church," he mused.

Several bystanders stopped my brother as we walked back

to Kuangchi, remarking they had seen him on TV or heard him on the radio. Although these interruptions were annoying to me, especially when we were in the middle of a conversation, they were not surprising since this was also a common occurrence during our two years together at the Fu Jen theologate. Jerry was always the focus of attention, and when I was with him, it was sometimes necessary for me to fade into the background. We were as close as brothers could be, but our paths were not always the same.

However, there is one area in which I shine a little bit brighter than my big brother—and that is in story books and art. A year ago, in addition to writing about my adventures on Orchid Island, I also produced an illustrated children's story called "The Fish Boy of Orchid Island" and sent it to a publisher in Taipei. During this stopover, I was delighted to find my story had already been published and was included in a tribal anthology that would be distributed to all the primary school libraries in Taiwan—including the ones on Orchid Island, for which I had specifically written the story. The publishers promised to send an extra supply of books to children on the island.

The editor told me she liked my story the best and hoped I would make another one for a future volume when I came back to Taiwan. I did not tell her it had taken me almost a year to produce just the dozen or so paintings for this story. And they did not even use all of them. While most of the other tales in the anthology had rapidly drawn cartoonish characters, I had painted slowly and tried to depict the Orchid Island people as realistically as possible. Maybe that is why the editor liked me, too—because I was "different".

~

No one can say that being in the Philippines is not exciting. When I arrived at Manila Airport, a thunderstorm caused the lights to go out just as I was passing through immigration. Then the taxi I caught outside the airport stalled in a flooded street and filled up with water. I piled my bags high on the back seat, rolled up my pant legs, and helped to push the car. When the taxi got out of the flooded area, the driver tried to dry out the wet engine by stuffing burning newspapers into its tubes. I thought for sure the whole car would blow up. But it worked! I reached the Ateneo campus safely that evening, happy to be back but totally drenched.

My classmates said I had not missed much even though, as usual, I was late for the beginning of the semester. The newly ordained priests in my class had been doing pretty much the same as I did, spending most of their time exercising their pastoral ministry. In less than a week, I said Mass for my community, for the diocesan seminarians, and for parishioners crowded into the Barangka church, where I gave individual blessings afterward.

In Barangka, I preached some parts of my homily in Tagalog, stumbling through the language fairly well until I made a mistake that caused giggles in the congregation. I was trying to say how Christ died on Calvary (*Calvario*) but used the wrong word, making it sound like Christ died on a horse (*kabayo*). After Mass and with much merriment, my friends in the barrio held a *Bienvenido* for me. No mistaking that word. It means "Welcome party".

The next week, I moved from Loyola House to the Barangka church rectory at the request of Father Nery, who wanted me to replace him while he went for a retreat. The so-called rectory was actually a tiny attic built between the roof and rafters of the chapel. Living in such close proximity to the people crowded in the streets below was a new experience. A constant clamor came up from the hordes of children outside and the motorized tricycles ferrying residents back and forth. It is hard to believe how so many people can live together in such close quarters. But except for an occasional fist fight or knife stabbing, there was relative harmony in the streets.

Six "*convento* boys" also stayed at the church. They were members of a tough gang ironically called the "Happy People's Society" that had nowhere else to live. Father Nery had given them odd jobs to do at the church, and they also prepared for the daily Masses. When one of them asked me if he could compose a song for Mass and I agreed, the talented boy wrote a new hymn every day. He also began directing the others in short dramas that served to compliment my homilies. Needless to say, these were very creative people.

Although I enjoyed my week in Barangka immensely, hardly a day went by that I did not reminisce about the time I had spent with my family, friends, and parishioners in San Diego following my ordination. That was certainly one of the highpoints of my life. And as nice as the people here are, and as fulfilled as I have been in my ministry to them, it has been painful to be away from those I love so much. Sometimes during the Masses in Barangka, my eyes would well up with tears as I imagined them there before me once again.

~

Now I am back at Loyola House after two weeks in the barrio, and I have been going full blast on my M.A. thesis. So far, I am half finished with the rough draft. It is not hard for me to write this thesis because the theme is so interesting to me. But there are days when I would rather "go out and play". The challenge during this fourth year of theology seems to be learning how to juggle a life of studies with the constant demand for Masses and priestly assistance.

In order to concentrate on writing, I have to restrict my active apostolate, which is difficult because the ministries here are so enjoyable. But when too much time is spent in serving others, there is no time for reflection. And writing demands reflection. So, my mind has to say "no" when my heart wants to say "yes".

My thesis is becoming clearer. The first part, which is already completed, is an anthropological study of the culture and native religion of the people of Orchid Island, showing how God the Father can integrate the indigenous spirituality of the Yami tribe with Christianity.

The next part concentrates on a slum area in the Philippines, showing how the sacrifice of Jesus Christ and His promise of justice and liberation can heal the wounds of the poor and suffering.

The third section is about ordinary Americans, who may be materially well-off but at the same time spiritually impoverished, and how the Holy Spirit can enrich their sometimes lonely and isolated lives with love and unity.

Since each of these three different situations comes from my own experience, my thesis is an experiment in a new method of theological reflection called "contextual theology". This means that instead of using the traditional way to understand God, which first starts with doctrine, I begin with actual stories of people and try to find God's plan in their lives through experience. Whether this experimental approach will be successful or not is questionable. The professor who serves as my mentor is excited about the idea. But some of my classmates have warned me that because my thesis sounds suspiciously like anthropology, the theology professors might not like it.

What is most important to me is that the thesis is about the needs of those I love in the different places where I have served. Hopefully, writing about these people and their search for God will help me understand the specific salvific love He has prepared for each of them. This seems more meaningful than researching some abstract theological concept that has no relation to my ministry. Besides, it is more fun.

~

Among my many pastoral experiences since coming back to the Philippines, two of them especially stand out. The first happened on All Souls' Day, when Father Nery and I concelebrated Mass for thousands of poor parishioners clustered beside the graves of their loved ones on the hills surrounding the Barangka cemetery. The scene looked so biblical that I would not have been surprised if Father Nery decided to multiply a few loaves and fishes to feed the needy people.

After the Mass, we trudged through the candlelit hills for several hours, blessing graves and praying for the deceased. During my final stop, I felt a fiery heat rising from one of the tombstones and was alarmed to see the bottom hem of my white alb was in flames. I had been standing too close to a candle placed on one of the tombs.

Several ladies standing near me rushed to extinguish the flames, and I was unharmed. But I was upset about the burned alb since that vestment had been an ordination gift from my mother. The kind Barangka ladies by my side quickly assured me they could mend the alb, and, true to their word, in a few days it was almost as good as new, with only a slightly discernible patch at the bottom to remind me of my All Souls' Day misadventure.

My second unforgettable experience happened at a Tondo high school in Manila's biggest slum area. I had received a phone call telling me I was urgently needed to hear Confessions and was given the address of a school. I rushed out to catch a jeepney without even changing my T-shirt and flip flops. I figured no one would see how I was dressed anyway if I was hidden away in a confessional.

But it turned out I was scheduled not simply to hear Confessions, but also to give the main homily at a grand outdoor Mass in honor of Our Lady of Fatima for five thousand Tondo students. It was big formal affair. When I arrived at the front gate, the school's honor guard stood at attention with swords raised as I passed into the school grounds to loud applause—in my T-shirt and flip flops—behind a towering statue of Our Lady of Fatima.

I was quickly "vested" in ornately embroidered priestly robes and seated on the side of a large stage at one end of an outdoor patio. Students packed the area in front of the stage, as well as in makeshift bleachers at the edge of the field, and even in the classroom balconies overhanging the patio. It felt like all the high school students in Manila were there—and I had no idea of what to say in my homily!

As I waited nervously in a hopeless attempt to decipher the Tagalog Mass readings, my eyes gradually began to focus on the statue of Mary that stood directly in front of me. And I prayed to her—like I had never prayed before—for help in this time of need. "Please give me the right words!" I begged.

When my turn came to preach, I still did not know what to say. My mind had gone blank. I approached the microphone, took a deep breath, opened my mouth, and these were the words that came out:

"When I find myself in times of trouble,
Mother Mary comes to me,
speaking words of wisdom, let it be."

There was an immediate reaction from the students as they recognized these lyrics from the popular Beatles song. And with their recognition came a thunderous ovation. I was almost swept off my feet by their overwhelming response. After that opening line, the rest of the homily simply flowed out of my heart, as natural as it could be. It was probably the best sermon I had ever given.

After Mass, the crowd of students practically suffocated me with requests for an autograph, as though I were a superstar. Someone tossed me a guitar, and I sang a few songs for the crowd, which caused more pandemonium. What a great day! And all because I had a little help from my friends—Mother Mary and the Beatles.

~

Speaking of superstars, Jerry visited me for a week during a recent trip to the Philippines—his first time here. He came for a meeting but spent most of his time with me and my friends in the barrio. We said Mass together, went home-visiting—and, of course, sang together as much as possible for the young people. What impressed me most about that week was how the two of us together seemed to multiply our individual talents—to create something bigger than both of us. There probably will not be too many more times like this when we can be with each other for as long as we were that week. I am grateful for every moment we had together.

After Jerry left, we began preparing for Christmas, which begins early in the Philippines. Every day for nine days preceding Christmas, there are Masses at 4:30 in the morning, and all the priests are expected to help out. Not being a "morning person", I found this hard to do. But the Filipinos consider these early-morning Masses to be especially happy occasions because of the sacrifice involved in getting up that early. Happiness is associated with doing something hard for God. So, I "sacrificed" and said all the morning Masses. After the Masses, we gathered at homes in the barrio for breakfast.

Just as last year, the day after Christmas I headed to Manila Harbor and boarded a boat, bound this time for the circular-shaped island of Bohol. One of my friends from San José Seminary had invited me to spend a few days there with his family. During the overnight voyage, I got to know some of the other young priests traveling in the third-class steerage. After landing in Bohol, they brought me to the residence of the local bishop, a grandfatherly figure who was the oldest of all the Filipino bishops. He welcomed me to join in their morning Mass and breakfast, where twelve newly ordained priests surrounded him—just like Jesus and his apostles.

Then I traveled by bus to a small town on the other side of Bohol, where my friend Joe lived. Along the way, it looked like the entire island of Bohol was made up of banana and coconut trees, until some two hours into the journey our bus passed by hundreds of cone-shaped mounds commonly referred to as the Chocolate Hills. Viewed from a distance, these velvety brown domes of earth looked like chocolate "kisses". The driver explained they were a natural wonder formed thousands of years ago. I would have liked to run up and down those hills, but they were too far away.

I spent a wonderful day and night at Joe's home on the outskirts of a small country town. Joe was the eldest of a dozen children, belying the youthful appearance of his warm and welcoming parents, who still acted as if they were newly-weds. Although both parents held government jobs, they appeared to combine work and family life with ease. Between having babies, Joe's mother traveled to different barrios, helping with home industries, hygiene, and community development projects.

Looking younger than I, Joe's father chuckled when I asked him how he had discovered the fountain of youth.

"Whatever happens, just laugh about it," he said with a boyish smile. "Wrinkles only appear on your face when you worry. Just relax."

I imagine the peace and beauty of the countryside was also a contributing factor. Joe's parents looked as if they had nothing to do but simply sit and talk. It was so different in this small town from the big city. Each time I traveled on Manila's streets, I found myself rushing around, trying to squeeze in enough time for everything. And if I stopped to wonder why I was running, I would not know why. Since everyone else is in a hurry, it gets into your blood.

During the day, I swam with Joe and his friends in the deep waters off a nearby ocean cliff. Later in the afternoon, we watched a basketball tournament in the town square beside a Spanish-style church. Then we spent most of the night singing. Since I could only stay for a day and a night, Joe said, "We will have to make the night day."

We drank coconut wine (*tuba*) and ate barbecued meat until the wee hours of the morning. At one point I remarked on how good the meat tasted and asked what it was. Joe's friends replied, "Guess." After going through almost every animal I could think of, there was only one left. When I mentioned my favorite four-legged friend, Joe's friends burst out laughing but did not deny it. I hope they were joking.

~

From Bohol, I took a boat to Cebu and from there to nearby Mactan Island, where the family of a classmate of mine had a nipa hut that they let me use to make my annual retreat. For the next eight days, I lived at the sea's edge in the little hut beside a coconut grove. The first few days, I felt lonely from being separated so suddenly from all the people and activities that had been occupying my life for the past few months. Then a gentle peace came into my heart that enabled me simply to sink into the calming presence of God in the quiet beauty around me. I almost felt guilty about enjoying the retreat so much. I neither saw nor spoke to anyone during the eight days, except to a village boy who came every other day to sell me fish and vegetables, which I cooked myself.

The highpoint of each day on retreat was the Mass. I loved saying Mass alone with God. Maybe after so many Masses in front of a congregation, which were wonderful, too, the chance to ponder the words of the Mass by myself and go deeper into their reality had more meaning for me. During my Masses, all the people I had ever known seemed to appear before me, allowing me to look at their faces one by one, thank God for them, and ask His blessing on each of them through the sacrifice of the Mass.

~

During the past few months, in addition to writing my thesis, I have also been preparing for the crucial final oral exam that will cover all four years of theology, affectionately called the *Ad Grad*. Some time ago, we fourth-year theologians were given 150 theological "theses" (propositions) to study. But during the oral exam, the professors will only ask us to explain four of those theses. Since we do not know which theses they will choose, we have to be ready to explain all 150 of them.

Although for some time I have been studying these complicated theological theses, which are gleaned from our four years of theology courses, during the month before the *Ad Grad* I did nothing else but review them. When the time came for the exam, I still did not feel as prepared as I should have been and was quite nervous, so naturally my prayers to do well in the exam were as intense as my studies for it.

There are two kinds of exams. For those who have done especially well in theology, a longer and harder exam called "Honors" is given. For the others, an easier exam is prepared. Since I did not think I had done very well in theology, I had not expected to receive the Honors exam—but I got it.

During the ninety-minute comprehensive exam, I sat at a desk, alone and tense, facing four professors who in turn asked questions about particular theological questions in Church dogma, the Bible, morality, etc. Each professor had a different style. Some would simply ask, "What can you say about this question?" And I would explain what I knew about it to the best of my ability. But others, especially the Scripture professor, asked more direct questions. Although I seemed to do well when I could speak freely, I did manage to stumble at least once when a specific question was asked.

"What does Saint Paul say about chastity?" the New Testament professor asked me. As I began to explain, he interrupted me by adding, "By the way, was Saint Paul married?"

Married? That was not part of my thesis preparation. The question was so direct that I was afraid to answer yes or no and stalled for time. But the professor was not fooled and quietly said, "So, we will go on to the next question."

Although most of us feared the *Ad Grad* only slightly less than the Last Judgment, my examiners were not as forbidding as I had expected. In spite of fumbling my answer on Saint Paul (no, he was not married) and losing some much-needed confidence in the process, the Scripture professor told me afterward that he thought I had done well. I think he was just being kind.

~

On Holy Thursday, a few days before Easter, I was watching some of the Barangka parishioners put final touches on their costumes for a Good Friday procession to be held the following day. One of the members of the Happy People's Society who lived at the church told me his gang would have its own pilgrimage in honor of Christ's Passion.

Freddy, the gang leader, asked me, "Do you want to come with us tomorrow, Father?"

"Sure," I replied. "Where are you going?"

"To Quiapo," Freddy said. "We will walk."

"Quiapo? That's ten miles away!"

"Yes," said Freddy, adding, "and with no shoes. It will be a *penitencia*, Father, a sacrifice for our sins."

A ten-mile hike. And barefoot. And in the hot sun! Why had I agreed to this? But as I thought it over, I realized that if they wanted to make a sacrifice for their sins, then I should make one for mine, too.

Early the next morning, Freddy and I, together with twenty-one members of the Happy People's Society, gathered at the Barangka church to begin our *penitencia*. After a short prayer, we took off our shoes, slung them on our backs, and started walking. Because of Good Friday, which is a solemn holiday in the Philippines, there was little traffic. The atmosphere among the gang members was casual. They talked quietly, laughed a little, and sometimes sang, but it was all low-key. After about an hour, we stopped at the home of a relative of one of the gang members for a little water—but no food. This was Good Friday—a day of fasting.

As we walked, my companions shared their problems with me since they knew I had time now to talk with them and answer their questions. We paused a few minutes at each church along the way to make a visit. We also stopped at each movie theater to see what was showing. And at the *sari-sari* stores for cigarettes. And sometimes at the little pineapple juice stands lining the road to get something to drink.

The sun grew hotter, and the road became harder to walk on, especially when we crossed an intersection. I could tell everyone was trying to pretend their bare feet did not hurt in order to keep marching stoically ahead. But sometimes one of the boys would yell out in pain while hopping across a steaming pavement. Wherever we could, we would huddle momentarily in the shade of a parked car, a storefront awning—or even a telephone pole.

Twice, we passed penitents clothed like Jesus in blood-streaked robes. They carried heavy wooden crosses as "soldiers" beat their back with scourges. At least we were not in as much pain as they were, I thought to myself.

Finally, we reached Quiapo in central Manila. We crossed the plaza to San Sebastian Church, where the famous statue of the Black Nazarene resides. The gang members went over and kissed the wounds of Jesus on the statue. Gazing at the miraculous icon, I was aware of Jesus' bloody feet in particular. Then we knelt on the floor in the back of the crowded church. When we came onto the street again, no one spoke. Some of the toughest gang members were wiping their eyes.

At the main Quiapo church, many worshippers were crawling on their knees to the altar, which is a popular penitential custom in the Philippines. The boys did not want to do that, though, because most of the penitents were women. So, we rested on some empty pews beside the confessionals. Some of the gang members went to Confession. After about a half-hour, we were out on the street again. But the faces of the boys had somehow changed. The Happy People's Society seemed happier now—even giddy.

We posed for photos, put on our shoes, and walked to nearby Luneta Park. Everyone was laughing now that the *penitencia* had been completed, and Freddy had to remind them that since it was still Good Friday, they should not be too merry.

After strolling through the grassy park and paying our respects at the bronze statue of José Rizal, the national hero of the Philippines, we caught a bus back to Barangka. One gang member had bought a large loaf of bread, and all twenty-two of us shared it. Somehow, that filled us, at least until we got home.

Back at the Barangka church, as we parted ways, Freddy looked at me with a glow in his eyes and said, "This is what the Happy People's Society is all about. If you want to be happy, you have to sacrifice."

~

My thesis, entitled "Salvation in Three Local Contexts", is finished at last. Yesterday, I sent copies to be reviewed by the professors, who will gather in two weeks' time for my thesis "defense". The defense is like a courtroom procedure, wherein the writer of the thesis sits in front of a board of examiners, who question various points in the thesis, which must then be "defended" by the writer in order to obtain his Master's degree. That sounds fairly simple.

Although my thesis turned out well, its length of 230 pages is quite a bit longer than most papers professors are accustomed to reading. I hope my examiners will make it to the end. Looking back, there are parts of the thesis that do not quite satisfy me and that might be misleading. But as a whole, I am happy with it because it is about the people I love and God's love for them. Since the thesis is contemporary and rather journalistic in style, perhaps it may also be of value to others in some way.

I probably will not need to prepare much for the defense exam since I have memorized almost every page of the thesis. So, what should I do during the next two weeks before the exam? My classmates are all relaxing at home during this Easter break. But that's not for me. I only have a short time left in the Philippines. And what better use of that time could there be than to travel again? There are still many remote places in the Philippines I want to see, and this might be my last chance. So now I am off to the islands for a whirlwind adventure once again!

~

In less than a week, I covered about as much ground as possible during my final voyage in the Philippines—exploring the distant provinces of Masbate, South Cotabato, and Davao. Bert, one of my friends in the Happy People's Society, had invited me to accompany him on a boat ride to his hometown in Masbate, a poor and relatively neglected island-province near Cebu. Since Bert's family lived close to the beach, we did a lot of swimming. But this was no resort.

Bert's family, as well as most others in his village, were dirt poor. They lived in stilt houses along a vast stretch of arid sand, where neither crops nor any vegetation could grow. It wasn't hard to see why Bert and so many of his fellow villagers had migrated to Manila for work. Even though he spent his days in Barangka as a "stand-by" (one who waits for any available work), Bert's livelihood in the crowded slums of the city was a step higher than in this desolate wasteland.

But there were compensations. In addition to beaches that were perfect for swimming, Masbate was also notable for the excellent *tuba* produced by its villagers. *Tuba* is like the "national wine" of the Philippines. And during my visit, I had an opportunity not only to imbibe this delicious drink but also to see how it was made. I watched, intrigued, as a slender young boy shinnied up a coconut tree to cut an unopened flower stalk and put a bucket under it to catch the slowly dripping sap. In a few hours, the bucket was full of deliriously sweet *tuba*, which resembled milky orange juice and had a real kick to it, especially when it was freshly fermented.

From Masbate, I took a boat to Cebu and from there flew to General Santos City in South Cotabato, a province rife with warring rebel groups but also home to some of the Philippines' most remote minority tribes. It was there, in a secluded forest of South Cotabato, that twenty-seven members of a primitive tribe called the Tasaday were recently discovered.

Since the Tasaday tribe could only be reached by helicopter, and the government had forbidden outsiders to enter their domain, I opted to visit the more accessible T'boli tribe that lived around Lake Sebu, only six bumpy hours into the mountains by bus. While there, I stayed at a sprawling mission compound run by Passionist priests, who ministered to the T'boli minorities in their jungle paradise.

Arrayed in colorful red dresses and turbans, with thick brass bracelets on their arms and ankles, the women of the T'boli tribe were a sight to behold. Even more exciting for me was seeing men on horseback galloping through the hills—and hitching a ride on one of the horses myself.

The T'boli villagers invited me to their fiesta, with horse fighting as the main event. Having previously witnessed cock fights, which seemed cruel to me, I was not sure I wanted to see horse fighting. But since an enthusiastic T'boli man was already pulling me to a wobbly set of bleachers to watch the show, I could hardly refuse.

Two young stallions were led to a waiting mare that was tied securely to the bleachers where we sat. When the stallions sensed the mare was in heat, they began fighting with each other in order to "win her hand" (or "hoof"). It was a ferocious battle, complete with bites to the horses' necks and rivulets of blood streaming down their legs. This show of violence shocked and repelled me, and I could not bear to watch the fight any longer. But before I was able to get up and leave, the horses in their excitement rammed into the bleachers, sending the entire group of onlookers racing for the exit. It was easy for me then to slip out from the fiesta area unnoticed and explore the rest of the countryside in peace.

The highlight of that day was not the fiesta, but rather my fortuitous discovery of a small evangelical mission church overlooking Lake Sebu, which was run by a sweet T'boli tribal girl in pigtails. She was conducting a prayer meeting with three or four youth and invited me to join them. Afterward, we had lunch together, talked, and sang. When it was time for me to leave, they called for a horse and rode back with me to the much larger Catholic mission. The horse was so gentle and obedient that I hoped he would never be sent to fight like the others. Better to be ridden than to fight.

The next day, I journeyed to Davao to visit my friend Cris once again. As before, we paddled a *bangka* to his parents' home on Samal Island, where I spent most of the time following Cris around as he showed me his now flourishing seaweed farm. I was so proud of how hard he worked and all he had accomplished for his family in such a short time. For sure, he had found his true vocation.

It was hard saying goodbye to Cris since he was my closest friend in the Philippines and most likely we would never see each other again. But I had to hurry back to Manila for at least a few days of preparation before my thesis defense. The defense should be easy, though, so I was not worried.

~

But I should have been worried—and better prepared—since my thesis defense turned out to be an excruciating experience for me, both mentally and emotionally.

A few days before the exam, I asked Father René Ocampo, a scholarly young priest who had successfully defended his own thesis only a week before, to take me through the defense process and give me some tips.

"Whatever you do, don't argue with the examiners," he cautioned. "Always act very humbly when you explain your viewpoint because professors do not like to be contradicted. It may seem they oppose what you have written, but they are simply trying to find out if you are sure of your thesis."

Alas, during the exam, I forgot every word of what Father René had said to me.

As the defense began, what first caught me off-guard was when one of the examiners quietly slipped three sheets of single-spaced type-written pages in front of me.

"These are the grammatical errors I found in your thesis," the examiner politely explained. "I'm sure many of them are simply typos, but all the same I think you should be aware of your mistakes."

My confidence was shattered. How could there be so many errors after months of careful proofreading? Following this opening salvo, I was appalled when the first professor to question me on my thesis apparently did not like it.

"Your thesis reads like a novel," he said. "But I'm not sure it's theology. It seems more like an essay in anthropology."

As I tried to explain what I had written, and the professor countered my reasons one by one, I found myself becoming more argumentative and at one point delivered the fatal remark, "Well, if you had read the whole thesis, you would know the answer to that question."

The professor glared at me as if he were going to fail me on the spot. "Read all your thesis?" he repeated. "How could I have time to do that? It is over two hundred pages long! I read the beginning and got the general idea. That's enough."

Fortunately, another professor stepped in before we came to blows, and he changed the subject. From then on, the defense improved, and I regained my composure. But I realized that after spending all that time writing my thesis, I had actually forgotten half of what I had written. I think my mind was still somewhere in South Cotabato, galloping through the fields on a horse, or in Masbate, swimming with my friends on a beach. It certainly was not there at the defense.

~

Against all odds, and in spite of my quarrelsome attitude, I passed the exam required for my Master's degree. Immediately afterward, I headed to Baguio for our community retreat.

At the beginning of the retreat, my mind was filled with nagging thoughts about what I had said and done during my thesis defense. I was remorseful for the way I had behaved and resentful toward at least one of the professors for the way he had acted toward me. Although I had received a good grade on my thesis, to me it was as if I had failed. My spirits continued to be burdened by these negative thoughts.

Then, out of the blue, a letter arrived from Father Rouleau, who always seemed to appear when I needed him. There is nothing negative in Father Rouleau's spirituality. Everything is about acceptance. And it was as if he had sensed from afar the turmoil that was fuming inside of me. His answer to me, without my even asking the question, was this:

"Even apparent failures have a part in the Divine plan. If you acted to the best of your knowledge at the time, then there is no need to feel bad now. Don't dwell on your mistakes. Learn from them, and they will help you grow. What is most important is to thank God for the bad things that happen to you as well as for the good."

So, I began to thank God for each of the "bad" things that had happened to me. And gradually my feelings of disappointment over all that I had said and done, and my resentment toward the professors, began to fade away. I was grateful for every person and event in my life.

As I thanked God for the few bad things, I became more

aware of the many good things God has given me. I had lacked humility in defending my thesis, acting like I knew more than the professors. But hopefully, I have grown in humility through that "bad" experience—and is that not most important? The "bad" has become the "good".

~

There are only a few more weeks before I go back to Taiwan and begin my priestly ministry there. I am getting anxious. I think I have been here long enough, and even though I have made good friends and enjoyed my studies and apostolates, Taiwan is in some way closer to me. An older priest once said to me, "The first place a missionary goes is always the place that remains dearest to his heart."

Father Bernard Chu, who was one of the first people I met in Taiwan when he was rector of Chabanel Language Institute—and is now our new provincial—passed through Manila a few days ago and visited our community. While here, he asked if I had thought about my future ministry in Taiwan. Although he is the "boss" and can assign me anywhere he pleases, Father Chu was considerate in wanting to know my preferences.

I told him of my interest in working with Taiwan's aborigines, either those in the mountains or migrant workers in the cities. I also hoped that my future work would involve the youth and the poor—two groups I seemed to relate with better than others. But I added that no matter where he sent me, I would devote myself to the task.

Father Chu glanced at me with an enigmatic smile and asked, "Aren't you forgetting something?"

I was not sure what he meant. Then the provincial reminded me of his recent visit to my home in San Diego.

"I saw the paintings you made for your mother," he said. "They were hung all over the walls of her house. It made me wonder about how you express your creativity."

Then we talked about my art and writing—and the songs that he had heard me sing the first day we met.

"So, your creativity is joined to your apostolate," Father Chu concluded. "And it seems you get your inspiration from the people you work with."

Although Father Chu's observation should have been evident to me, at the time it was a revelation. I had not thought of "creativity" as a form of ministry. Father Chu encouraged me to continue to express what I see and feel and love—creatively. I do not know what this will mean in my future work, but I pray that God will let me know when the time comes. I am sure He will.

EPILOGUE

Fresh from my last two years of theology studies in the Philippines, and after a grand total of thirteen years of Jesuit training, I was looking forward finally to receiving my first official assignment as a priest. When Father Bernard Chu asked me to meet him at the provincial office in Taipei, my heart pumped with excitement. A long-awaited mission was at hand—and most likely a lengthy discussion beforehand on where I should be sent.

But there was no discussion. Father Chu simply told me, "You will be going to Chingchuan." Then, putting his hand on my shoulder and looking me in the eye, he added with a smile, "Do you have any questions?"

The provincial knew, of course, that I had worked in Chingchuan before and often visited that beautiful and remote mountain village. It was a place already close to my heart.

And now, following all the years of preparation and unforgettable experiences that had taken me to the ends of the earth—how could I express my joy in receiving such an assignment? I needed to choose the right words to answer Father Chu. But my first response after being missioned to Chingchuan was anything but profound.

"I suppose I can have a dog there," I replied.

I do not know why I said that. And I doubt if Father

Provincial did either. His smile grew a bit fainter as he led me to the door, his hand still on my shoulder.

"Very well, then," he said quietly. "Go now—and trust in God."

And with that I had my mission.

~

I have been in Chingchuan now for two months—and I do have a dog. The former pastor left before I arrived because a typhoon was coming, and he wanted to get out before it hit. Not being as experienced in typhoons as good Father Miguélez, who almost lost his life in one many years ago, I merrily set off for Chingchuan just as the storm was approaching, only to find the tunnel leading to the village had caved in.

An alternative path involved lugging all my earthly belongings over a long mountain trail in the wind and rain. Fortunately, I was helped by some villagers returning from the city. At present the tunnel is still impassable—which means I am pretty isolated here in Chingchuan.

Now that I am their pastor, the people here look up to me much more than when they knew me as a seminarian. Before, I was a Brother. Now I am a Father. Living a poor life-style used to be a priority for me, and though it is still my preference, the more involved I become with the people here—studying the Tayal language, organizing a youth club, visiting parishioners, caring for those who are sick, or painting murals on the church walls—the less relevant my former priorities seem to be.

I have been too busy lately to think about "being poor". Anyway, my church does not have much money, and I have fewer worldly goods than any of my neighbors. My job now is to serve others. What is important are their needs, not my own. The kind of life-style I lead is something the people here do not seem to care about one way or the other.

It is a fresh and exhilarating experience for me to be responsible for an entire parish. I am already making plans on how to beautify the church and improve the spiritual and material lives of the villagers. Despite advancements in their economy, the people here still have deep, underlying problems that are likely related to the gradual loss of their tribal identity. Of all Taiwan's tribes, the Tayal have retained the least in the way of material culture, folklore, and traditions.

I would like to help this tribe experience a cultural rejuvenation. So far, I have discovered ancient stories that could be made into murals. I have heard traditional melodies that could be sung at Mass. And I have watched the women weave and the men hunt and the young people express their deepest longings through ethnic songs and dances. In the future, the people of Chingchuan will hopefully be much prouder of a tribal culture that once was theirs and could be theirs once again.

I am not sure how long I will stay here in the mountains. It could be for just a short period—or for a lifetime. But for however long it lasts, I want to work as if there is no tomorrow. The needs are enormous, and who knows how many years I have left.

It is time to get started.